I Am Here You Are Not I Love You

Aidan Ryan

I AM HERE
YOU ARE NOT
I LOVE YOU

Andrew Topolski, Cindy Suffoletto, and Their Life in the Arts

University of Iowa Press, Iowa City

University of Iowa Press, Iowa City 52242
Copyright © 2025 by Aidan Ryan
uipress.uiowa.edu
Printed in the United States of America

ISBN 978-1-68597-006-2 (pbk)
ISBN 978-1-68597-007-9 (ebk)

Design by Nola Burger

Printed on acid-free paper

Anne Boyer, *The Undying,* copyright 2019 Anne Boyer. Published by Farrar, Straus & Giroux, and used by permission. John Cage, *A Year from Monday*, copyright 1967 John Cage. Published by Wesleyan University Press and used by permission. Chris Kraus, "No More Utopias" from *Where Art Belongs*, copyright 2011 Semiotexte. Published by Semiotexte and used by permission. Eric Siegeltuch, postscript to letter to Wynn Kramarsky, December 22, 1989. Courtesy Werner H. Kramarsky Papers, I.555. The Museum of Modern Art Archives, New York. Andy Topolski, letter to Wynn Kramarsky, September 27, 1990. Courtesy Werner H. Kramarsky Papers, I.555. The Museum of Modern Art Archives, New York. Andy Topolski, letter to Wynn Kramarsky, February 15, 2000. Courtesy Werner H. Kramarsky Papers, I.555. The Museum of Modern Art Archives, New York. Jessica Berwind, letter to Wynn Kramarsky, January 5, 1993. Courtesy Werner H. Kramarsky Papers, I.555. The Museum of Modern Art Archives, New York. Molly Brodak, *Bandit*, copyright 2016 Estate of Molly Brodak. Published by Black Cat and used by permission. Excerpt from "The Apache Dance" from *The Painted Word* by Tom Wolfe. Copyright 1975, renewed 2003 by Tom Wolfe. Reprinted by permission of Farrar, Straus & Giroux. All rights reserved.

Catalog-in-Publication data is on file with the Library of Congress.

for Mom

Contents

Selves Portrait

SHE LETS HIM help her move the armchair from its spot against the pale plaster wall. Really, Cindy does the lifting—tugging, stutter-stepping to clear a space. Opposite, the upholstery sags, straining beneath his fingers. When she moves to lift the framed drawing from the wall, then inch out the nail that held it, he rests, laying his palms flat against the chair's faded arms. Still and splayed like this, his hands look white, like enormous summer moths.

Four months ago, Andy had been built like a laborer—eating well and breathing mountain air, putting in shifts at his studio beside their home in Callicoon, a hamlet tucked in the Catskills. He lifted bricks and stones for sculptures, practiced joinery with heavy beams meant for dining sets that friends and neighbors had commissioned. But now, back in the city for appointments with specialists, stairs dizzy him, elevators give him vertigo. Small talk leaves him breathless. Budweiser still sits well, but even simple foods, favorite foods, can make him nauseous.

Cindy manages. She manages the double-mortgaged house in Callicoon, the dark rented apartment on Withers Street in North Williamsburg. She manages the correspondence—friends checking in and galleries from Buffalo to Basel inquiring. And she manages the hospitals. With weathered eyes and wiry hair from her own second round of chemo completed in the fall, Cindy knows the hospitals, knows the right people at Herbert Irving and Weill Cornell and Columbia. She knows all the sallow hallways, the exits and the dead ends.

For twenty years, Cindy has managed for the both of them. She has managed Andy and Andy's career—the recognition received for his beautiful, precise, complicated, recognize-it-anywhere art. She took pride in it until, one day, pride was an indulgence that exhaustion wouldn't afford her. And now this. Now Andy needs her more than ever, and in new, rewardless ways. They are alone in love and knowledge of each other. Cindy manages because she must, for the both of them.

But with them it has never been just about surviving. They learned to be alone together first inside ideas.

The purple T-shirt hangs loosely from Andy's shoulders. His shrinking body is a factory of bones, new protuberances emerging from him every day. His own unfamiliarity makes the shirt difficult to remove. Cindy steps to him, her small hands finding the hem hanging blousily where his stomach used to be. He looks away as she lifts, letting his arms drop and loping to the tripod as soon as he's free.

He fiddles with the camera, an old Polaroid. The same one that has been with him all these years. Funny. He earned his MFA in photography and came up in the world with a group the critics called the Pictures Generation. He had been a leader among them—the far-out one, the star to catch—once. But when the coffee-table books were finally written, Andy was relegated to the appendix. The reason was simple: Andy stopped making pictures. For a period of years he stopped making art altogether.

But now pictures are all he can talk about.

"The surface..." Andy says, speaking to himself, staring through the viewfinder to the open wall. "A loaded gun..."

When he sways it feels like the room moves with him.

She thinks: he's paler than the walls. Under the brutal shop lamp his bruises glow like bar signs. Outside, snow falls and music fills the street when a car door opens. "No One," Alicia Keys, one of the first hits of the new year. Cindy starts to hum along, but as soon as she begins the song is gone.

"A little more," Andy says. His rumble now a rasp. Cindy tugs the chair another inch, another inch, then straightens up.

Still bare from the hips, holding his waistband with one hooked hand, he shuffles into the light.

Cindy sees it now. Where the blank wall ends and the canvas begins.

When he turns, he doesn't look into the camera. He looks to her. Their eyes shine like a river in the moonlight.

"Wait," he says. Straightens his body to the camera. It is a minor struggle even to lift his own chin. To face, in a way, his own gaze. The cheeks behind his beard slacken, eyes go hard.

"Maybe this is it."

The voice—his—or hers—is lost inside the *click*.

Eulogy.Doc

And the truth must be written for someone, a someone who is all
of us, who will exist in that push and pull of what bonds of love
tie us to the earth and what suffering drives us from it.

—ANNE BOYER, *The Undying*

LIKE A MAGIC TRICK, the nightly fires at Cindy and Andy's place in
Callicoon are something we expect but never see coming.

Maybe we're down the hill, picking up fresh bread at the
quaint Callicoon Pantry or pacing the chill fluorescence of Peck's
Market for chicken and frozen shrimp. Cindy, my aunt and godmother, might take my sister, Talia, and me for a swim in the
Delaware River; we spread a towel out on the small bank below
the gravel parking lot and afterward get ice cream cones at the
Callicoon Creamery. We might stop by the furniture shop
Karkula, a little Appalachian-chic place that sometimes sells
tables and chairs Uncle Andy makes, or we head to the top of
the hill where some friends live, with a view northeast into the
Catskills, turning orange and chalky indigo in the sunset. Or
maybe we'll just have been sitting on the front porch at 69 Seminary Road, listening to Mom and Dad and Cindy talk, watching
through the white and green wooden railings as cars pass up
and down the steep hill—lifers in pickups and weekenders in
Audis and Benzes, the families escaping from New York City, just
seventy miles to the south.

But at a certain point in the late afternoon we inevitably turn
back through the house and walk out onto the rear wooden deck,
which overlooks a short yard falling to a stark, glacial ravine

Andy, Aidan, Cindy, and Talia on the porch of 69 Seminary Road in Callicoon, early 2000s.

already covered in dusk. And there we see Andy walking toward us up the sloping lawn, in a T-shirt and knit beanie rolled up above his ears, behind him blue smoke beginning to rise from a well-made hutch of different woods, barked logs from the forest and splintered planks from his workshop in the garage, some still curling with paints that give brief green flashes in the fire. We stay out until the dark makes a dome above us, constellated by an endless stream of embers.

Sitting around the fire, Cindy draws my sister and me into breathy, indulgent reviews of what we've read and listened to lately, or, in my case, impromptu manifestoes built like card houses out of whatever I've retained from last semester's classes—Andy only occasionally interjecting with an observation in tectonic bass-baritone. We play dangerous made-up games around the fire with the neighbors' kids after the adults retreat inside to talk over the dining room table Andy had recovered from the abandoned convent across the road. When we pass through the kitchen to grab Cokes, or when Andy opens the glass deck doors for a smoke, we catch fragments of conversation about movies, real estate, politics. And when we go to bed—Talia to a spare room on the second floor and me to a blow-up mattress in Cindy's attic studio—I can still see the fire's glow warming the corner of the northeast window.

A high school teacher once remarked to my class that, given enough time, we will forget almost everything the people in our lives said or did, but we will remember the way they made us feel. When I heard this, I dismissed it as cliché.[1] Now I know it was a warning.

Whether you measure the absence in days or decades, after a person leaves your life, a person who gave color and shape and velocity to your life, the echo of the feeling they left in you will yearn backward for specificity, for the color and shape and velocity that made it. And every time that feeling-tone reaches back into the past, it finds less. The echo's echo returns to the present less certain.

I haven't lived long enough to test the limits of this theory, but I have lived long enough to sense a terrible trajectory. Eventually, I suspect, these echoes will be like the pockets of absence uncovered beneath the floodplains of quiet volcanoes. We can tap into them, cast them in plaster, and study the shapes, but this will never amount to more than speculation—when what we want, all that we want, is to walk again with the dead in Pompeii.

This could help explain why I remember the fires in Callicoon so clearly. I am holding onto a shape in myself. In it is captured and conveyed into the present the way that my aunt and uncle made me feel, made so many of their friends and family feel: welcomed, warmed, held, heard, safe—present with them in a living dream, a bright space apart from the wide wastes of the fast-passing world on the other side of waking. Theirs was a fire always going, a conversation waiting to be picked up where the last breath left off.

This is how I remember them.

And when the memory fades to fuzz, a final exhale, what I'm left with is the waiting.

Andy Topolski passed away on February 14, 2008, after a brief and one-sided fight with lung and kidney cancer. His wife and partner, Cindy Suffoletto, follows him on May 1, 2012, succumbing to the return of a cancer she'd beaten back during Andy's illness. It is three weeks short of my nineteenth birthday, finals week of my second semester at a small Jesuit college in Buffalo. My father tells me that the family—my mom, Sandy; her siblings, Dave and Tom; and my grandparents Hank and Annette—have decided I am best suited to give Cindy's eulogy. I am a writer; I am her godson; but more importantly I have a reputation for coolness, even distance. The job is mine because I can do it without crying.

I sit at a wooden hutch in a sixth-floor room in Bosch Hall, one of the first-year dorms. Behind me, my roommate, an eccentric redhead I hadn't chosen, plays Minecraft on his laptop, occasionally sending a horsey laugh into his headset. Sodium lights just above our window mark the quad in overlapping rectangles of glistening silver, and instead of writing I watch other freshmen crossing it: ghostly girls in T-shirts and gym shorts, guys shuffle-strutting in white tube socks and slides.

There's something capricious in the way neural circuits form without conscious input, without direction from a congress of foresight and sentiment. We can strain after impressions, ghost sensations from events that we know we experienced… and touch nothing in our inner dark. And at other times memory will—on its own—storm the conscious mind with sounds and images, terrible or merely mundane, that we never would have elected to keep.

I remember, for example, Cookie Crisps.

We were visiting Cindy and Andy's apartment in North Williamsburg in the mid-'90s. I would have been a toddler—serious, unnaturally talkative, with a face like a heavy melon. At that point, an only child. I don't remember how we filled those long summer days, what we talked about, whether we passed beneath the Twin Towers or visited the Statue of Liberty. I remember the vivid green of their rooftop garden, filled with potted plants and raised beds built over the rolled tar as hot in the afternoons as the surface of Mercury. And I remember Aunt Cindy reaching into a kitchen cabinet on our first morning in Brooklyn to pull out a box of Cookie Crisps, something I knew (and knew to desire) from TV but hadn't experienced in real life.

Cookies—for breakfast? Back home in Buffalo, Cap'n Crunch was my highest indulgence. That Aunt Cindy would have stocked in the cereal cabinet of her faraway apartment a box of bona fide cookies, and that one could eat these first thing in the morning, was entirely consistent with the view of my aunt and godmother that formed early and that I still carry today: full of fun and a simple largesse, free from the flimsy and conventional scruples I associated with other adults.

Seventeen years later I watch the slim black bar blinking at the top of an empty Word doc, a rectangle of artificial white suspended in the trapezoid of fluorescence that my dorm desk's built-in lamp casts. I know what I want to say about Cindy, what I want to tell the people who will gather at St. Martin's Church in South Buffalo this weekend. I want to tell them that Cindy was fun, that she was generous—that she was as free as she was caring, a paradox. I remember the way she made me feel, but when

I try to ground it in something specific, in a story, I come up with Cookie Crisps.

I feel the clamp of panic in my throat. Panic at the thought of the role I must perform for the family, for Cindy's friends, for strangers—panic at the possibility of failing them all. But beneath that, an even stranger and vaster sensation of encountering not the sudden loss of Cindy as a living person, a *present* presence in my life, but a silent entropy, a steady attrition of specificity that has been happening from the moment my earliest memories of her had formed.

Other family members want to help. They don't know that I'm struggling to write the eulogy, but they are processing grief in their own ways, free-associating fragments, scrolling Cindy's Facebook feed, opening shoeboxes of photographs—an attempt to collage her back to life. They share what they find.

My father texts me a picture of another laptop screen open to another cell phone picture of a film photograph that Cindy had posted to her timeline shortly after Andy had passed four years before. I recognize myself, but the image doesn't jog any memory. In the picture, taken during that trip in 1995, I sit next to Andy on a couch covered in a pink slipcover below the windows in their Brooklyn apartment, wrought iron and the garden's greenery visible through gauzy cream curtains behind us. Andy leans into me, holding in his large hands a comically tiny children's book. On Facebook, Cindy had added a comment meant to be in Andy's voice—but that I hear now in her own voice, dropping an octave to imitate him: ... *and see, Aidan, that's why we entered WWII.*

I don't remember the moment, but it helps me to free-associate, too.

I remember images: Cindy as the center of our hysterical attention on countless occasions; Cindy and my mother and grandmother tight to each other's shoulders like their own kind of Holy Family, three beings in one person, united in infectious, wildfire laughter.

I remember eras—remember the eight years of the Bush presidency through the polarity of my father and Cindy debating, with dazzling intelligence and unfailing respect, over holiday dinners.

I remember episodes or borrow ones that others relate to me. My little sister tells me about a time when she was six or seven years old, sitting on Cindy's lap in our grandparents' living room and drawing a simple figure on a notepad. The head sat oblong and horizontal like a resting watermelon. Gently, even hesitantly, Andy—then a Parsons art professor—leaned over. "You should turn the head around. The head slopes down to the chin." Cindy laughed and chided him as Talia sat in silent terror. "Let her draw it the way she wants," Cindy said.

But mostly I remember feelings. The feeling of fun. Of wonder and mystery. Of being seen and being really loved. Of a door always opening onto a much wider world than I knew as a child in Buffalo. Mostly I remember the feeling so familiar from Callicoon, where Cindy and Andy had moved in 2001—the feeling that it's always too early to leave a fire still burning.

Cindy and Andy left Buffalo for New York City almost a decade before I was born, depriving us of casual contact. My impressions of them would come entirely from "occasions"—our visits to New York and later to their house in Callicoon and their trips home for holidays. I grew up learning to keep in touch with other out-of-town relatives, but Cindy and Andy were different because they left Buffalo for different reasons. Andy and Cindy were artists. Even as a young child I understood this—understood that their lives were structured around people, dreams, challenges, economic exigencies, and conversations that didn't correspond to anything I could recognize in my own life in Buffalo.

Andy's art was a presence in our house growing up. Countless times, inhabiting different versions of myself, I stood before two of Andy's works hung one above the other in our back room. The larger was a Christmas gift to my parents, signed and dated 1997. In it, a portrait of my parents is doubled, side by side, manipulated with different tints. Finely drawn black lines and arcs frame this, giving way to arrows, then floating numbers and shapes. Letters spelling TALIA and AIDAN appear in red below—and are doubled in pencil, in Andy's own hand, block capitals. I recognized certain numbers as Mom and Dad's birthdays (in fact, I sometimes used the artwork as an emergency reference), but other numbers were harder to identify. A black string and a red string attached to screws in the backing cross directly over Dad's face, with a slightly menacing effect. The second piece, a thinner rectangle, incorporates a musical score, one-half delicately julienned; over this there is layered what appeared to be a topographical cross section in a faded blue; this again is crossed with red string, like the view from a bomber over a nuclear test site. In pencil Andy wrote what could be a key to a musical score, and below that other letters and numbers in a code I never tried to crack. I didn't "understand" the work but even as a child I recognized at once its elegance, the precision of the apparent collage—and could feel a sense of vicarious daring in imagining the hand bold enough to annotate in common pencil over shapes as cool, correct, and finished as these.

We grew up with Cindy's art, too. In the living room, above a record cabinet, my parents had hung one of Cindy's wooden sculptures. The piece is a rectangle carved lightly with three arches, suggesting the transept and apsidal chapels of a cathedral. The body is topped with a ridged lintel and two curved wooden pieces forming a crowning arch, and appended to the front is a smooth, dark piece of wood that, in contrast to the architectural elements behind it, seems like it might have come from an unlucky cello. It had none of the textual complexity of

Andy's work, but it appeared to me even more mysterious, the shapes bypassing the conscious mind, the resistant surface swimming with faint blooms of color that might have been intentional or might have been due to aging—an aspect that deepened the piece's suggestion of ancient origin.

Their work was never comprehensible to me. Some days I passed Andy's works without a glance, heading to get my bike from the garage. Cindy's sculpture disappeared every year behind the Christmas tree. If anything, the works' literal nearness more precisely articulated the distance between us—me, my sister, the rest of Cindy and Andy's families—and their world of art and artists.

Then, something changed.

In high school I realized that the act of reading I had always loved to excess yielded naturally to the act of writing—essays, stories, rhyming couplets, utter nonsense—and in turn I realized that the act of writing was really a way of *being*: being different, being heard and admired, being larger than life—being myself in infinitely variable ways. At the same time, I rushed toward other modes of expression and identification. I drummed in garage bands and discovered Herbie Hancock, made dozens of idiotic skits in the first days of YouTube, read the *Republic* and took umbrage at Plato's treatment of the poets. When our family took vacations, I lingered stubbornly in every gallery—Chicago's Art Institute, the National Gallery, the Kreeger—until my more easily sated parents ran out of patience. By the time I took the SAT, I knew I wanted to live a life in the arts.

Only two people I knew could tell me what that meant, what it required. And shortly both were gone.

I'm not thinking about any of this in my dorm room that first week of May in 2012. I am thinking about honoring my aunt.

The problem, I realize, isn't a deficiency of memory in the present. It is a deficiency of attention in the past. As a child, myopic, expecting all comfort to last forever, I passed up opportunities to *know* Cindy and Andy. Forced to consider for the first time the nature of my relationship with both of them, I come up with Cookie Crisps.

I save the file—"Cindy eulogy.doc"—a second time, though I still haven't put a single mark on the page.

After all the thousands of hours of writing—poems and satires, sophomoric autofictions, weekly columns for the college paper, even the simplest class assignments packed with pointless pyrotechnics—I sense that this is the first time I might produce something that matters to other people. Maybe the first time I might produce something that matters to me.

And I don't have the words to do it.

I think, then, that if I don't have my own words to work with, I might start with Cindy's.

A few months earlier she'd sent me an unexpected package. It was a padded envelope with a CD—Creedence Clearwater Revival. Cindy knew I was playing in jazz and jam bands; she watched and liked every video we put online. In college I was beginning to get paid gigs and had just recorded a demo as a session player for a much more talented guitarist. At just barely nineteen, music is only one of many doors into another life. Cindy knew what this feels like. She sent the disc with a short note, just one line: *I heard this, and thought of you.*

I took it, the gesture and her message, for the eulogy. Cindy had been dying even then, secretly, when she heard a song from the album—probably on the radio, one of the indistinguishable small-town classics stations she would have picked up between Callicoon and chemo appointments in the city—and thought to dig out the album and mail it to me. A piece of herself she knew she wouldn't need anymore. Cindy meant only the CD as a gift, but she had given me the words, too. I realized even then that they were mine to keep—and to keep handy.

I didn't realize how often, as the years passed, I would echo them back to her.

I heard this, and thought of you.

Each time waiting for an answer.

Beginnings on Essex

A DARK-HAIRED, DARK-EYED girl moves across the torn court-yard, passes under the corrugated tin overhang of a loading dock heavy with snow, and steps through a door—a door cut out from a set of bigger double doors—into a scene of ecstatic bric-a-brac. She wears a loose corduroy coat and a man's plaid shirt, her short hair pulled back by a broad bandanna, and a resting smile as contagious as a radio single. Heads turn at the change in the air—particulates of snow pulled in with the door's opening make it a wobbly foot-and-a-half into the cinder-block studio before evaporating in the heat from a wood-burning stove, captured and channeled by a complex architecture of clear plastic sheeting that lines and subdivides the space. An artist, she notices the walls first, hung with a mix of work by different hands—nude figures, abstractions, canvases with fragments of complex systems, in oils and carbons, pencil and ink, metal and gauze, alongside Polaroids, postcards, clipped advertisements, scraps of inspiration or in-jokes. Patches of Sheetrock that don't have anything taped or tacked to them are reserved for stacks of frames of all sizes and in every state of assembly. Next she notices the smell: a familiar and inviting mix of sawdust, stove smoke, charcoal, wool coats, and Marlboro Reds over an unmistakable undertone of American lager and warm bodies. And last she notices the broad hand gently press against the in-curve of her back, feels her small shoulder fit into a much bigger one. The scuff of her shoes across the loose charcoal on the floor sounds like a needle dropping into a new record.

. . .

Cindy and Andy at the Essex Art Center, 1980s.

I make my hands into a visor and press my face into the glass of the barn-style double doors of Essex Art Center Studio 30F. It's sunny, bone-warm, mid-August—and about forty years after Cindy first crossed this threshold.

The white rigid top of a pickup bed sits between me and the doors to 30F. Beyond it is a new, unpainted wooden ramp and covered patio leading to Big Orbit, a small art space, carrying on a tradition of exhibits and performances here nearly half a century old.

But this isn't the Essex Art Center of the '70s, once the unexpected nexus of everything of any interest in the arts community. The studio of the sculptor Larry Griffis Jr., who purchased the complex, once an icehouse serving the large Victorian homes of Buffalo's West Side, in 1969 and opened it to other artists, is gone. The pioneering DIY, mostly student-run gallery Hallwalls, the center's other famous tenant, is gone, too, moved into fancier digs downtown.[1] Green placards hang against the baking brick and tell stories of Griffis, Hallwalls, Big Orbit, and some of the other artists and organizations that have passed through this place.[2]

To my right, a freestanding sign designates a stretch of space as a parking spot for 19 Ideas, a boutique marketing firm, now the complex's anchor tenant. Behind some of the glass doors I can see renovations under way. Along the far wall of the sun-whitened dusty court, new sanctioned graffiti in electric gelato colors cover the corrugated doors of treasure-and-scrap-filled bays that once housed painters, sculptors, new media artists, and even some writers. Now the whole place seems to be waiting to be reborn as a microbrewery—a familiar postindustrial apotheosis. But some artists and originals are hanging on.

I run through the names of a dozen of Cindy and Andy's friends who lived and worked here, placing each inside the space they had occupied. I know their voices well enough now to set the whole complex echoing.

A month earlier I had missed a call from the photographer and publisher Mark Dellas. We had been playing phone tag since the spring and I knew what he wanted: new writing.

About once a year, Mark and I collaborated on a piece for his magazine, *Traffic East*. I profiled musicians and writers, opened up forgotten chapters of local history, found pockets of uncommon enterprise to praise, and Mark paired the words with his signature portraits, stylish and evocative. Our partnership began in 2012, when I sent him a short story. It was loosely autobiographical fiction, based on then-recent events: set in Callicoon, New York, it involved a quiet child, a death in the family, an emptying house, and a bonfire that burned for days. Mark liked the writing but not the piece. I sent him something else and he published it. We became fast friends and favorite collaborators.

But in the summer of 2020, mostly homebound because of the coronavirus pandemic, I was empty-headed and exhausted. Around the Fourth of July my fiancée, Rachelle, and I had booked the lower level of a barn outside Skaneateles, and planned to spend a long weekend reading, swimming, talking. Not writing. I let Mark go to voicemail.

In a moment of weakness, I thought of asking him to publish the first story I'd sent him, the one he'd been sitting on for eight years. I hadn't reread it but I thought of it often—that final image of a bonfire burning in the middle of an afternoon, the insatiable hunger of the ash heap.

Then I reminded myself why he hadn't chosen to publish it the first time: because it was a failed piece of writing, a false gesture in the wrong direction. The piece came from a persistent sense of loss—the loss of two real people I had known and loved—but it didn't bother to say anything about them.

One of the best pieces I had written for Mark was a profile of Karl Ove Knausgård, the product of interviews and observation during the writer's visit to Buffalo in March 2015. I couldn't write like Knausgård, and probably didn't want to, but I admired his lonely courage, his commitment to driving at his most difficult subject matter, asking blunt questions of himself at his most vulnerable moments.

I thought of another writer I admired, George Saunders—specifically that for decades he had been afraid to address the subject matter of his greatest book, *Lincoln in the Bardo*. I had interviewed Saunders five summers before, while he was finishing that book. The best writing and revising, he told me, amounted to a process of steering toward complexity and away from certainty, of always asking, *Can I be kinder?* and *Can I be braver?*

As I navigated the country highways that snake among the Finger Lakes, Rachelle scrolling Twitter in the seat beside me, I tried to put the certainty that was emerging into words. It was this: I thought of Cindy and Andy not merely often, but *always*. Memories of them were woven into the backdrop of so many of my encounters with the world—particularly the world of art and artists, the world that had once been theirs and the world that, years after they left it, I too called home. Cindy and Andy had left behind marks and messages—in their art but also in accidents, little bits of personality that survived them—that have served as guideposts to me as I moved through that world. And sometimes their memories have been a filter through which experiences of that world reach me.

This was my certainty—my starting point. What I had to do next—what I had to *write* next, I understood by then—lay in the opposite direction.

I could tell the story again. Not my story, but their story—my way. This time I could tell the truth. And if the truth proved out of reach, I could at least steer toward the difficult questions.

· · ·

By August 2020, I had asked plenty of questions and answered a few. I began on July 2 in Skaneateles, emailing my mom a battery, more than she was ready to answer. To buy time she offered names and pictures of our family trips to Brooklyn and Callicoon. "Start with Peter Muscato and Charlotta Kotik," she said. Start somewhere else.

Peter was a framer and a Buffalo kid whose movements through the art world corresponded with Andy and Cindy's a surprising number of times; they'd lived either in the same building or next door for more than two decades in Brooklyn. Charlotta was a Czech expat and curator, first at the Albright-Knox Art Gallery in Buffalo (now the Buffalo AKG Art Museum), later at the Brooklyn Museum. They were among Andy and Cindy's oldest and closest friends. I spoke with Peter and Charlotta over the phone, at length and on multiple occasions. They were excited—moved—to hear from me. Impressions and stories poured out of them—old wellsprings tapped. They gave me more names.

I interviewed members of Buffalo's 1970s avant-garde, some who stayed, others who followed or preceded Andy and Cindy's move to New York, and others who dispersed even farther: Robert Longo, Petr Kotik, Charlie Clough, Larry Lundy, Linda Brooks, Joan Posluszny, Bob Gulley, John Toth, Brian Duffy, Bill Maecker, Don Metz, and Marilynn Deane Mendell and two of her sons, Michael and James Tunkey. I interviewed the critic and gallery director Anthony Bannon, the German art insurance executive Christiane Fischer-Harling, and the art handler Tom Holt. I interviewed Andy's colleagues from Parsons, like Ann Ledy, Jim Osman, and Raymond Saá. I found close friends from Brooklyn and Callicoon: Janine Tramontana, Tom Kotik, and Ian and Amy Milner. I spoke with the gallerists Eric Siegeltuch, Jessica Berwind, Christel Schüppenhauer, and Stefan von Bartha. I reached people close to the great collector Wynn Kramarsky, including his daughter Laura and his right hand, Michael

Randazzo. I tracked down some of Cindy's high school friends and interviewed her employer in New York, the architect Richard Furman. I called and emailed their friends in Europe, like the artist Petr Mayr and the collectors Pieter and Marina Meijer. I interviewed Andy's brother Thomas and his nephew Alex, along with members of my own family.

Some sources in the art world declined to participate, for reasons that complicated my search as they became more apparent.

Where oral histories ended I consulted written and material history, particularly Andy's papers at the Burchfield Penney Art Center, but also archives at MoMA in New York and the Brooklyn Museum. I contacted town clerks, examined topographical maps and tax records, and paged through the digital archives of galleries in the US and Europe.

And I visited landmarks from Cindy and Andy's past, starting with the Essex Street Art Center's Studio 30F.

Beyond the glass my hands are now pressed against, 30F seems just-yesterday abandoned, and in haste: lathe, carpenter's paper, and cables have crashed down from the ceiling, and scrap metal and a mini fridge have been pushed to the center of the swept floor, apparently to make room for someone to park a clean green Elmwood Village Association utility cart. Two liters of Diet Coke stand untouched among the wreckage—and a gash in the plaster wall leads into 30E and someone else's history.

The scene is as crowded and senseless as the Redweld folder of notes I've been building out for a month—stuffed with articles, printed pictures, and transcriptions on yellow legal pads of two dozen hours of phone calls. More overwhelming than what I've learned is what I still don't know—a storm of relentless, uncountable questions.

The first was deceptively simple: Why are these two people still so present to me?

The questions that lay beneath it were not meant for a godson or nephew to ask. I had to ask them as a writer.

Why did Andy and Cindy leave friends, family, and a city that seemed poised to offer them everything?

What does it mean to "make it" as an artist?

What does it take?

And what does it feel like to live—and to die—on the border-line?

These lines of inquiry led me on an underground tour of some of the most interesting moments in late twentieth-century art history. I became intimately familiar with the interplay of personality and economics that made Buffalo in the 1970s the avant-garde of the avant-garde—a history essentially unknown to most who live here today and not even terribly well understood by most surviving participants. I toured the art markets of 1980s SoHo, Paris, and Berlin, and enjoyed a front-row seat for the implosion of the '90s—an American story of speculation, a tide of Wall Street money summoned by members of the art world's glamorous priestly caste like Larry Gagosian and Mary Boone, who lifted some artists to canonical status and left others beached in Brooklyn.

Relative and writer fused in the questions that followed.

Why did Andy—one of the great artists of his generation, with a singular mind, unsurpassed technical talent, and prolific output—end up as a footnote in books about lesser lights?

And why did Cindy—who sacrificed everything to become an artist—end up sacrificing her art?

This work has barely begun as I stand in the sunny courtyard of the Essex Art Center, peering through a dusty window, trying to squint past my own reflection. I try the handle but the door is locked.

I'm only beginning to sense the scope of the task ahead—just now perceiving that I won't be writing an *article* for Mark. The questions are too big for that.

I don't have many answers yet.

But I'm certain that soon, if I keep driving in this direction, I'll be able to see into this locked room, see past the wreckage of the decades—see it the way it looked one winter night in 1980.

Byway: A Fractional History of Money, Ideas, and Art in Buffalo

START SOMEWHERE ELSE, my mom had hinted. She meant that she needed time to think about my questions, to think about her sister. She didn't realize that she was giving me a method, a technique for bypassing the story I thought I wanted to tell and entering the story that I needed to tell.

Writers, detectives, and genealogists understand this. If you start from one point and walk into the past, the field of inquiry expands exponentially, soon becoming too much to put your arms around. The center appears farther away than it did at the beginning.

To get to the center of events in the past, you need to find the perimeter. Cover as many points as you can and march inward from each of them. The trick is start at all the somewhere elses— to start everywhere at once.

I

Scrape of six wooden folding chairs on a concrete floor. Snick of a Zippo. Rustle of papers—a mimeograph, two pages, stapled, on a simple letterhead: HALLWALLS, it says.

The two men at the head of the room—an empty, nearly square studio, clutter pushed back to the walls, center cleared for six chairs and a single folding table—present a diptych of a decade in transit. On one side is Charlie Clough, in a flannel shirt and corduroys, parted hair mussed from the day's work, his gentle face completed by a pair of round, bookish glasses and a mustache as though a small bird just now alighted on his lip. If Charlie is a product of the sixties, Robert Longo, beside him, leans full-tilt into the eighties. His beard is thick and sharply trimmed, like a fastidious guerrilla's. His hair is edging toward a pompadour. He's heading toward the intersection of Mel Gibson and Elvis Costello.

Looks are deceiving. Charlie is the guerrilla. At twenty-six, he is the oldest here, and the most hardened.[1] He's been to New York and back again. He spent a year at Pratt and another in Toronto at the Ontario College of Arts, waiting for his draft number to come up. He was also one of the first artists to move into the Essex Art Center, cutting a deal with the sculptor Larry Griffis to act as his assistant in exchange for space. And he had made a mark on Buffalo in a way that none of his generation, at that point, could claim. Under cover of darkness on Halloween night, 1972, Charlie and his friends Linda Brooks and Joe Panone snuck onto the grounds of the Albright-Knox, the region's preeminent art gallery, and installed an enormous wooden arrow—painted stop-sign red—piercing the limestone pediment of the temple.[2]

Charlie clears his throat. Now, it seems, the notorious prankster is getting serious.

"We intend to provide local access to the network that circulates information about developing ideas of art," he says, reading from a sheet in his hand.

Beside him, Bob Longo bores holes into the opposite wall with a brooding two-thousand-yard stare. But the others read along.

There's Michael Zwack, pensive like an apprentice monk, straight dark hair pulled back and big square glasses resting on an aquiline nose. Beside him is Nancy Dwyer, elbows on her knees, hair tumbling down her shoulders, broad mouth pulled into a tight, straight line as she parses each word. Around the circle is Diane Bertolo, brows knitted together, deceptively—she's dating

Charlie and has already read the draft. And finally Cindy Sherman, immediately recognizable with her short shock of cropped hair—her latest in a series of regular transformations.[3]

Michael raises his head and nods at the open door. Charlie, catching him, looks up to see Zwack's friend Pierce Kamke entering.

"Sorry," Pierce says, dropping into a squat against the wall.

Charlie's eyes fall back to the page.

"The network is individuals, publications, galleries, and museums—"

Laughter echoes from the hallway.

Nancy and Michael both laugh at the laughter. Then another head pokes around the corner—Larry Lundy.

"I was an hour ahead," he says. "Or an hour behind."

Larry slides in next to Pierce.

"Should we take roll call?" Diane asks the room. "Linda? Kitty? Joe H?"

"Andy?" Michael adds.

Bob speaks—quickly, sharply, out of the side of his mouth, a faint Brooklyn accent announcing itself.

"Let's take it from the top and run straight through, Charlie," he says.

The Essex complex is a venue for jokes and pot smoke, plenty of bullshit and a number of love affairs, but there is a seriousness to the kids from Buffalo, too—a seriousness, a savvy, a sense of timing, and a need filed down to a keen edge.

Charlie clears his throat again.

"February 2nd, 1975," he says. "We intend to provide local access…"

Charlie's arrow had made the news on November 1, but by November 2 the Albright-Knox had disassembled and discarded it. Less than three years later, however, Charlie, Robert, and the friends who had begun to gather around them weekly in the studio on Essex Street were poised not merely to make a mark on the cultural establishment—and the wider world of late twentieth-century art—but to become one of art's unruly appendages.

"Let's get together and call ourselves an institute," Paul Simon sang on "Gumboots," off 1986's *Graceland*. This was the spirit of the preceding decade in the arts—a gang of students and recent graduates in Buffalo had done exactly that. Hallwalls, the freewheeling exhibition and events collective formed in the old icehouse on Essex in 1975, would do exactly what its founders intended. Through shows, performances, and lectures featuring some of the most famous artists of the day, it would weave Buffalo's grassroots arts community into the wider networks of access and influence in the art world. At the same time, it would position its founders to capitalize on that access.

Many of the artists who joined or associated with the first Hallwalls cohort would go on to make names and make a living in the art world. Five of them—Cindy Sherman, Robert Longo, Charlie Clough, Nancy Dwyer, and Michael Zwack—would become permanent members of the Pictures Generation, as canonized by curator Douglas Eklund in a 2009 show at the Met. And two among the original cohort, Sherman and Longo, stand with the most celebrated—and best-compensated—artists of their generation.

Other participants—like Andy Topolski and Cindy Suffoletto and countless contemporaries—would both benefit from and be stifled by their association with Hallwalls in complicated ways as the decades unfolded.

II

Start somewhere else. What happened in late 1974 in a former icehouse on Essex Street in Buffalo was possible because of events set in motion in February 1913 in New York City on Lexington Avenue between Twenty-Fifth and Twenty-Sixth Streets.

The International Exhibition of Modern Art at the 69th Regiment Armory—later simply called the *Armory Show*—imported the latest European art, and the latest European art controversies, to the United States. Thousands of Americans encountering modern art for the first time swiftly took up impassioned positions for and against.

On the side of the moderns was one son of Buffalo, A. (Anson) Conger Goodyear. Born June 20, 1877, and raised in high Victorian style at 723 Delaware Avenue,[4] Conger was heir to a business and political dynasty that reached from Buffalo to Bogalusa to Washington, DC.[5] He completed his undergraduate studies at Yale in 1899 and followed in his father's footsteps—first into the lumber and rail business, and then in 1912 succeeding him as director of the Buffalo Fine Arts Academy, the parent organization of the Albright Art Gallery. Presumably this responsibility and his own growing taste for the modern art coming out of Europe drew him to New York for the fateful encounter the following year.

At the *Armory Show* the young Buffalo industrialist saw Marcel Duchamp's *Nude Descending a Staircase No. 2*,[6] and Constantin Brâncuși's *The Kiss*. He returned to the Queen City and to his post at the head of the Buffalo Fine Arts Academy, with limitless cash and a powerful itch.

"It's a mockery."

"I think you're being a bit high-minded. Uncharacteristically, I might add."

Frank Goodyear Jr.'s glance says everything. Across from him, E. B. Green Jr., son of the famous architect Edward Brodhead Green, blushes and lifts a tall sweating glass. Ice avalanches to his waiting lips. He frowns, shakes the glass once, and sets it down beside the cards they've forgotten.

"It's—"

"Whiskey highball, sir?"

"That's right," E. B. Jr. nods once to the man behind the bar at the back of the tiny room, which shimmers with cigarette smoke and heat from a cozy fireplace.

" 'Nother for me, too, Louis," Frank says.

"But it isn't a social club," E. B. Jr. presses on. "And it isn't a *bordello*."

"What about here? Would you hang it here? At the club?"

"No, no, listen—it's a *museum*."

"This is your father speaking."

"This is your *nephew* we're talking about."

And here, at least, they can talk freely. Frank and E. B. Jr. sit at a small wooden table over an abandoned game of bridge. The exposed beams of the ceiling hang low, giving the room a conspiratorial feel. The walls are bare except for a single framed portrait of two rows of young men.

The house, 164 Elmwood Avenue, belongs to E. B. Jr. In three years he will sell it to the Pack Corporation, or the Pack Club, an exclusive fraternity that Frank Goodyear Jr. recently helped to found. Already in early spring 1926, it is transforming into a clubhouse.

Ever since Bill Donovan's Prohibition raid on the Saturn Club in 1923, the habitual drinkers among the Buffalo elite had to search for safer harbors. Frank Goodyear and a few friends rustled up a membership of fifty-two and capped participation there—at the number of playing cards in a standard deck.

The Pack Club's founders' grandfathers had formed the Saturn Club in 1885 as a relaxed and somewhat mischievous alternative to the Buffalo Club, established in the starchier times of 1867. Now in 1926, the great-grandsons of Buffalo's first formalized social elite are shaping a still more exclusive and still less conservative klatch, chiefly for the purpose of bridge playing and hard drinking without drawing attention.[7]

But "liberal" and "conservative" are slippery labels—always, but especially toward the end of the Roaring Twenties, between the wars, and especially in Buffalo, a rich city far from the influence of Atlantic tides.

"You're being a Brodhead," Frank quips.

"And you're a bit tight."

E. B.'s bright face betrays the truth: he's the tighter of the two. Still, he waits until Louis sets down the fresh whiskey highballs and retreats behind the bar to snatch his up.

"This Picasso's terribly well known," Frank says.

"I don't particularly care," E. B. says, taking pains to enunciate each syllable. "Picasso…he's a pornographer with…with *no technique*."

"That's rather an insupportable assertion, Ed. I don't pretend to understand the new style but…"

"It's—"

"It has character. It has…it has *life* in it, Ed."

"Giving old Ansley a hard-on isn't the sort of 'life' I think we should be bringing into the—"

E. B. cuts himself off. The room is small. A few heads have turned up from other card games at the mention of the esteemed reformer Ansley Wilcox, an avuncular eminence universally beloved.[8]

But the issue isn't—strictly—the erections of septuagenarians. The issue is *La Toilette*, a painting by Pablo Picasso completed in 1906 and just acquired by the Albright Art Gallery and its Fellows for Life Fund, at the direction of Conger Goodyear. Freshly post–Blue Period, the painting depicts a naked woman using both hands to tie (or untie) her hair, standing toward the viewer and before a mirror held by a handmaid in classical profile, the latter's face (androgynous and curiously suggestive of the artist's own) inscrutable, staring past her mistress and as if beyond the left edge of the canvas.

The acquisition catalyzes the first great controversy among the gallery's directors. They have put up with Conger Goodyear's modern tastes—and his generosity—so far. At first he focused on sculpture; and though E. B. Green Sr., the architect of the neoclassical Albright Art Gallery, had opinions on sculpture (he would convince John Albright to pay extra for caryatids commissioned from the Beaux-Arts master Augustus Saint-Gaudens to complete the temple), he and the other directors kept quiet while Conger emptied the center courtyard of its plaster casts of Greco-Roman glories and replaced them with new works by Epstein, Despiau, Dobson, Bourdelle, Haller, Maillol, Poupelet, Rodin, Brâncuşi, Noguchi, and Lehmbruck. These were, at least, originals, and restricted to the courtyard.

Conger's donations and acquisitions in the realm of painting were somewhat more contentious.

Between 1920 and 1964, Conger would acquire and donate to the Albright 361 works of art. These included Paul Gauguin's *Spirit of the Dead Watching*, Giacomo Balla's *Dynamism of a Dog on a Leash*, Salvador Dalí's *The Transparent Simulacrum of the Feigned Image*, Camille Pissarro's *Peasants in the Field, Eragny*, Jean-Baptiste-Camille Corot's *Italian Monk Reading*, Roger de La Fresnaye's *Still Life with Three Handles*, Honoré Daumier's *Laundress on the Quai d'Anjou*, Vincent van Gogh's *The Old Mill*, and comparable works by Henri de Toulouse-Lautrec, Edgar Degas, Pablo Picasso, Mary Stevenson Cassatt, Paul Klee, Pierre-Auguste Renoir, Juan Gris, Amedeo Modigliani, Henri Matisse, and Suzanne Valadon, along with countless of their studies and sketches.

But in 1926, Picasso's *La Toilette* hits a trip wire. This year Conger has a nomination to serve as president of the board. Fearing an expansion of his campaign to modernize the museum, longtime director E. B. Green Sr. makes every effort to scupper his candidacy. Green secures the support of other archconservatives on the board. He activates proxies, like his son. It is a war fought largely out of sight for most of the city—with pitched battles and quick sorties in the Buffalo Club, the Saturn Club, and the Pack Club—until finally it resolves in Conger's defeat and ouster from the board.[9]

Conger doesn't wait around to take his punishment. He takes himself—and his ideas, his collection, and his still-plentiful reserves of cash—to New York City. There he meets with Abby Aldrich Rockefeller, Lillie P. Bliss, and Mary Quinn Sullivan along with their friends Murray Crane and Paul Sachs. All share a taste for modern art, and mutual friendships with some of the leading modern artists. All understand that at the time, the United States lacks any gallery dedicated to collecting modern art. And each one is richer than Croesus. Abby and the others know Conger had attempted to rectify this in Buffalo and had failed—had been ostracized. So they invite him to serve as the first president of the Museum of Modern Art.

III

"Time forks perpetually toward innumerable futures," Borges wrote. In one of them, MoMA's hundredth anniversary, in 2029, happens here—in Buffalo.

But time forked in 1913 and again in 1926.

Nineteen twenty-six was the year Conger Goodyear founded the Albright's Fellows for Life Fund, tapping a wellspring of cash for the unrestricted purchase of contemporary art.

It was the year Conger directed the gallery to purchase Picasso's *La Toilette*, triggering an outcry and his ouster.

It was the year, in the depths of Prohibition, that our frontier town's silk-stockinged Saturnalia moved into a nondescript white house at 164 Elmwood Avenue, a discreet place to drink, debate the modern, and foment social coups.

And it was the year that Seymour H. Knox II, eleven years

Conger's junior, heir to the Woolworth's five-and-dime fortune, and already a vice president of the Marine Midland Bank, joined the Albright board—and, at Conger's urging, the Fellows for Life Fund.

Down one path we might have found Buffalo, the acknowledged mecca of the modern—with Frank Lloyd Wright houses, a perfectly preserved Pierce-Arrow showroom, F. Scott Fitzgerald's childhood home, an Eero Saarinen concert hall, the towering grain silos that inspired the International Style—and, of course, *the* Museum of Modern Art.

But taking the other tine—the one we're following now— instead we find MoMA in Manhattan and Seymour Knox in a helicopter somewhere over Paterson, New Jersey.

The relentless percussion of the chopper blades had faded over the Finger Lakes. The closer Seymour gets to New York, the easier it is to forget he's in a metal bucket in the sky. Beside him a tall, square-jawed man sits focused on the pages in his lap— flipping between a copy of *Art in America* and the latest *New York Times*, cross-referencing names and dates in each. They've flown this route so many times now—nearly every other weekend for a year. The silver spires of the city soar before them—Seymour feels as if he could touch them, pick them up like polo sticks and raise them high above his head.

From 1926 to his death in 1964, the exiled Goodyear, serving as president of the explosive MoMA, continued to send extraordinary gifts back to Buffalo.

And as Conger approached the end of his life, his younger friend Seymour began to think about his own legacy. He had funneled millions to the Albright Art Gallery. But, approaching fifty years old, he hadn't made a *mark* on the city—not the way Conger had in New York, starting a museum of his own, according to his own tastes.

The problem was that Knox didn't know his own tastes.

In truth, there is disagreement on this point. The party line among the art intelligentsia, echoed by *Buffalo News* critics and docents for decades, is that Seymour had exceptional taste in art, taste that was adventurous and ahead of his time.

But this didn't become evident until Knox was half a century old. For more than three decades he had carried out his charge at the Buffalo Fine Arts Academy like a foot soldier, rarely opining on acquisitions.

Buffalo News critic Jean Reeves, quoted in Knox's obituary, leaves a clue: "His outlook was always youthful and adventurous, and he was unfailingly receptive to new ideas and techniques."

Receptivity was the key. For in 1955, Gordon Smith replaced Edgar Schenck as director of the Albright and brought a clear vision to revivify the museum with a mission to collect the art of its time. To that end, he recruited the affable, pliable, and fabulously wealthy Knox to serve as president.

Knox was a businessman, a banker, a retail magnate sitting on a fortune from the Gilded Age, a squash enthusiast, and a world-class polo player.[10] But Smith guessed he had the potential to become one of the all-time great patrons of artists and the arts. The record doesn't reveal where the new board member stood amid the dustup over *La Toilette*, but under Smith's influence, Seymour would prove as simpatico to his own time as Conger had been to his.

"Art should be acquired to be seen and enjoyed, not to be stored in a warehouse," Knox once remarked. "There is no point in buying more for myself. Where would I put it?"

In their frequent helicopter trips to New York City, Smith would guide Knox toward the newest artists of the emerging postmodern schools: Willem de Kooning, Arshile Gorky, Jackson Pollock, Robert Motherwell, Philip Guston, before these names became famous.

To a significant degree, Gordon and Seymour *made* them

famous. It was the Albright, not MoMA or the National Museum or any other regional gallery of note, that first collected and canonized these artists.

They had help from another expat aristocrat. Martha Kellogg Jackson had left her home and her husband, John Anderson, in Buffalo, and in 1953 opened a gallery in New York City—first in a brownstone at East Sixty-Sixth Street and then, after 1955, in a modern glass-fronted space on East Sixty-Ninth. Drawing on a considerable inheritance—her grandfather was Spencer Kellogg, a baron of Buffalo's silo-dotted waterfront and founder of what was once the world's largest linseed oil company—Martha quickly made a name as a discerning dealer and promoted dozens of up-and-coming artists from the US and Europe. A former member of the Albright's acquisitions advisory committee, she kept in touch, cut deals, and served as a guide for Seymour and Gordon on their helicopter trips to the city.[11]

Following Martha's taste and Gordon's tactful urging, Seymour became the leading proponent of the modernist and abstract expressionist movements.[12] He aggressively acquired these works and donated them to the museum in Buffalo—so many that in 1962 it became the Albright-Knox.

By 1969, the Albright-Knox was home to the world's largest and best collection of the art of the American 1950s and '60s.[13] This was so widely recognized that artists who wanted to cement their reputations in that canon didn't wait for Seymour to come with his checkbook—they donated their works, an investment in their legacy. Most notably, Clyfford Still donated a virtually unheard-of thirty-five pieces to the gallery—a significant number even against the grand total of seven hundred works that Knox would acquire and bequeath in his lifetime. The Pop Art sculptor Marisol would bequeath her entire estate to the Albright-Knox in 2016—likely because of Seymour's early and sustained support.

Gordon Smith and Martha Jackson may have shaped Seymour's

tastes. But Seymour shaped the times he lived in; his tastes became the tastes of the nation, and then the world.

And, to his credit, he did more than merely acquire works. He was also a friend and patron to numerous artists—even Andy Warhol would produce his portrait. And he brought those artists home, not merely as guests to show off at the Saturn Club or in private salons, but as teachers and ambassadors to the people of Buffalo.

In the summers, Knox put on free festivals that brought the world's most famous modernists and most exciting new names. Marcel Duchamp, Jackson Pollock, and Jasper Johns all visited, gave talks, praised the many charms of the Queen City, and left their art behind. The Festival of the Arts Today, held in 1965 and 1968, brought together Gordon Smith's Albright-Knox and the Buffalo Philharmonic Orchestra, then under Lukas Foss's baton, into a dizzying collision: John Cage, Merce Cunningham, and Marcel Duchamp all performed, exhibited, and talked over the course of an action-packed six weeks.

Whether one knew it or not, to grow up in Buffalo in the 1960s and '70s meant to come of age at the swirling center of the world of postmodern art and artists.

Banker, businessman, and tastemaker, Seymour Knox was also an ally to Governor Nelson Rockefeller and chairman of the governing board of the University of Buffalo, a private medical college founded in 1846. In 1962, the same year that the Albright became the Albright-Knox, Rockefeller and Knox hatched a plan to merge the private university into the state system and transform it into a powerhouse research institution, the SUNY flagship, a "Berkeley of the East": the University at Buffalo (UB).[14]

Under Rockefeller—one among a rising class of second- and third-generation centimillionaires and billionaires who leaned left (from the right), collected art, and believed in directly funding its creation—philanthropy and state funding reached dizzying postwar heights.[15] For UB to succeed under Knox's and Rockefeller's plan, it would have to function as one of the state's— if not the nation's—biggest spigots of funding available to artists, scientists, philosophers, and critics. There was money enough for a medical school and a law school; for mechanical, civil, and aerospace engineering departments; for the NPR affiliate station that would launch Terry Gross and Ira Flatow; for the nation's library of record for twentieth- and twenty-first-century poetry in English; for the laboratories of Nobel laureate Herbert A. Hauptman, revolutionary in the fields of mathematics and chemistry; for a nuclear fission reactor. And there was money enough for a jewel of a liberal arts college,[16] one equal to the radical spirit of the early '60s and flush with the no-strings cash needed to attract the era's brightest academics and cultural exponents.

Cash—in the form of endowed professorships, residencies, and project funding—began to draw artistic talent from across the country, and this constant influx of academics and artists made Buffalo more attractive for homegrown talent, too. The faculty of the '60s and '70s—both visitors like Jacques Derrida, Michel Foucault, J. M. Coetzee, John Cage, Gregory Corso, Roland Barthes, Hélène Cixous, and Charles Mingus, and long-term members like Julius Eastman, Tony Conrad, John Barth, Leslie Fiedler, René Girard, and Robert Creeley—created prolifically while in Buffalo.

More importantly for the purposes of sustaining that creativity, many seized grants and endowments and set up funded fiefdoms dedicated to their chosen crafts.

The Fine Art Department looked outward into the broader Western New York community and offered three-month intensive summer sessions open to matriculated and nontraditional students. With state and Rockefeller money they offered summer stipends to faculty and star student teachers alongside national names—like the abstract expressionist Robert De Niro Sr., who taught in Buffalo for several consecutive summers.

In 1964, UB music department chair Allen Sapp and Buffalo Philharmonic conductor Lukas Foss approached Howard Klein, executive director of the Rockefeller Foundation, with an idea. The notion was to create a fine arts institute couched within, but distinct from, the university—they would use it to attract the greatest living musicians and composers. The catch was that these artists wouldn't be faculty members, wouldn't even have to teach graduate seminars. They were to come to Buffalo and *create*. Their presence alone would benefit the university and the city. Local music lovers would attend their concerts—free or discounted—and because of the location of the institute on campus, university students might bump into the leading creative minds of the day on their way to class.

"Great—how much do you need?" Klein asked.

He gave them $300,000 on the spot—closer to $3 million in today's dollars—to found the Center of the Creative and Performing Arts.

Foss—a German prodigy and recognized genius, friend and peer to both Arnold Schoenberg and Leonard Bernstein—tapped his network and made good on his promise to bring the best to Buffalo. Fellows at the CCPA were called the "Creative Associates"; these giants of contemporary composition met regularly, pushed each other and pushed each other's buttons, and put on nearly 300 concerts and as many as 400 additional smaller performances between 1964 and 1980.

In 1971, a medieval literature specialist named Gerald O'Grady, sucked into the swirl of fast-opening faculty positions, switched his focus to the nascent field of media studies. He founded Media Study / Buffalo, a nonprofit exhibition space that put on film workshops and offered students and artists access to equipment. By 1973 he'd persuaded the University at Buffalo to open its own Center for Media Study and to fund five additional tenured faculty positions. O'Grady hired Hollis Frampton and Paul Sharits (pioneers of structuralist film), Steina Vasulka and Woody Vasulka (already famous as the founders of The Kitchen in New York), and Tony Conrad (noted minimalist musician and video artist). Leading lights like Peter Weibel and James Blue soon followed. It is no exaggeration to say that the center of new media shifted overnight to Buffalo.

Almost simultaneously, the photographer Robert Muffoletto, who had earned his MFA in visual studies at UB (and who also had a workshop at the Essex Art Center), founded the Center for Exploratory and Perceptual Arts (CEPA), the first photography-focused exhibition space in Buffalo and one of the first of its kind in the nation. One of its earliest exhibitions featured Ellen Carey and Cindy Sherman, then a student. To this day, the Denver-based artist Roger Rapp keeps a CEPA flyer from 1975 tacked near his desk. It was the very first time, he tells me, that he saw an institution put out a call for *digital* art.

The writers and critics at the university never did agree on a new name for themselves, but they were almost as effective as the artists and musicians in expanding tenured faculty positions and funding visiting professorships. The leading literary critics came to UB and established Buffalo's place in the network of postmodern literary studies. The experimental and deconstructivist fiction writer Raymond Federman held a position from 1964 to 1999, and he brought and kept close visiting peers like Walter Abish. Leslie Fiedler brought friends like the science fiction writer Samuel Delany for repeat visits. Meanwhile Robert Creeley and other poets, bringing the flame of Black Mountain College to Buffalo, held weekly—*weekly*—readings at the longtime pub at the corner of Essex and Rhode Island, the obvious watering hole for tenants of the icehouse. In 1975, Buffalo's Debora Ott hosted the poet Diane di Prima at the Allentown

Community Center; this event birthed Just Buffalo, a literary organization focused on readings and opportunities for members of the community—working writers and hobbyists—to learn and share work. With help from Creeley and other connected academics, it would go on to host Ed Dorn, Allen Ginsberg, Diane di Prima, Peter Orlovsky, Alice Notley, Ted Berrigan, and other writers for community readings and workshops.

The professors bought or rented inexpensive homes tucked snugly among the brick roads and maple, linden, and crabapple trees of Central Park, Parkside, Elmwood Village, and an emerging neighborhood called University Heights.[17] In the '60s, professors from around the country and the world flooded into these affordable Foursquares, Craftsmans, and bungalows below their College on the Hill—often on mortgages the SUNY system subsidized.

And, though lacking, perhaps, the same prestige, and certainly lacking access to the biggest spigots of state cash, other no-less-talented artists and critics and innovators secured professorships at Canisius College and SUNY Buffalo State (affectionately known as Buff State), which started hiring more and more faculty to accommodate enrollment surging on the GI Bill and the baby boom. Tenured and visiting luminaries from every institution held court with students in their parlors, offering liquor, books, encouragement, and occasionally a department travel stipend—sometimes even offering connections to agents and collectors and gallerists and postdoc fellowship committee chairs at other institutions—and their students would disperse, late at night, flush with pot and philosophy, back to their rented three- and four- and five-bedroom apartments, back to their parents' houses, back to shared West Side studios.

Much of this is public record—available if you know where to look. But over the course of several visits and phone calls, Tony Bannon, Don Metz, Charlie Clough, Linda Brooks, and other living beneficiaries of Buffalo's postwar cultural boom helped me to connect the dots from UB to other cultural institutions, and in the process adumbrate the valent influence of these networks of money and power on the individuals actually *producing* the culture.

Among the students and artists who stayed in the region, many secured their own professorships or gigs at emerging galleries like Buff State's Burchfield; they strove and often succeeded to create in new, formal and informal associations the same heat and pressure they'd found in Creative Associates concerts and professors' salons.

In 1960, with Governor Rockefeller's support, Knox also helped to orchestrate the founding of the New York State Council on the Arts, an expensive proposition that "Rockefeller Republican" state senators had to ram past considerable opposition. It had an immediate impact that reached far beyond New York.

Knox was an outlier—in means and duration of focus—but he wasn't alone. A critical mass of the state's and the city's moneyed elite and elected politicians were genuinely interested in the contemporary arts in this period. Members of the Buffalo Common Council like Ned Regan and Bill Hoyt were regulars at art exhibitions—and they took their interests and advocacy to higher offices, like the state assembly and comptroller's office. Businessmen like Sheldon Berlow, a commercial real estate broker with close ties to the University at Buffalo and its foundation, or Charles U. Banta, "dean of Buffalo stockbrokers," or Armand Castellani, the emperor of supermarkets, assembled their own salons of artists, critics, and fellow collectors. The artist Roger Rapp recalled a couple living near Delaware Park who turned the second floor of their home into a small gallery, with regular exhibitions open to the public.

And to the north in Niagara County, the powerful Republican operative Earl Brydges, a state senator from 1949 to 1972, championed the creation of Artpark, which finally opened in '74 on a former industrial waste dump beside the breathtaking Niagara River Gorge. An unprecedented experiment in state-sponsored large-scale and continuous public art, Artpark commissioned and hosted hundreds of avant-garde artists to experiment and execute site-specific projects on its 108 acres. It attracted dancers, sculptors, orchestras, earth artists, new media and performance artists, and more[18]—and it paid them all.

Each of these stories is remarkable. But it's the simultaneous emergence and convergence of them all that made this time so explosive. The region wedged between the Great Lakes Erie and Ontario birthed Hallwalls, CEPA, Artpark, and Just Buffalo in fewer than eighteen months. And even that tally leaves plenty out of frame. This is the environment, I came to understand, that fostered Andy's and Cindy's earliest artistic ambitions.

"It was a congeries of people who were in positions to make things happen," Tony Bannon remembers.

IV

The room is dim, the beige linoleum floor reflects a starry night of track lights, and the gauzy curtains over the windows put in mind an infirmary or a nursing home—but the energy is so high that there might have been a Tesla coil tucked in a corner. It pricks the skin, makes the lungs work like altitude. It's opening night.

The first Hallwalls show isn't at Hallwalls. The collective famously took its name from the hall that ran between Charlie Clough's and Robert Longo's studios at the Essex Art Center: the walls would be their gallery. But before they could welcome the world into their own space, they needed to get their name out.

First Bob and Charlie invite the artist Robert Irwin, then in New York, to give a talk at Buff State. To their surprise, Irwin agrees—he flies up on his own dime on December 18, 1974, while

Bob and Charlie work the phones, telling everyone and their cousin where and when to show up—and Hallwalls's MO takes shape.

Construction begins in earnest on Essex, and everyone does something: Pierce Kamke, a welder, installs track lighting, while Michael Zwack hangs drywall, all with a little bit of the nonprofit Ashford Hollow's money. Meanwhile Bob and Charlie scheme to keep up momentum. Hallwalls has strong ties to both Buff State and UB, and the founders know those ties will be essential to their plans.[19] Charlie and Bob approach Judy Treible, coordinator of Gallery 219 in UB's Norton Hall, and she quickly offers her space for their debut exhibition.

Spatial Survey, a small group show of sculpture and situational work, opens at Gallery 219 on January 22, 1975. The featured artists, which Charlie curates, are Robert Longo, Roger Rapp, Joe Panone, and Andrew Topolski.

The space is less than ideal. Sixteen by thirty feet of reflective linoleum, one wall features a thinly curtained window onto the Norton Hall parking lot, a palisade of sodium lamps in the icy dark, and the opposite wall is punctured with huge glass cutouts, like the space was formerly a kindergarten or an undergraduate science lab. These allow only glances from passersby—flyers for basketball games, Valentine's socials, and beer blasts are taped to the opposite side, framed by the interior casing as if these, too, are part of the exhibition.

But the artists are unfussy. If anyone cares, they don't mention it.

Andy takes the left wall and hangs half a dozen of his line drawings—simple and elegant, invented runes referring to architecture and the Earth's surface, already a recognized style.

Robert Longo takes the opposite end. He stretches plastic sheeting floor to ceiling, wall to wall, and isolates a volume of the room.

Joe Panone also plays with conceptual space; on the floor in front of Longo's sheet he defines an eight-foot square in neon, using the play of light through the room for various demarcations in two and three dimensions.

Roger Rapp, an MFA student in sculpture at UB who joined the lineup at Andy's suggestion, brings three sculptures in wood and brick—each a cube comprising twenty-four pieces of material, four to each of the six sides, arranged on the principle of rotational symmetry.[20]

The room fills up quickly by quarter after seven. Liberal arts professors in corduroy jackets and fine arts professors in pleated jeans; plenty of shaggy students; and what seems like every aspiring artist in the region.

Linda Cathcart,[21] curator at the Albright-Knox, shows up early. She taps Charlie Clough's arm and says something that makes him giddy with laughter. But everybody's a little giddy tonight, helium-high. She asks for introductions and Charlie leads her in a circuit around the room.

Charlotta Kotik, Linda's colleague at the AK, shows up after her kids are in bed. Hi Bob, hi Andy, hi Joe, hi Roger. She's already spent many nights on Essex getting to know these artists. She thinks they'd benefit from a different light—and a little more of it. She'll compare mental notes with Linda to bring to the AK's new boss, Bob Buck.

Tonight the students, tastemakers, and gatekeepers are all part of the same crowd. The featured artists clown around. Andy snaps pictures with his treasured Hasselblad, making three-by-three slides of the show. Along with the work, he captures Roger recumbent inside Joe's neon, aping the arrangement of his own rotational symmetry sculptures.

For Charlie, world-wise and hip to the import of the first impression, the selection of artists for the first Hallwalls show would be a matter of aesthetic leavened with politics—not something to leave to chance. The exhibition would set the table and the tone, he knew: it had to be contemporary, cool, ecumenical, unapologetic, a little bit messy, and definitely headed elsewhere.

I visit Charlie Clough at his East Aurora studio on May 31, 2021, around six in the evening. He's in the basement of the Roycroft Campus, the former printmaking studio of the Arts and Crafts movement. We greet each other in the hallway, unmasked, when this still feels like a big deal. He's dressed in black, with gray hair combed back, and Van Halen fills the hall from a Bluetooth speaker in his studio.

First he gives me the tour. On the second floor, enormous Clough paintings dominate the Great Hall. They're characteristic of the practice he developed around 1971, which imitates finger paints—but on a bigger scale—using appendages of various sizes made from thick wooden sticks and plump pads of tape or another material, applying latex paints to plastic canvases. On the next level is his private office and library—filled with books on countless movements in art, on philosophy, on the *I Ching*; and also brilliant minerals of every size. ("I'm a rock guy, too," he tells me.) This was once Elbert Hubbard's office.

Before I ask him any of the questions I've prepared, he takes me back downstairs and I suit up in a plastic bib and elastic boots slipped over my socks. Across the narrow hallway is another studio where Charlie has set up one of his canvases, several small man-made "thumbs," and a table of paints. For the past three years he's invited members of the community and visitors passing through to take part in an art project, an experiment in authorship and collective creation. Each visitor paints a new layer onto the existing work, covering up any evidence of the previous visitor under thick layers of latex. Then, at the end of the season, Charlie gouges deep into the canvas, like the glaciers that shaped this landscape, revealing by chance the many layers of intention beneath the surface.

It's my turn. While Charlie waits across the hall, I look into the buckets of paint, test the awkward applicators in each hand. I think about the first mark I want to make.

I barely consider the painting that I'm covering up. I pour pools of true blue, Barbie pink, electric lime. I roll and swirl the wooden thumb to fill the canvas, a kind of cosmic look. After a few minutes I discover other ways to use the applicator. I can rotate the stick to twist colors together. I can use the narrow edge, like a fingernail, to trace bright arcs through fields of other colors. I cover up my own work several times before I'm finished.

"Sorry," I say, shuffling back into the main studio and loosening the bib's plastic strap. Charlie lifts his readers to his forehead and appraises me kindly. I start to explain why I took so long—learning to use new techniques.

Charlie is benignly unconcerned with my artistic journey. Maybe he's heard the same story before.

"Some people take three minutes, some people are in there for an hour," he says, standing to turn off the music.

It's interesting that someone so curious about chance and blurred authorship is the same artist whose precision, consistency, and cunning got Hallwalls off the ground and forever altered the fates of artists in Buffalo.

But in the beginning, at least, Hallwalls wasn't really *about* Buffalo.

"It was an import-export model," he says to me.

Charlie had explained this for a *New York Times* reporter a few years before. The concept was "to figure out which artists ahead of us we were interested in and to bring them in, and those artists got to know who we were, so that when we went to New York, we'd have an audience. And the fact that we were in proximity to the Albright and Artpark and Media Studies meant that we could bait them," he told the reporter.[22]

He puts it a little more colorfully to me. When Charlie and Bob

Longo found out about a major artist slated to visit one of Buffalo's established institutions, they'd buttonhole them at the airport or even accost them in New York.

"Or we relied on Buffalo's winter weather to waylay folks here for a few days, and give a talk or do a show. And plenty said yes."

Charlie and Bob tightly controlled the programming.[23] They did so to make the right impression on Buffalo tastemakers and visiting artists—but mostly to build their own networks.

Their aesthetic was established in the debut at Gallery 219, with Andy, Bob, Roger Rapp, and Joe Panone. Just three weeks later, on February 22, 1975, the cleanup and drywall and track lighting at Essex were finished, and Hallwalls—first an idea, now a place—was ready for the public. The collective—twelve core members now, with another dozen regular helpers—mounted a huge exhibition of 100 works by 26 artists. They followed by announcing an ambitious slate of upcoming events—incredible, in retrospect.

Working on Paper: Developing the Idea, they called the home-turf debut.[24] Reputation established, they could play a little looser, raise the volume. They basically invited "anybody who had any sort of avant-garde reputation," Charlie had told the *Times*. Bill Baer, Linda Brooks, Jeff Catalano, Charlie Clough, Peter Frank, someone named "Georgenes," Duayne Hatchett, Joe Hryvniak, Pierce Kamke, Les Krims, Richard "Link," Robert Longo, Larry "LP" Lundy, Philip Malkin, "Marcus-Tamalonis," Joe Panone, Barbara Jo Revelle, Paul Sharits, Keith Smith, Peter Sowiski, Alex Sweetman, Andrew Topolski, Kurt White, Michael Zwack, and two others uncredited to this day.

The twenty-six comprised scenesters and newcomers, loners and hipsters, some of the biggest names in the local arts and some complete obscurities, prominent faculty and students who would eclipse them.

The exhibition was huge. It was a smash.

It reached up and grabbed NYSCA's purse strings.

It spelled the beginning of the end for the founders' time in Buffalo.

But most importantly, it signaled something significant to the generation rising behind them: there's space for you.

There's money.

There's time.

There's a playbook.

Or not.

You can do it with us or you can do it on your own.

And if you want you can get the hell out.

I Blame You for All the Good in Our Family

A painting is not a record of what was said and what the replies were but the thick presence all at once of a naked and self-obscuring body of history.

    —JOHN CAGE, "Jasper Johns: Stories and Ideas"

FOR A MOMENT, the breathy rattle of the M train on Broadway is all that she hears. Then, when it's passed, the compressed energies of the evening reform around her. The dry, warm lilt of Chris Wallace's voice on *60 Minutes* in the next apartment. Running water, high heels clicking clockwise around a table as plates and silverware go down. Peal of beer bottles crated on a handcart moving up the street. Everywhere people are preparing for the end of the decade.

Dear Grandpa, she writes beneath the date—*Dec. 31, 1989. You have always been the most amazing person to me. It's hard to find words to describe you.*

Cindy is freshly back from Buffalo, from a week living with Andy out of a suitcase in the little back bedroom of her parents' house that she'd shared with her sister for nearly eighteen years. Now twenty-seven, an established expat, coming home for Christmas is like stepping into the past. She is twenty again, sixteen, twelve. Passing the same dishes in the same direction to the same waiting hands beside her at the big dinner table. Laughing at the same jokes. Getting snippy at the same little familial irritations. Even the biggest changes in their lives seem retroactive at Christmastime, written back into the record. Cindy had always lived in New York, it seems now. Her sister, Sandy, had just married that

August—and it feels as if Danny, the gentle wisecracking Irish boy with his enormous glasses and stick-on mustache, had somehow always been a part of their tightly packed Italian family.

This year is different. This year the doctors have discovered cancer in her grandpa, John Donaruma. Leukemia. One of the best-known barkeeps in Buffalo since before the Second World War, her grandfather's presence more than filled up any room—it seemed to fill up the city, reach even to her new home in New York. Now that presence is palpably diminishing.

John Donaruma is a great-grandfather now. The infant, Michael, Cindy's brother David's son, sits on his lap like so many infants before him; he calls him "Grandpa GG"—double grandpa.

Everyone stops over—Uncle Tony and Aunt Dorothy, Uncle Al and Aunt Mary Jo, the Scirris, the Farbers, Lucy and Larry and Donnie and Lucille, Kathy, Steve Polichetti, innumerable Deniscos—and everyone wants to talk to John.

Cindy's grandmother Anita watches quietly from the seat beside her husband, attuned to signs he might be tiring out. His face is drawn, sharp lines running from his cheekbones to the corners of his mouth. His frame is thin, and only a soft gray fuzz covers his crown. But he keeps on smiling. He doesn't want to let his great-grandson go.

Now, in Brooklyn, Cindy tilts the little top-bound spiral notebook beneath her fingers and begins again.

I blame you for all the good in our family, she writes. *You have a way of making people stop their hectic, hard lives to laugh—even strangers, giving everyone a feeling that someone cares.*

She flips the page, glancing at the clock beside the sink. Peter and Beverly Muscato will be coming soon, more friends from the building. Bob Gulley might be stopping by, though you never can be sure with Bob—and maybe Charlotta Kotik and one of her girlfriends visiting from Prague. The food isn't out, the apartment isn't ready—Cindy spots a pair of black socks laid over the lip of the magazine rack next to Andy's favorite chair. But she looks back to the notebook. She wanted to say these things over the holiday—but when? It came and went, imploding into pools of wrapping paper, a sprint through a four-course dinner, the bare tree waiting at the curb. Back in Brooklyn, she's accepted that she might not have another chance.

In her haste, conscious of the cleaning still left to do before their friends arrive, Cindy's pen slips into a slightly stilted, interior voice—leaning on the sort of odd, almost antiquated turns of phrase that spring to the minds of irregular letter writers.

> *For you were a wise man. You had a way of teaching without sounding like a teacher or an old man.*
>
>   ...
>
> *So many words, simple sentences that you said to me over the years are still held with me. And I am sad that I could not be closer to you to gain more of that knowledge.*
>
>   ...
>
> *Even when you were ill or feeling bad or scared or tired, you would tell a joke.*
>
>   ...
>
> *I am so immeasurably proud to have been your granddaughter. And I know that your name will live on forever in our family. You will be very missed some day.*
> *But as I do now every day, I will always have you in my heart. And always try to be the remarkable giving person that you were, to always have your passion for living and your strength to stay forever young.*

A door shuts down the hall and Cindy lifts her head, concentration breaking. Winter boots on the tile. It will be Andy with a case of Budweiser and a bag of ice. She draws her lips flat, regards the smoothness of her favorite scarlet lipstick. Silently runs through everything left to do. Flips shut the notebook, stands, and tucks it into the end of a bookshelf on her way to the door.

· · ·

I didn't meet my great-grandfather John Donaruma. He died on Monday, March 19, 1990, a little more than three years before I was born. Cindy was right, though: he lived on in our family.

I knew that he was born in Italy in 1912 and moved to Buffalo as a boy; he took his first job at the Lafayette Theater downtown. Head usher by the time he turned seventeen, the year of the Great Crash, the owners trusted him but instructed him not to hire any other Italians.

He was a bartender at Manella's Tavern on Swan Street and eventually married the proprietor's daughter, Anita Manella, my great grandmother.[1]

I knew he was loved for his humor—that he made the guards at Buckingham Palace break face, and that he was known to hundreds in Buffalo because of a long-running prank.

"Do you have my card?" he'd ask friends and newcomers alike from across the bar.

Hearing "No," he'd open his wallet and give the patron a business card. One face was blank and the other simply said "My card."[2]

How many people have your card? Cindy had written to him, New Years Eve 1989.

But she never delivered the letter.

My grandmother brings out the stenographer's notebook to show us one evening in 2017. She'd been cleaning out the back room, what had been my grandfather's office until his death in 2012. We pass around the notebook, plain and spiral-bound with a bright yellow cover. If it had seen more use we might have missed the letter altogether, but the New Year's Eve message is one of only two entries. The other is a puzzling list.

> *you left the empty cake box and milk*
> *carton on the counter*
> *beer cans*
> *socks   pants on floor.*

over coat.
shaving things out
clothes in magazine basket
clothes on chair by desk
the wax pan

Sitting around my grandmother's dining room table in 2017, I imagine that Cindy wrote the letter here, in this house, in a few quiet moments snatched from the happy fervor of the holidays.

But four years later, revisiting the note, I ask my mother to confirm the hunch. Was Cindy still in town? What would you have been doing New Year's Eve '89? Dinner at home, then a cab downtown? Dancing at the Statler? Standing in the frigid night, in the windy canyons of the city, to watch the ball drop from the Electric Tower?

No, she said. Cindy would have been back home in New York by then. And in New York she would have been entertaining.

At first I'm amazed at the journey the tiny book took—from 440 Broadway to 211 North Seventh in Brooklyn up to 69 Seminary Road in Callicoon—and from there, salvaged from a two-week-end blitz of cleaning and burning, into my grandfather's den in Buffalo, and finally resurfaced from a filing cabinet in 2017.

Considering the twisted transit of the letter leads me back to the intention that sent it into the world in the first place.

What had drawn Cindy so close to her grandfather?

And if she wanted to be closer—if she had such powerful ties to her family—why had she left?

Then, given three more months between the time she'd put pen to paper and her grandfather's passing, why hadn't she delivered the letter? Why hadn't she mailed it?

And finally, what was so important about the notebook's only other entry? Why had she felt the need to make a similarly private documentation of domestic messiness?

· · ·

Born July 30, 1962, into a big Italian family that had settled as if by accident in the Kelly-green heart of Irish South Buffalo, Cindy Suffoletto had always been inventive, with an early talent for crafts and drawing.

This is what everyone tells me. Creative, loving, and independent are the words that come up again and again.

The Facebook response I get from Theresa Ewing, one of Cindy's friends from St. Martin's School in South Buffalo, is typical:

> wow...cindy was the best person that i ever met...
> cindy and i were best friends from grammar school thru high school
> and beyond...she was carefree, lovable and did her own thing...
> not only was she talented with her art she was "cool" as a person...
> i miss her so much
> ps...even my children know who cindy suffoletto is...i still talk
> about her

Friends and family noted that Cindy started taking her talent more seriously at Sacred Heart Academy, the girls' high school run by the Sisters of St. Francis. Starting in 1976, Cindy (and soon her sister, Sandy, eighteen months behind) would take the number 31 bus from McKinley Parkway all the way across the city, fourteen miles up Bailey to Main Street, stopping at the edge of the South Campus of the University at Buffalo. From there the Suffoletto sisters would walk another eighth of a mile past the university and the Grover Cleveland golf course—except in the worst winter weather, when they'd transfer to another Main Street bus—until they reached the grand switchback steps of Sacred Heart. There Cindy took studio art, three-dimensional art, advertising art; she painted the backdrops for all the school plays; she filled her free time with painting, illustrating, and collaging with images snipped from *Vogue* and her father's *National Geographics*.

I asked my mother, my grandmother, and some of Cindy's

friends when it became clear that Cindy wanted to be an artist—and when it became clear that she'd have to leave Buffalo to do so. None could tell me.

But I find an answer in the cedar chest in my parents' house, where my mother kept a clipping from the picture pages of the *Buffalo News*. It's undated, but the context suggests 1979 or '80.

Cindy and a classmate (Suzanne Gregory, the caption says) sit on the floor of Hengerer's, the department store on the other side of Sacred Heart's parking lot, which boasted a Tea Room on the fourth floor that seniors with "campus privileges" loved to visit.[3] On a clear day you could see from those windows as far as the mists of Niagara Falls, seventeen miles northwest. In the picture the girls wear plaid skirts, dark cardigans over white blouses; they wear their hair closely cropped over their ears and blush high on their cheekbones—Suzanne's styled herself after Mia Farrow circa *Rosemary's Baby*. With big pads on their laps they sketch late '70s versions of Gibson girls, working from Hengerer's mannequins dressed in summer fashions—enormous costume pearls, headscarves, and sunglasses bigger than the TVs in many Buffalo homes then—an obvious contrast to the frontier Catholic schoolgirls. The picture says what the caption can't: they are dreaming of New York.

Cindy dreamed but didn't leave after graduating from Sacred Heart in spring 1980. She started a fine arts degree at Buffalo State, moved out from the back bedroom on the first floor of her parents' house and into a small apartment on Essex Street on the West Side, started working at the corner bar—then called the One World Kitchen, later the Essex Street Pub, a hangout for the artists in the area, with a jukebox, dartboard, and seven-foot pool table. Around the tin ceiling hung license plates and photographs of neighborhood celebrities, crossed skis, old political posters, a carved wooden rooster. Tall windows pushed the glow of neon beer signs into the quiet residential night, but the dark inside—especially among the hundred-year-old watering hole's conspiratorial nooks and corners—shimmered with wood polish, full pints, and leather jackets. They served burgers, wings, and loaded nachos until two, drinks until four—or, for favored faithfuls, even later.

Most of the local crowd in the late '70s and early '80s were artists—artists like Cindy, who lived in cheap apartments on Essex, Massachusetts, Nineteenth, or Chenango—or they were the artists of the in-crowd's in-crowd, who occupied every hallway, office, loading dock, and storage unit of the old brick icehouse—the Essex Art Center—that hulked between Cindy's apartment and the pub at the corner.

I know the pub on the corner well. It still stands, still serves a similar crowd, even though the neighborhood's changed. For a few years in the late 2010s, some of my best friends lived nearby on Nineteenth, and I spent several nights a week at Essex—playing pool, raiding the jukebox, talking shit, placing bulk orders for pitchers of Pabst. And every time I visited I thought of Cindy working there, drinking there, dreaming there—Cindy even younger then than I was.

The scene today is similar to what Cindy knew, but not the same.

For about a decade in the latter half of the twentieth century, a critical mass of Buffalo's most buzzed-about artists worked—and in many cases lived—at the Essex Art Center. The established sculptors Duayne Hatchett and Larry Griffis Jr. (who, recall, owned the whole complex) had large studios there, and employed younger artists at the center as assistants. Some of those students and assistants founded Hallwalls there when Cindy was just a freshman at Sacred Heart. By the time Cindy stepped on to the scene, the Essex Art Center was a melting pot, a low-rent Alexandria, with a painting wing, a sculpture wing, a film wing, and even a literary wing. Professors from the local art colleges were stopping by, celebrity artists from elsewhere were exhibiting, and at least three of the Hallwalls founders—Cindy Sherman, Robert Longo, and Charles Clough—had already left Buffalo for New York City, trailing legend behind them.

Cindy had made a place for herself in a new world—that's how the rest of the family saw it. When Cindy started to exhibit at Buffalo State, Hallwalls, and other upstart galleries around town, the entire family would troop in for the openings: her father and mother, Hank and Annette; her grandparents John and Anita; her aunt Molly and uncle Joe; and of course her siblings, Dave, Tom, and Sandy. The entourage sometimes swelled to include even great-aunts and second cousins.

The menagerie of Manellas, Suffolettos, Donarumas, and Deniscos may have been immiscible with the hipsters of Essex Street—the music, the radical attitudes, the pot smoke detectable from storerooms and alcoves—but Cindy didn't mind. She didn't come from money, connections, or other conventional forms of privilege in the art world, but an aspiring artist couldn't have asked for a more supportive family than Cindy's. Yet it was a family she knew she had to leave. To be an artist, a measure of departure from the safe, from the known, would be necessary. Like so many others in that place and at that time, Cindy—at just eighteen—arranged her life so she could be near that bright and accessible nexus, the place where things happened, where it was happening all the time.

He—Andy—sees her—Cindy—passing up the street, headed to the corner where Essex ends at Rhode Island. A cigarette, pointed downward, traces his strong fingers with slow smoke. From the cracked door behind him comes the sound of Roxy

Music's *Manifesto*, a record he's heard a dozen times already. Elsewhere around the courtyard, the sounds of old jazz, rock, and blues records: Skip James, the Byrds, Coleman Hawkins.

He recognizes the figure—five-foot-one in a loose coat and trademark bandanna—from around town. Maybe from an opening at the Burchfield Penney Art Center in Buff State's Rockwell Hall. Or maybe at the Albright-Knox's Western New York show, the only juried exhibition open to locals. Maybe it had been in this very courtyard, for a show at Hallwalls—nobody missed a show at Hallwalls. Or maybe—it clicks—maybe it had been across the polished bar at the corner pub, where she's just now headed for a shift.

Buffalo's art scene—the real art scene, the one made up of the makers, not the benefactors—is small, so small that no one can stay anonymous for long. Sooner or later you meet everyone. And if you can't remember where you met, chances are it was over a pint at the corner.

Maybe he'll check. They're out of beer at the studio, his eyes ache from working in the uneven light, and he's heard the record—all the records—too many times before.

Maybe it was this way. Or maybe another way. Maybe they'd spoken already, or maybe they'd only exchanged a few frank looks.

The truth is I don't know. Few people I spoke to remember exactly *when* Cindy and Andy walked into the same picture frame. Several offer contradictory accounts, dates that don't add up, or demonstrable falsehoods.

Brian Duffy offers my favorite memory. He says Cindy, at Buff State in 1980, was part of a student show in the former Buffalo State Asylum for the Insane, cleared of its last patients only four years before. The students occupied a long hallway in the dark brick and copper-capped H. H. Richardson–designed building, each one with their own "cell." Brian and Andy, friends and fellow professors at Villa Maria College, attended—and stopped at Cindy's section. Cindy was doing abstractions in oil, resembling bridges, Brian recalled to me—almost landscapes, but without the features that typified that mode. He and Andy were both taken by the art—and Cindy.

Brian didn't remember a date and I wasn't able to find any booklet or review. But an equally important question, after their first meeting, is when one of them decided to meet again—to force that second conversation. So, I imagine it at Essex.

It had to have been a winter night.

In the summer, people here are too busy enjoying themselves—drinking on patios, reading languorous books, stretching weekends in Crystal Beach or Sherkston out over three, four, five days—to do much of any importance. Only when we're forced inside by the weather, into our tight Queen Annes and converted studios, with the heat turned up and cold beers in the fridge and our elbows on our knees, do we experience those collisions that change the course of a life.

Mark-Making

THUNDER ROLLS ACROSS Greater Philadelphia. Heavy clouds have covered the sunset, turning the western skyline into a Phlegethon, a band of murky magma beyond the Schuylkill. The fire disappears only when the lightning cracks, flooding the full clouds white.

From the balcony of her new row house in Old City, Jessica Berwind watches the spectacle and speaks to me. She texts me a picture of the apocalyptic view while we're on the phone.

A former gallerist and a friend of my aunt and uncle, I had tracked her down to get her perspective on their careers, their partnership, their personalities. She had operated a gallery in Philadelphia, first at 1618 Latimer Street and then at 301 Cherry Street, from 1985 to '95, and showed Andy's work many times. After leaving the art world and losing touch with many friends in the process ("I had to slam that door shut to walk through a different door," she tells me), she's returning to the old neighborhood and unboxing powerful memories—precisely at the time I make contact. In our first minute on the phone she gives me something I hadn't expected: a method—a set of assumptions and a style—through which to talk about Uncle Andy and his art.

"Being with Andy and Cindy was always so fucking stimulating," she begins.

She illustrates a typical scene—Andy's immediate presence, at once powerful and approachable, and Cindy, beautiful in an unfussy way, with her red lipstick and cigarettes, radiating a warm, protective intensity.[1] Both of them "incredibly intelligent,"

Jessica remembers, and often funny and light, but with an undercurrent of seriousness about art and ideas, a seriousness sometimes attenuated into an anxiousness.

"He just had such a strange way of communicating," Jessica says—and then remembers something: "Didn't he have some kind of speech impediment? So he would put words together that were easier for him to navigate than they would have been for other people—which was consistent with his work."

I think back to the previous summer, when I was just beginning my research for this book and had visited the vaults of the Burchfield Penney Art Center to see the Topolski collection. The art handler pushed the white hanging latticed walls along their tracks to open up row after row of his works, spanning four decades. Music and geometry mingled most frequently in his works on paper—fine, precisely rendered lines that expressed some idea, obscured in translation from its original tongue, sonics or arithmetic. But as time went on, bits of chemistry, geography, astronomy, anthropology, and literature entered his work—GCS coordinates directing the hand that marked the paper, transmuted mathematically into the notes of the treble clef, making a map you could read and even play as music, colliding with scraps of text from a report by the Department of Energy—and all of this, perhaps, punctuated by a puzzling smudge along the edge of some Pythagorean ideal, a reminder of the human hand behind it all.

"When I see work that I like I get a pit in my stomach," Jessica tells me. "I get a strong physical reaction even before I get an emotional or intellectual reaction."

When she saw the work, some of the same work that I had stood before in the basement of the Burchfield Penney, "I just fell in love with it. I didn't care what it was about. Andy's mark-making was just so rich and so beautiful and so poetic.

"I'm attracted to a work of art before I know what it means," she explains. "Over time as I began to understand what Andy was intending, I fell in love even more." But, she adds, "If it's all right there, there's no reason to look again."

Speaking again about Andy's technical ability, Jessica notes something I know but never have put into words: Andy's "huge, gentle presence," she says, contrasts with the "delicacy" of his work.

She takes the notion further, tying it back to Andy's funny way of putting things into language: "He was expressing a part of himself in his work that didn't come out in his presence."

Of course she's right. All true art expresses something that an artist could use no other means to express. That's what distinguishes, say, a novel from an entry in a diary, a song from some lucky utterance in the course of a late night of beers and bullshit. But some artists tap only a shallow well of expression beyond the reach of intention. Andy had access to a vastness, cold reaches far below the surface of his personality. This is partly the reason language so often failed him, and why representational and even the prevailing modes of abstract art failed (and failed to interest) him.

My realization is this: to write about Andy and Cindy, about their lives and about their art, I have to borrow their methods and materials. History. Geography. Economics. Poetry. Architecture. Anthropology. The language of scientists and bureaucrats. Elemental shapes appealing to the prerational mind. Music composition, sculpture, and performance—all at once. Only in the collisions of these vast systems can I hope to find them.

Collisions defined Andy's art. In a different way they influenced Cindy's art. And collisions made their lifelong partnership possible. Collisions in Buffalo are a matter of climate, architecture, economy—but also urban planning.

Many have compared Buffalo's radial street pattern to the spokes of a wheel, with broad avenues beaming in every direction from the center, Niagara Square, across a more familiar orthogonal grid laid underneath. The work is Joseph Ellicott's. The Holland Land Company surveyor and freelance city planner cut his teeth in Washington, DC, before turning north to Buffalo in 1804, falling in love with the tiny town tucked in a Great Lake's frigid armpit.[2] While the earlier DC plan, known for its radial "grand avenues," is both practical and dazzling—a scrap snatched from the night sky above the Potomac, a constellation of many bright points in balance—Ellicott's application of the concept in the 1804 plan for Buffalo is at once less ambitious and more inspired, an effort not to impose order onto an undeveloped environment but to pick a starting point and to suggest promising directions for future development. Ellicott's map looks like the Buddhist dharmachakra, with a "public square" situated favorably near the mouth of Buffalo Creek on Lake Erie, and spokes, wide radial avenues, extending symmetrically in eight directions.

But this analogy ignores the position of the wheel, snugged between a creek, a lake, and a river. Because of these natural boundaries, four of Ellicott's eight original spokes terminate only a few blocks from their common origin. In the 1804 map, south, southwest, and westward avenues end at the water, and the northward spoke of the wheel extends only to the east–west of Chippawa, the pattern reemerging above this as a rigid grid of rectangular five-acre lots stretching upward into farms and unsettled lands before colliding with the cruder graticule of another inland port town, Black Rock.[3] The only streets that really *radiate* look to the east. Though Ellicott's original grid was made a palimpsest by the progressively heavier hands of Fredrick Law Olmstead and Robert Moses, the original eastward streets—today named Genesee, Sycamore, Broadway, William, and Clinton—

still make straight, radial lines, like the beams of the sun drop-ping each night like a coin into our enormous wishing well, the lake.

Considered this way, the Buffalo plan recalls a wheel less than it does the waveform theorem of the seventeenth-century phys-icist Christiaan Huygens. In a principle depicted memorably in most junior-high science textbooks, Huygens predicted that when any wave traveling in a straight line encounters a small opening, its passage will transform the planar wave into a spher-ical wave. Provided several apertures, a single planar wave will multiply into as many overlapping spherical waves, colliding, diffracting, and propagating endlessly outward.

Taking our map as a diagram of Huygens's waveform theo-rem, we can imagine the tides of Lake Erie colliding again and again with Ellicott's radial grid, traveling eastward in great arcs, multiplying at the apertures of avenues, irrigating the forests and scrublands and flooding the great limestone pits that built the city.

People propagate in waves, too. In Buffalo—or more precisely, in the region east of where Lakes Erie and Ontario meet—successive immigrant groups have developed, outgrown, and abandoned communities in a cyclical manner determined in equal parts by the landscape, by Joseph Ellicott's radial grid, and by the rising and falling of the local economy.

What is today Buffalo was once a popular crossroads common to many indigenous groups. The French found the Wenrohronon common in the region in the early 1600s, but these shortly fell into conflict with the Chonnonton peoples to the west and the Senecas, part of the Iroquois Confederacy, in the East. By the middle of the seventeenth century, these enemies virtually elim-inated the Wenro peoples east of Erie.[4] Tenuous control of the region passed from the Iroquois to the French to the British prior to American independence. After the War of 1812, which saw Buffalo sacked and burned, that independence was cemented, and the passage of new peoples through the fertile frontier region would be a story not of conquest, but assimilation.

In the floodplain of the city's East Side, first Germans, then Slavic Jews, then Poles settled, building homes and houses of worship, building businesses, building fortunes. A small Black community that had existed around William Street almost from the beginning of the city's history bloomed in the 1950s with the arrival of economic migrants and social refugees from the South and followed the same pattern, pushing out the Poles who had pushed out the Jews who had followed the Germans.

Like waves pulsing through the apertures of Genesee, Sycamore, Broadway, and William—and beyond, flowing into Walden and swelling far north to Kensington—middle-class wages and middle-class cars took the Poles farther east than any immigrant groups before them, bringing Polonia finally to rest in the inner-ring suburb of Cheektowaga, "land of the crab apples" in the Erie-Seneca tongue.

Under the crab apple and the constellation Virgo, Andrew L. Topolski was born. The son of Lorraine Pokrywczynski and John Topolski, he entered into the world on September 21, 1952, and grew up with his younger brothers Ronald and Thomas at 101 Claude Drive. A single-story Cape Cod, the house was in the southeastern extremity of Cheektowaga, just off William Street, in a tract-style subdivision wedged between the village of Sloan and the Lovejoy and Kaisertown neighborhoods of Buffalo, bounded by CSX railroad tracks to the north and the New York State Thruway to the south.

Nothing like the rural expanses of Clarence or the quaint village of Williamsville, this was a postwar suburb, with life, for many families, centering on its major blue-collar employers: the

Westinghouse Electric Corporation plant on Genesee, Joy Manufacturing on Union, or the Curtiss-Wright airplane hangars. Cheektowaga's thoroughfares were lined with the warehouses of distributors, and residential streets were pocked with scores of small machine shops serving the suburb's light industry and the CSX Frontier Yard off Broadway, which packed 63 tracks on just over 300 acres, coordinating 1,083 trains a day. The land of the crab apples became progressively less bucolic as Andy aged. In 1956, Interstate 90 replaced the New York Thruway, and three years later it joined with the new I-190 at a minor spaghetti junction just a five-minute walk from the Topolskis's front door.

Andy suffered a severe stutter as a child, and perhaps because of this his father, a postman, bought a child's art kit, put a pencil into his son's hand, and taught Andy the elements of drawing. Embarrassed by his tongue's unruliness, Andy took to drawing as another form of communication. He didn't commit to sports, didn't join any garage bands, wasn't the most popular kid in his grammar school—he was too reticent, too inclined to self-editing for that—but those who witnessed his early illustrations found a voice that was confident, singular, and arrestingly clear.

Some in the family will say without hesitation that Andy, the firstborn, was the favorite of the three sons. Whether or not this was true, John and Lorraine let him turn the family's basement into a studio, and Andy spent most of his free time creating there. As a senior at John F. Kennedy High School, Andy joined an after-school drawing program, testing a hungry talent. There he met Don Metz, a baseball player with an interest in art and music; the two drew close and shared their influences. While he sketched, Andy's mind also drifted to collection and collage, and the basement filled with detritus from magazines and newspapers. He followed his talent into the BFA program at the University at Buffalo.

Andy and buddies like Don had been attending campus Vietnam protests while they were still juniors and seniors at a high school already named for the president who'd wanted to end the war; even before graduating they had watched their friends get drafted or disappear into Canada. Protests were happening weekly on UB's campuses when Andy attended, and these attracted the fine arts and new media students (and their teachers). The political climate of the Nixon era—and its teeming universe of images and information—exerted a gravitational influence on Andy's art as on his life, but even in high school and college he resisted the temptation to make the obvious "protest" art that was becoming so popular.

Andy would be a lifelong learner, but it was also evident early that he felt called to be a teacher. In September 1975—nine months after abandoning a graduate degree at the University of Michigan because of a scholarship mix-up[5]—Andy stood in front of a class of UB undergraduates as a teaching assistant. He had returned to pursue his MFA, focusing on lithography, serigraphy, and photography, while supplementing his income as a substitute teacher in the Buffalo Public Schools. UB's art department was housed in Bethune Hall at 2917 Main Street, a former factory,[6] and Andy assisted John McIvor in the basement printmaking studio. McIvor was the established artist,[7] but Andy's was the presence that held the students at attention. Six-foot-two, with a heavy black beard and a voice like a talking bear's, he passed between the basement studio's long tables and under the slant columns of autumn light that fell in from Main Street. Studio critiques of students' first screen prints turned into miniature seminars—floor space quickly filled up by other classmates listening in, hanging on every word.

Graduating with his MFA in '77, Andy earned a spot as a part-time lecturer, teaching "Introduction to Screen Printing" at UB, before finding a full-time position at Villa Maria College, just three miles from his childhood home.

On this spot—a few acres of green preserved between the freight yard and the Polish cemetery—authorities in Cheektowaga had redirected the tiny and long-abused Scajaquada Creek, which starts in a green pond in a subdivision of Lancaster to the east, into a culvert. From Pine Ridge Road it flows beneath the college campus—and through four miles of buried toxic sludge—emerging in the tonier Protestant cemetery of Forest Lawn in Buffalo, where it begins the last leg of its journey to the broad Niagara River, which precedes its apotheosis at the crush of the falls.

And it was here, at Villa Maria—its front windows saluting the disappearing Scajaquada—where Andy first found the institutional support that would enable him to make art, teach art, and talk about art in every waking minute of his life. He passed word of another opening to his friend Brian Duffy, who had been a GI Bill undergraduate at UB when Andy was McIvor's teaching assistant.

Villa was surrounded by highways, interstates, and train tracks, each suggesting innumerable futures. But for an artist—young and undiscovered, but comfortable—Villa was on the road to nowhere in particular.

At Villa, safely tenure-tracked, Andy's mind began to turn away from Cheektowaga's changing landscape—where the factories, machine shops, and warehouses of his childhood had given way to a great shopping mall, an interstate, endless plazas of transit, and multiplying brownfields of outmoded light industry. Instead, like the Scajaquada, his spirit plunged into the corrupted earth, heading westward, seeking answers in the past.

EBMA

A SIDE DOOR bangs open onto Playter Street—the heart of the East Side of Buffalo, beating with a pacemaker—and out comes a gang the locals would have called hippies (even though this is the start of the Reagan era, and the last of the hippies got tenure two years ago). But they have long hair, and at least since the days of Rupert and the Cavaliers this has signaled a certain laughing disregard that engenders suspicion in the Roundheads of every time and place. So, on the East Side of Buffalo in 1981, they're hippies. They flash cigarette smiles and wink with Budweiser eyes, wear hip-gripping Levis and straight-legged Dickies, Chelsea boots and cowboy boots and Chuck Taylors and second-hand Boston-cracked black loafers; they're covered in corduroy, armored in leather, laughing at the last line of a riff pinched short as the doors swing shut behind them.

John Toth—tall, talkative, bare-armed in a black T-shirt and oblivious to the cold—turns to his girlfriend, Lisa, and picks up the thread of a conversation started two, three weeks ago, with seemingly infinite ground left to cover—something about a canvas as content instead of context, *see* ... something about reactivating postindustrial spaces ... the contradiction of intention in indeterminate music ... something about the launch of CNN, a cable TV channel broadcasting all news, twenty-four hours a day. *Crazy, right?* Michael Basinski, with a dark mane, thrifted leather vest, sterling silver bolo tie, and gym teacher's mustache, walks ahead, humming a line from a poem he'd just performed over a Julius Eastman composition. Don Metz hangs back, kicks a brick to keep the door from latching behind them, the honks and ululations of a Rahsaan Roland Kirk album flowing through the gap into the halogen night.

And at the front of the pack, a couple that fits together like parquetry—a contrast perfectly balanced—Cindy Suffoletto and Andy Topolski.

Andy—black-bearded, big-framed, heavy features capped with architectural eyebrows—lights a cigarette and gestures up the street. Sattler's department store, a locally owned institution, a postwar juggernaut that for decades signified middle-class comfort and dignified discounts in the "bargain basement" style, has just closed its flagship store. The ghost-shapes of its neon name, spelled in Streamline Moderne block lettering, are still visible on the thrusting vertical of its paquebot façade, and beneath this sags a vinyl banner announcing the building's new tenant: 998 CLEARANCE CENTER.

Cindy—thick, lively curls of dark hair cropped close to her neck, frost-burnished apples above her slanted cheekbones, lips marked out in a confident red—looks as if her frame could fill the one beside her two-and-a-half times over. She stops at the corner and the group turns on this small pivot—Cindy, with Andy serving as the lever—to cluster loosely on Broadway in front of the main entrance to Buffalo's Dom Polski, the "Polish House."

The Essex Art Center on the West Side may have been the locus of new visual art in Buffalo, but in the twilight of the '70s into the early '80s, the avant-garde's avant-garde—across all genres and media—was here, at 1081 Broadway.

Andy and Cindy's friend Don Metz tells me this when we connect over the phone on August 20, 2020. As he speaks, I pull up the address on Google Maps and look at a corner I'd passed dozens of times before. A four-story, red-brick, Renaissance-style building designed by the East Side's own Wladyslaw Zawadzki, the Dom opened on July 16, 1905 as a community hall with space for singing societies, political clubs, and ladies' groups, all aimed at helping Polish immigrants settle and assimilate while protecting their traditions. Toward the end of the twentieth century, tenancy had dwindled to just the Mazur classes and serious drinkers—but, starting in '76, the dziadzias and laskas made room for a new crowd: weekly, nightly, then, the old temple welcomed poets, composers, musicians, visual artists, prophets of new media, students and faculty, hipsters and immigrants—people hoping for any kind of break; people desperate for something other than disco.

If you were to place a pin in a map of the city of Buffalo to mark the position of this gaggle of artists laughing on a street corner in the cold spring of 1981, you might wonder why they congregated here, in a neighborhood on the wane, far out from the city center, nowhere near the major galleries, not even close to anyone's studio.

The answer is simpler than the question suggests. In Buffalo, at least in the last hundred years, any explanation, no matter how detailed, as to why an event plays out precisely the way it does will always be an elaboration on one of just two possible "first causes." Simplify any causal equation in Buffalo history and you will discover them, the underlying laws of the region.

They are: *cheap rent* or *cheap beer*.

By the mid-'70s, many of the East Side's old Polish cottages were abandoned, whole blocks turned to urban prairie, and fewer congregants were driving in from the suburbs each Sunday to attend mass at St. Stanislaus, St. Adalbert, and Corpus Christi. But the Polish powers in the ward and their allies in City Hall strove against time, pumping a little money into the old cultural organs of Buffalo's Eastern Bloc—like the meeting house of the Chopin Singing Society, the Ukrainian Center, and the Dom Polski.

Andy's aunt Genevieve Zielinski had long been involved in the Polish Arts Society. As an MFA student, Andy had limited interest in the nineteenth-century and folk-arts focuses of the PAS, but his aunt kept him informed of cultural goings-on in old Polonia. When she told him to stop by the reopening of the Dom Polski in 1976, he did.

He was sitting in a folding chair, Joan Posluzny, artist and gallerist, tells me over Zoom, 8:00 a.m. on a Thursday, July 15, 2021. I reach her in Sweden where she's lived since 1989. Like Andy, she had grown up in the Western New York Polish diaspora, and her family had always been involved in various Polish American cultural efforts. She had graduated from Boston College in 1976 and had studied in Poland and Austria. Naturally she showed up at the Dom reopening. She didn't know Andy then, but she remembers they waved to each other from across the room—possibly recognizing something in each other, a quality of being simultaneously at home and out of place.

Joan took a job as assistant to the new director at the Dom; shortly, within a few months, she had taken over as director.

"There was a revival going on in the East Side at that point," she tells me—a brief but brilliant reversal of its decline.

Joan scored NYSCA grant funding for a theater group that performed in the top floor and additional funding for a Polish film festival—bringing a major Polish director to Buffalo and screening classical and contemporary films to substantial and enthusiastic crowds. But as a visual artist, Joan's chief goal was to open a gallery.

Teaming up with two contemporaries, Monica Pavlov and Andy Topolski, Joan went after more NYSCA funding for an exhibition space. It was Andy's idea to call it the J. C. Mazur Gallery, honoring one of the great artists to come out of Buffalo's Polonia—a painter, sculptor, and stained-glass worker whose windows are still visible in churches from Massachusetts to Detroit—who had died in 1970.[1] Joan, Monica, and Andy found themselves with a little bit of municipal cash, free space in the Dom, and a mandate to revivify the Polish cultural scene. They started to host visual art openings and interdisciplinary events, and Andy tapped his old high school buddy Don Metz—who'd pivoted from artist and baseball player to musician and composer, then studying composition at UB—to take an arts coordinator position.

"Let's show them what's really going on in the community," Andy said.

Though the gallery had no reputation, no cachet, the friends discovered it wasn't difficult to bring visual artists and composers to share their work. There was little chance of selling pieces that displayed at the J. C. Mazur Gallery, which lay well outside Buffalo's small collectors' beltway, but Broadway was close enough to just about everything, and more importantly its inner doors opened onto the Dom Polski bar, where there was plenty of room to fill in among the tattered rearguard of old Polonia (and where eighty cents bought a Krakow and a shot of Schenley's).

The artists had become accustomed to a certain tacit animosity moving through buttoned-up Buffalo in the '70s, a time when complimentary brochures in the airport advised business travelers on how to dress to match the manners of the conservative frontier town. Like their contemporary Patti Smith, they felt "confined by the notion that we are born into a world where everything was mapped out by those before us";[2] the old ways were not working, the paths mapped for them, they could see, did not lead to happiness. They got mixed up in antiwar protests and civil rights protests, worked blue-collar jobs where bosses called them communists for wearing hair that touched their collars. But the old Poles at the bar out on Broadway didn't bother them.

The NYSCA funding ran out and the Mazur Gallery closed in 1980; Joan, by then an MFA student at UB, moved on to manage the Bethune Hall Gallery, and for a time she and Andy moved north, sharing space in a studio Brian Duffy rented on the second floor of a commercial space on Hertel Avenue. But the Mazur Gallery's short life seeded other important happenings in the city's art scene, and Andy again looked east. The conversations sparked at the first Mazur showcase setups and tear-downs, Dom community workshops, and late-night bull sessions at the bar had led Andy and Don to cofound the East Buffalo Media Association (EBMA) in 1977, aiming to bring together formally the composers, musicians, writers, sculptors, and video artists who had begun to meet regularly on Broadway. Don admits to me that he had initially wanted to call it the East Buffalo Music Association, but Andy pushed him to include the visual arts and new media. Andy and other visual artists like John Toth had started mixing nightly with musicians and composers that Don, a connector, helped to introduce from UB's high-powered electromagnet of a music department: Lukas Foss, Morton Feldman, Petr Kotik, Julius Eastman, and scores of their students.[3]

The visual artists joined in the fun of experimental concerts held regularly at the Dom Polski (even after the Mazur Gallery closed) and at the Albright-Knox, making Buffalo a hub for intermedia. The term, which the artist and theorist Dick Higgins had adapted from the Romantic poet Percy Shelley, referred to art that operated within and across several media at once.[4] Like its conceptual older siblings—Dada, Fluxus, the new collage, and John Cage's indeterminate music—it often prioritized process, collaboration, audience involvement, and chance. "Pop and Op" art were dead, Higgins had declared in the first volume of his *Something Else Newsletter* in '66, confined to "older expressions of art... decorating and suggesting grandeur." Abstract expressionism was *really dead*, fundamentally irrelevant, in Higgins's estimation, by the time that Seymour "Shorty" Knox II was establishing its privileged place in Buffalo's Beaux Arts temple to culture. In contrast, and befitting a period characterized by rapid flattening of the earlier social order (he thought), intermedia attempted to occupy a place between established forms, where nothing is tacked on, and all elements contribute to a whole— even including the viewer or the audience and their movement through space.[5] And it was *fun*. "Some things having a quality of invitingness seem to invite almost anything," Higgins had written.[6] In this vein, the EBMA put on exhibitions, performances, and happenings at the Dom, Buff State, and the International Institute, and later even in New York, in a shoestring operation, run from a war room in Buffalo, that involved chartering discount buses to shuttle people between tiny exhibition spaces in Greenwich Village and Red Hook.

The mix of the old forms and the new, the high and the low, the DIY and the heavily grant-subsidized—this fecund upheaval defined a way of life in Buffalo in the late '70s and early '80s. It was a time that everyone who lived it remembers with a kind of fond amazement that it happened at all.

Lukas Foss was fusing the standard repertoire of heavies like Bach, Webern, and Ravel with the possibilities of electronic music powered by the supercomputers available at UB—and as director of the Buffalo Philharmonic, he was bringing this fusion to the city's "mainstream" classical music fans.

The media studies department at UB would put on public shows of their own avant-garde work in film—and Andy and the Hallwalls crowd, artists operating in completely different disciplines, would march in as a troop, all dressed in black, and sit in the front row, attentively watching and listening to Hollis Frampton's flicker films—harshly oscillating black-and-white frames over an accompaniment of shrieking and industrial cachinnation.

At one of Petr Kotik's performances, the composer took a fourteen-foot birch tree and thrashed it on an electrified floor until none of its leaves remained—and then walked off stage.

On February 5, 1976, Larry Lundy, an early macher at Hallwalls,[7] decided that instead of celebrating the nation's bicentennial, he would celebrate the sixtieth anniversary of the Dada movement. In a frigid frontier February, he pulled off an elaborate prank and an unforgettable party: A made-up international reporter named Stuart Temple appeared alongside two mysterious figures dressed in black with Parisian chapeaus and cardboard exoskeletons, each spelling out "DA"; without securing anyone's blessing, Hallwallians welcomed the party at prominent Buffalo sites including the airport, the train station, and the Albright-Knox, holding mock interviews. At the icehouse there was a screening of Hans Richter's *Ghosts Before Breakfast* and René Clair's *Entr'acte*, while members of Creative Associates performed amid an exhibition of works by locals and the likes of Marcel Duchamp.[8] To cap the night off, the participants took to Hallwalls's hidden courtyard and set fire to donated artworks and a crude effigy spelling out "ART."

Was it music? Was it composition? Was it visual or performance art? Was it Dada? Was it just a party?

I don't know. I've participated in Buffalo's art scene for more than a decade, lived through another period that observers and promoters took to calling a "renaissance." And I've never seen anything like *that*.

Larry Lundy related the DADADAY story over the phone in July 2021, a ninety-degree night, far from the "Scandinavian" cold of the February he remembered. He summed up the whole scene this way: "I knew what you were doing, you knew what I was doing, and there's this other group of people doing something interesting that I'm going to tell you about."

The mode of Andy and Cindy's Buffalo was collaborative and aleatory: by leaving themselves open to each other's influence—and leaving central elements of their art up to chance—composers, performers, filmmakers, sculptors, and poets found they could challenge the basic assumptions that undergirded their disciplines and chosen media and put constraints on expression. So they beat the floors with birch trees, invented new languages, consulted the *I Ching*. They kept challenging, kept collaborating, left more up to chance. And then got together for spaghetti dinners at the icehouse or in professors' dining rooms and hashed out what had happened, what was happening.

It wasn't just the artists in those days, either. At the *Buffalo Evening News*, Paul Weiland, a reporter hired just to cover the "space beat," took to calling out at random—*next paragraph with a Z!* And at every desk, from crime to cooking, from sports to the opinion page, reporters would hit Return and start their next paragraph with a Z, weaving a secret meaning-making game into an edition that would soon land on welcome mats from Wheatfield to West Seneca.

When I asked Don Metz how Andy felt playing a part in proximity to such an incredible confluence of cultural currents, he gently corrected my frame of reference.

"Andy was the catalyst that it all grew from," Don said.

I didn't read the tributes published after Andy died. At least, not then.

But a decade later, as I learned from firsthand accounts that Andy was more than a prolific studio artist and a favorite teacher—that he was "the catalyst" for a period in Buffalo's cultural history that most would call a high-water mark—I sought out the record of written remembrances. Most read like the panegyrics of heroes.

"He was partner and friend to the Buffalo luminaries who will acknowledge that he was the most inventive of the bunch," wrote Anthony Bannon.[9] The decorated critic, art historian, and gallery executive served two stints as director of the Burchfield Penney, spending sixteen years in between as director of the George Eastman Museum in Rochester.

In the mid-'70s, Bannon was lead art critic at the *Buffalo News* and art section editor for the Sunday paper. With the responsibility of reviewing fine art exhibitions, architecture, film, photography, even theater and dance—all produced in Buffalo at peak postwar levels—Bannon was among the best-equipped to say in which direction influence flowed. But something about his pronouncement wouldn't settle with me. *Who* exactly were these Buffalo "luminaries"?

It takes until November 2020 to get through to him. By then I've interviewed more than a dozen of Andy and Cindy's contemporaries. I have educated guesses about the identities of these bright lights, but need Tony to confirm them. He calls me at half past ten on the twelfth, a Thursday night, returning from a late dinner at Storm King Art Center, the sculpture park about an hour outside Manhattan. I am surprised to find Tony—three weeks from his seventy-seventh birthday—more than happy to talk well past midnight. I sit at my dining room table transcribing his memories, mixed with gossip and asides, filling half of a legal pad by the light of a standing lamp. Finally I read him back the quote from his 2013 tribute.

"Who did you mean," I ask, "specifically?"

Tony rattles off the names without a moment's thought.

He meant Toth, Metz, and other visual artists like Michael Zwack, Nancy Dwyer, Charles Clough, Larry Lundy, Joe Panone, Duayne Hatchett, Larry Griffis. Pointedly, he says, he meant the more famous Hallwalls founders, Cindy Sherman and Robert Longo.[10] He meant the composers: Kotik, Foss, Sapp, Eastman, Feldman. He meant language poets like Mike Basinski and acolytes of Ontario's Four Horsemen. He meant all the people who gravitated toward Andy at UB, Villa Maria, or Buff State, at the East Side's Dom Polski, or the West Side's Essex Street Art Center. (And, yes, Tony includes himself.)

This squares with the evidence I've by now amassed but hadn't yet put in the right order.

Andy had been an influential Hallwalls tenant. An influential instructor at UB. An assistant to Hatchett.

Andy had been in the inaugural Hallwalls show.

He had exhibited at Upton, Bethune, 219, the Castellani.

He had been a director and chief curator at the Mazur Gallery.

He had cofounded the EBMA and performed with the day's leading composers.

He had even begun to work with Joan Posluzny in 1980, on a space he'd wanted to call the Howl Gallery, after Allen Ginsberg's poem.

All this before he'd met Aunt Cindy.

Andy's artistic vision and drive drew followers as much as an arrangement of additional qualities that spoke to something other than an artist's character: his attention, his sincerity, his eagerness to connect and to build—his predilection for collage and collision, collaboration, even confrontation.

But the tides of Lake Erie were beating at the breakwall, sending pulses of energy into the emptying city. With each concussion, little columns of air moved subtly but insistently down the steel and concrete canyons Ellicott's dream had made destiny. Energy funneled down the unbroken avenues of Genesee, Sycamore, Broadway, and William—cracked, crossed, cacophonated in new directions at every intersection. They reached the drinkers in the Dom Polski bar, artists who felt something just on the other edge of *happening*: a word we use for a wish, waiting to feel a tip over into the present tense. Over time it built up into a roaring in the ears. It whispered: *east.*

Where to Begin?

ANDY TRIES TO brush away the light dust of ash that fell from his last cigarette, but the broad edge of his hand only grinds the grains into the weft of the white tablecloth, leaving a gray smudge like charcoal on canvas. As he lights another he looks up into the big windows beside the table and finds a face there, a transparency in another dimension, seeming to look past his shoulder and into the restaurant. But the woman across the table, who casts her image into the glass, isn't appraising the lunch crowd and isn't looking at the street scene. She is looking at Andy.

"Well?" she says.

Charlotta Kotik—fashionable, frank, petite, with a face like a book perpetually falling open—an émigré from Prague, curator of prints and drawings at the Albright-Knox—tries to find the right expression to meet Andy's. He is visibly nervous, self-distracting. She settles on an all-too-familiar look of concern: eyes wide, attentive—but armored. Armored against the reach of a man's need.

Charlotta hesitates before telling me any of this—the scene in the restaurant that day in the middle 1980s.

She reaches me late in the morning on July 20, 2020, a Monday, in my office in downtown Buffalo. The pandemic seems to be at an ebb now—the worst yet to come—and short-sighted employers (like mine) are experimenting with inducements for workers to return to their desks. My window looks due east from Main Street; straight ahead is the clocktower of the Central Terminal, the abandoned art deco train station that defines the East Side skyline. One click to the left, the Dom Polski. And all around, the spires of Russian, German, and Polish churches, originally Catholic and Orthodox, some now home to AME congregations, and more each year rededicated as mosques. Like the landscape, the voice that leaps from the phone is a product of flight, sea change, and persistent memory.

Kotik's husband, Petr, had left Prague for Buffalo in 1969—he was twenty-seven—to join Lukas Foss on the faculty at UB's Center of the Creative and Performing Arts. Charlotta followed in 1970—she was thirty—with their infant son, Tomas. Though she "barely spoke English," she told me, she found work almost immediately at the Albright-Knox Art Gallery—"on a fluke," through an internship funded by the newly minted NYSCA. This was a time when the region's biggest gallery had a total staff of five, an all-hands employment arrangement where everyone helped to paint, hang, frame, change lights, make marketing materials, court the city's gerontocracy for legacy gifts—where everyone knew each piece of the collection. And in the '70s, that collection was growing at an astounding rate. For Charlotta, the internship—which evolved quickly into full-time employment—provided an inimitable education.

Charlotta was a connector. She knew she would never be part of Buffalo's established art elite, so she gravitated toward the emerging artists, the striving artists, the group who all seemed to be coming up at the same time, who claimed their own spaces and made Buffalo in the 1970s the *place to be*. Charlotta connected them with each other and with galleries; she encouraged them to submit to the *Western New York Show* at the Albright-Knox, a biannual juried exhibition and one of the few events that could bring together artists from across the stark lines of the city's segregated neighborhoods. Sometimes she influenced an acquisition.

As I pored over Google results, my due diligence before our

conversation, I found a friend who described her curation, connecting artists and individual works, connecting people, like writing poetry—there was a sense in Charlotta's exhibitions of a singular voice, the friend wrote, and each of the pieces on display a note in its song.

And, like the best poets, Charlotta is a very good listener.

She listened to her friends, most of whom were artists. A few years older than the cohort then at the top—two decades older than Cindy—she was an approachable source of wisdom and perspective for many who found those qualities lacking in their inner circles, in themselves. She listened to dreams, to troubles, to silences. Now she listens to me, as I struggle to explain my project, my relationship to Cindy and Andy, what I need from her—*why* I'm spending my time this way.

"Do you want to hear this?" she asks me, after a beat. "I don't know if you do."

Before I can answer, she has decided for both of us.

"I'll tell you," she says. "I don't know everything. It's just what I remember."

Charlotta cuts Andy short—he has rambled his way into an explanation about a minor argument with a gallerist over payment for the printing of postcards to promote an upcoming show.

"Andy—" Charlotta says, and he falls silent, bored with his own story. "Where to begin?"

"I'm sorry," he says. "I wanted to ask you…"

Charlotta can see Andy working himself up into another roundabout approach. A server in black had circled the table twice and hadn't stopped to take their orders—scared off by a sudden movement from Andy, wrestling cigarettes from his pocket or snapping his head to one side to check the tables around them. Charlotta is hungry and had long ago decided on the ahi.

"Maybe," she says, flashing her eyebrows at one of the wait-staff, "start with the end?"

Andy's posture slackens. She's right. The ending is the place to begin.

Andy had married Patricia Zylka in 1973, when they were both twenty-one—Andy was finishing his undergraduate degree at UB and Pat was working as a nurse, fresh out of training at Millard Fillmore Suburban Hospital. Things were looking up in the mid-'70s: Andy got the full-time gig at Villa Maria, and they moved into a comfortable rented house in Elmwood Village, at 85 Inwood Place, walking distance from the storied cemetery, Olmstead's park and parkways, the Albright-Knox, and pubs like Cole's and No Name. By 1980—the year Cindy Suffoletto graduates from high school, moves out from McKinley, starts at Buff State, and gets a part-time job bartending by Hallwalls—Andy has been teaching undergraduates for nearly six years, he has been married for seven, and he is the devoted father of two children, James and Julia.

If he could have found the words, he would have told Charlotta this: It started at the student show in the asylum—Andy looked up from Cindy's face, his cheeks flushed beneath his beard at the abrupt realization they'd been talking for a quarter of an hour, standing in front of one of the exhibited works so that no one else could get a straight-on look. His eyes went wide and black as he clocked one, two, three other artists dropping gazes, leaning in to whisper with one another—*shit*, he thought, he'd pissed someone off again—until a touch at his arm broke the record, stopped the soundtrack of howling doubt. Cindy smiled at him, laughed at their obliviousness, tugged him away from the wall. And he saw now that the others were smiling. The conversation with Cindy started up again. It carried on well into the morning.

In Cindy he found an electric intellectual connection, a spiritual connection. Cindy understood the drive that kept him in the studio at every available hour. Cindy saw and wanted to support the part of him that needed to be there. And Cindy saw more: she saw where he was headed. He would have to leave—not just his familiar haunts, the Essex Art Center, the Dom Polski, Villa Maria, but all of Buffalo. She felt the same wind at her back, the same rushing in her ears.

But what to do about his family, their life together? Charlotta only shook her head. She could offer Andy nothing but aphorisms, mangled up or truncated to sound less trite.

"You know what you need," she said. "There isn't any…" she waved her hand over the table, as if sifting in another medium for the word.

Getting around it, she meant. But she didn't say this.

"This will get worse," she said.

To Andy, Charlotta signaled more than she might have intended.

Hard Choices

CINDY'S GIVING HAIRCUTS, the story goes. Half the artists in the icehouse line up outside Studio 30F for a turn, happy to save a buck. In exchange they bring beer, bring food, make conversation.

John Toth is back—he and Lisa, now his wife, had shared the space with Andy, Cindy, Bill Maecker, and Eric Knerr, but things got crowded, mixed up, briefly acrimonious, and so they moved into another studio down the hall. John, soft-spoken, raises his voice above the music—the creaks and growls of Tom Waits's *Swordfishtrombones*—to crack a joke aimed at Eric, who's bent over to mop up the beer he'd spilled before the puddle reaches the stack of fresh-stretched canvases in the corner. Andy watches and laughs from his folding chair in front of the woodstove—keeping the corner of an eye on the double doors so he can tell the next one of his friends coming through to double back first and grab him a fresh Budweiser from the snowbank outside.

Cindy stands in a space cleared at the center of the studio, the aluminum-hooded shop lights clamped above easels and workbenches all turned now, trained on her. She wears one of Andy's denim work shirts with the sleeves rolled up past her elbows, her own hair back in one of the bandannas she loves. She isn't trained to cut hair; this is just the sort of thing that Cindy does—with confidence. The concrete around her is carpeted in a napped shag of natural colors.

Bill is slouched in the wooden seat, asleep. He's just returned from a trip to New York, where he'd been trying to make connections at galleries. It's a familiar circuit for all the artists in 30F. Bill was so tired from the drive that he'd fallen asleep almost as soon as he sat down—lulled by all the familiar voices, the familiar records, the warmth of the woodstove. He wears his coat—the long wool one from his Navy days, comically heavy for Vietnam but perfect for Buffalo winters—like a blanket or a sleeping bag, fists balled in the pockets, chin snugged down into the crossed lapels. His long hair spills over the collar. Cindy watches his eyes flicker under their lightly wrinkled lids, his Adam's apple bob beneath a prickly scrum.

"You should cut it all off," someone says.

Laughter ripples outward from the stove.

"He'll kill ya," Eric warns.

Bill had started growing his hair out after he'd returned from the Navy, where—he claims—he flew bombers armed with nuclear warheads. It was his way of saying *fuck all that*. He'd been growing it out for a decade.

"His head's too heavy anyway," someone says. "You'd be doing him a favor."

Cindy's eyes flash against the shop lights, lock onto Andy's.

"Everybody," she says, "could use a little change."

Change was everywhere, then—and with the exception of Cindy's appearance on the scene, Andy saw that change in Buffalo was mostly ugly.

Things were slowing down, emptying out. Less and less could you rely on a friend to say yes when you needed it. Friends were careful with their yeses these days, counted them like coins.

It was a matter of the way people moved through the world.

And the way people move through the world is a matter of money.

Money cleans you. We often think of money accumulating, but that doesn't get at the truth of it. Paper money might accumulate, but *wealth* works the opposite way. It smooths your edges and leaves you pure like moving mercury, to slide wherever you please.

Now, a *lack* of money—that lack accumulates. It's an absence that appreciates. Lack latches on and sticks to you; sticks you where you are.

Buffalo was getting sticky. This was particularly true for the artists, and for them it carried particular complications.

Artists, critics, collectors, and philistines—they're all typically quick to point out the "commodification" of art, an observation most often flavored with a remote condescension aimed at one of the other parties in this standoff. The collectors turned art into an asset class. The critics enabled it, gave it cover. The artists embraced it. And the philistines, because of their mass consumption of downwardly mobile cultural memes and discounted reproductions, allow this commodification to continue, force it to seek new, undemocratized sources of cool. The thing is that no one can say definitively where this process begins.

In October 2018, it seemed everyone online had a take on the latest Banksy prank. Sotheby's had put up a copy of the British "street" artist's famous *Girl with Balloon*, a version spray-painted on a canvas and placed in a heavy, overelaborate golden frame. Moments after the austere auction house had recorded the sale— for $1.4 million, a record for the artist—an alarm sounded and the canvas descended through a shredder built into the frame. Banksy intended to play on a common understanding of the commodification of art—art as a vessel for value, rather than meaning or enjoyment. He meant the prank simultaneously to emphasize and undermine the notion of transaction in the art world. The spectacle offered a brief but satisfying thrill for the many thousands of virtual onlookers who likely never could have afforded to be in the room where it happened. The famed graffito was pulling one over on an archetypical aristocrat, and the rest of us could enjoy the victory (if not Banksy's earnings) vicariously.[1]

But something about the stunt, to me, seemed off.

Denizens of art's most rarefied echelons found themselves plunged again into the deepest snake pits of trending Twitter topics the following year. At Miami's Art Basel, the Italian artist Maurizio Cattelan purchased bananas from a local grocery—thirty cents each, he later approximated—and duct-taped one of them to a wall in the gallery Perrotin. Three versions of the work, titled *Comedian*, each sold for an average of $120,000. Unlike Banksy's, this prank demanded attention to the *thisness* and the *thusness* of art, an inquiry with aftershocks that tickled broader political and social sensibilities: What mechanism raised the value of a piece of fruit from thirty cents to $120,000? And what do we make of the ethics of this mechanism when millions in the world are going hungry? And what do we think of the short causal chain (we cannot ignore it) connecting the banana taped to the wall to workers whose labor made the fruit available, first to the artist, then to the purchaser-investor?[2]

These events produced hundreds of articles and thousands of quick takes on Twitter, the latter dismissing the artists or decrying the influence of money on art, and the former mostly attempting to explain the phenomena as "critiques" of the same. All this tepid discourse rehearsed (like the fungible banana) long-established beliefs about art and money.

But these popular beliefs, whether or not they serve as valid descriptions of cultures and marketplaces at large, fail utterly to understand the experience of *the artist*. From this vantage, the commodification of art doesn't happen at the point of valuation or sale, as the Banksy and Cattelan stunts suggested.

The commodification of art is really a prerequisite to its creation.

All art begins with that most elemental commodity: time.

. . .

I've often described my childhood in Buffalo as like growing up in a land of antique shops. Specifically, I grew up in North Buffalo, off Hertel Avenue, a quiet, mostly residential part of the city, a melting pot of Italian, Irish, German, and Russian-Jewish influences, home to the zoo and to Delaware Park, full of friendly neighbors in eccentric old homes.

My description was literal. In the late '90s, Hertel Avenue, North Buffalo's main commercial strip, was flush with antique shops and businesses that might as well have been antique shops—a jeweler, a Victorian furniture store, a secondhand bookstore, two framing shops, and one place filled entirely with ornate ceramic lamps—with pizza-and-wings joints in between.

One Friday night each winter, my sister and I would bundle up and accompany our parents on the "Hertel Walk," a local initiative to support small businesses during the frigid months without foot traffic. Darkness descended by 4:00 p.m., but all of the stores would stay open late and put out treats for visitors—trays of cheese and crackers, bowls of candy, Crock-Pots of meatballs in sweet sauce, bowls of hot spiked punch, and shining carafes of coffee and Swiss Miss hot chocolate. In the way back, wine and Labatts. We walked the entire street those nights, both sides, never in the cold for more than one or two dark storefronts, but still ducking in each bright doorway with red, runny noses, my sister and I picking our way past glass cases and precarious towers of stacked treasures to find the appetizers at the back of the room. Our parents talked to neighbors while our attention turned to cufflinks and oil paintings, silk smoking jackets, crystal decanters, Mod clock radios, each tagged with handwritten prices.

But there's a deeper truth in the description. Like the proprietors of the antique shops that once stretched from our front doorstep to the horizon, all Buffalonians tend to invest in memories, to treasure trinkets that in the right light might trick us into thinking the best of the past endures.

We are a city of architectural treasures, we say. But we've razed more than half of what we had, mostly to make way for abominations of design, parking lots and enormous concrete obsolesences.

We are the best-planned city in the world, we say. But we turned our downtown inside out, filled it with spaghetti junctions and block after unwalkable block of windowless empty buildings, transformed a Paris of the New World into a frostbitten Potemkin Village.

It takes twenty minutes to get from anywhere to anywhere in Western New York, we say. But our subway runs only 6.4 miles in a straight line, far from the people who need it most; our buses are always late; we built expressways straight through the middle of our park and through historic, middle-class, and predominantly Black neighborhoods; and we lack the political will and bureaucratic competence even to time the lights on Main Street. If you can get from anywhere to anywhere quickly in Buffalo, it's probably because we lack the density to clog our streets. We're like a hermit crab living in a conch shell, a people saddled with crumbling infrastructure meant for a population three times our size.

We love to talk about Jim Kelly and Teddy Roosevelt and Frank Lloyd Wright, as if one day we might simply shake off our mistakes and again be champions, exemplars, protectors of the most prosperous little city in the world.

Today, Hertel Avenue is filled with chic boutiques and craft cocktail bars. Our waterfront is accessible and downtown warehouses converted into lofts are filling with millennials making low six figures. In 2020, for the first time in seventy years, the census does not show a population decline.[3]

But we're still a city of antique shops.

. . .

Time—and money—were running out in Buffalo long before I was born. In truth, they were running out even before Andy was born, in the best of the postwar years, but few people noticed until the late '70s. By the mid-'80s, it was obvious.

The arts in Buffalo Niagara were growing as the region was shrinking. You might even say it was happening at the same pace, reversed. At a peak population of 580,000 in 1950, Buffalo would see a decline in every subsequent census: 532,000 in 1960; 426,000 in 1970; 357,000 in 1980; starting to level off two decades into the new millennium at 278,000—a people halved in half a century.

One of the oldest sectors of the Buffalo economy, shipbuilding, vanished in 1962, a victim of the St. Lawrence Seaway and the obsolescence of the Erie Canal. The grain mills, wholly owned by outside interests by the '60s, were quick to follow, most shifting operations to other port towns. Manufacturing employment overall had fallen from 180,000 jobs in 1954 to 154,000 in 1967; the trend continued, and in '71 Bethlehem Steel laid off half of its 18,000 workers.

Unemployment reached twelve percent in 1975, when, on February 9, the *New York Times* ran a Sunday cover story called "Down and Out in America," with a montage of faces from Buffalo, recalling Dorothea Lange's Dust Bowl portraits.

And just thirty minutes away, the city of Niagara Falls would suffer an even worse fate, plummeting into a poverty maintained by mob-controlled construction unions, unscrupulous and short-sighted hospitality developers, and a corrupt and ineffective local government—all while Niagara Falls, Ontario, boomed, raising glittering, popular casinos, hotels, and attractions to taunt Western New Yorkers from across the canyon.

Competition in the arts peaked just as the state funding that fueled it (funding from outside Buffalo's battered economy) fell off sharply, pinched by the Ford and Carter recessions. New York, like other states, realized that higher education was the easiest expense to reduce, as tuition hikes could help to cover shortfalls.

UB President Martin Meyerson and his successor, Robert Ketter, had prioritized the arts and innovation for two decades, but Steven B. Sample, an engineer by training who assumed the presidency in 1982, was no advocate for culture. Under his tenure the university shuttered interdisciplinary programs like Domus, a performance space the artist and philanthropist Calvin Rand had opened on a leased floor of the old Pierce-Arrow factory on Elmwood. Unimpressed by flicker films, Sample slashed the media studies budget. Experimental colleges and degree-tracks closed, written off as relics of '60s and '70s excess. Sample upended the train of renowned writers and musicians who had paraded through the university's music and English departments for a quarter century. Cost cutting cascaded—the jobs and fellowships and grants dried up. And Buffalo artists turned to a private sector unprepared to support them.

There are only so many collectors. Only so many little galleries, like Nina Freudenheim's that opened on Franklin in 1975 and later moved into the Lenox Hotel, that would actually *represent* artists.[4] Only so many friends and family willing to sit through only so many cacophonous, esoteric intermedia performances at the Dom Polski (a venue suddenly without funding and less and less appealing to first-time visitors because of perceptions around accelerating "white flight" and rising crime). And there was really nowhere to go after showing work at the Albright's Western New York exhibition, where the out-of-town juries might—*just might*—pluck a rough diamond from the Rust Belt and make introductions in New York.

In the late '70s and '80s, introductions were the new currency in the Buffalo art world, where opportunities were disappearing and stagflation was limiting how far one could stretch art's wages. Introductions—introductions in New York—were a form of credit: they could be exchanged for time.

I reach the artist John Toth by phone at his home in Chester, New York, on the morning of August 2, 2020. He and his wife, Lisa, had followed a path remarkably similar to Andy and Cindy: from studios on Essex Street in the '70s to Brooklyn in the mid-'80s and finally to a quieter home tucked in the mid-Hudson counties in the 2000s.

I feel twice transported as we talk—first to John's Chester backyard, poolside under murmuring pines—and then into the heady '70s, drinking Budweisers and wandering under illuminated fabric installations in the humid ruins of the steel mills. In a soft, almost strained voice he bashfully begs forgiveness for the beginnings of dementia, but the scenes he brings to life are brilliant with multisensory detail. After an hour, I ask him the question I'd written on the first page of a legal pad now nearly filled: *Why*, I begin, *does it seem like an entire generation of artists left Buffalo at the same time?*

The Hallwalls cohort had cashed in first, John explains, around 1976. Cindy Sherman, Charlie Clough, and Robert Longo left their startup gallery in trusted hands and tried to establish themselves in New York, frequently sending new friends from the big city back to Buffalo to exhibit there, maintaining the "import-export model" they had established for just this purpose.

Clough and fellow Hallwallian Larry Lundy are able to add some color when I track them down nearly a year after speaking with Toth: Cindy Sherman won an NEA grant, they explain, and Bob Longo, though no longer an "item" with Cindy, tagged along—he knew his train by its whistle. He and Cindy had spent many nights discussing exactly what it would take to make the jump—where they would have to exhibit, whom they would have to meet—and they executed their plan with swiftness and precision. In New York they showed at Metro Pictures and other up-and-coming galleries, started hanging out at the Mudd Club, and found themselves in a swift, exhilarating current unlike anything that had been possible in Buffalo.

Charlie, Diane Bertolo, Nancy Dwyer, and Michael Zwack left next. Shortly after it had begun, Hallwalls was in the hands of a second generation.

Not all went to New York, where success was far from certain. In those years the city was still wracked with violent crime; you worked multiple jobs to make ends meet, wasting precious time in commutes among the boroughs; apartment buildings changed hands and new landlords yanked leases. In '78, Larry Lundy took an $800 commission he'd made on illustrations for a Buffalo bank and headed west, settling in Chicago. A few followed him. Others went to California. Joan Posluzny, after stints managing the Mazur Gallery, the Essex Gallery, the Bethune Gallery, and the Tralfamadore, had tried with Andy and Brian Duffy to open a new gallery in an abandoned chair factory (on the aptly named Old Chair Factory Road in Cheektowaga), but they ran out of money and Joan, too, started to look outside the region. She took a grant from the Polish Ministry of Culture to study with the artist Władysław Hasior in the tiny mountain town of Zakopane, and later at the Warsaw Art Academy.

But most moved to New York. A decade after the departure of that vanguard—now in the middle '80s—the migration of artists from Buffalo to New York had become a popular narrative. Buffalo, birthplace of the baby boomers' avant-garde, was in decline, while New York, essentially bankrupt in the '70s, seemed to be turning a corner.

"It's gone," Petr Kotik rasps, interrupting me.

His voice is warm, grained, with a rich Czech accent. I had

asked him to explain the forces of economics and personality that made Buffalo the center of the cultural world for two decades in the middle of the last century—and what caused its undoing.

I might have mistaken his abruptness for impatience. He listens, he hums assent—but he gives the impression that a total understanding of Buffalo's cultural rise and fall came to him in a flash many years ago and hasn't bothered him since.

"Now the bureaucrats run the place," he says. "They think they know everything, they think they can justify everything, they write the grant applications...and it is a desert."

I think of the Buffalo of my childhood, in the '90s and early '00s: dark storefronts, barren streets on winter nights, elevated expressways weaving around empty office towers, a light rail to nowhere. He isn't wrong.

"That's what it is if you want to talk about money," Petr says.

He would offer his laurels to Seymour Knox II. No one, it seems, surpasses Knox's contribution to Buffalo, in Petr's estimation. You need limitless money, the right friends, and some vision. The Knox family kept producing Seymours—but our region ran out of patrons of his stature.

"In New York there are always personalities to support something," Petr explains. "That's what keeps it alive. And if it dries out, it will become another Berlin. What is Berlin now? It is provincial."

Speaking to Petr, I have two words in mind. They come from a file John Toth had sent me moments after we had last spoken almost a year earlier. It was a photo of an article from a Sunday *Buffalo News*, February 17, 1985. The headline stated in simple, all-caps block lettering what Buffalo artists then faced: **HARD CHOICES.**

The correspondent, Mack Mahoney, was covering a subject already familiar in the arts pages: the difficulty of making a living as an artist in Buffalo and the powerful attraction of New

York.[5] The piece is a triptych of interviews with Bob Gulley, Andy Topolski, and John Toth—Buffalo artists who at the time, respectively, had just moved to New York City, were in the process of moving to New York City, or were contemplating a move to New York City.

The sculptor Robert Gulley departed on September 2, 1980, borrowing five thousand dollars on a student loan through UB and securing a teaching gig that would give him—in lieu of an apartment—twenty-four-hour access to a cold-water flat in the Westbeth Artists Community on West Street in Manhattan.

Andy occupied the middle of the "hard choices" triptych: he had been four months in the city at the time and still didn't quite feel his feet beneath him. In the article he mentions in a circumspect way a pending opportunity to meet with a gallery that might represent him. There's a sense of regret in my uncle's comments—the clear feeling that he should have left earlier, that he might have *just* missed some vague opportunity in New York.

"Bob [Gulley] didn't hang around long enough to get anything going in Buffalo," Andy told Mahoney. "He was wise enough to size up the situation and move quickly." After thirty years in a rent-controlled apartment on the Lower East Side, Bob picked up and moved back near his childhood home in Peoria, Illinois. When I track him down on a tip from Charlotta Kotik, he explains that Andy's assessment was overly simple. By '81, Bob had secured space—a bed, a cramped kitchen, and a twelve- by six-foot clearance for his sculpture and drawing material—on the fifth floor of a building on Stanton Street. But he had to work full-time in construction to feed himself and make rent. Between that and his sculpting he struggled to schedule time for visiting galleries with slides and photographs, doing the networking necessary to "make it" in the city.

"Hard choices" follows the artists, but the tug of New York reached Buffalo's curatorial class, too. Linda Cathcart moved to

Texas. The Albright-Knox director Robert Buck left for a position at the Brooklyn Museum in 1981. Charlotta would follow him not long after, taking a position in the new Prints and Drawing Department. By '85, she would help to found and then chair the Department of Contemporary Art. Like Sherman and Longo from the Hallwalls cohort, Charlotta stepped out from under the low ceiling in Buffalo and found unimaginable success: the Czech immigrant and former NYSCA intern went on to serve as US commissioner for the 1993 Venice Biennale.

The next to leave, in 1983, was Peter Muscato, another of the Albright-Knox's small staff and a close friend to Cindy and Andy and dozens of others in the Buffalo art scene. Peter had spent years meeting artists at gallery openings or at the Albright's *Western New York Show*; he got to know them more closely off-hours in their studios, where he photographed pieces for the 35 mm slides they mailed to contacts in New York, usually staying for a can of beer and a little conversation. Peter knew better than anyone where the wind was blowing.

Peter, who calls me one evening from his framing shop in Williamsburg, describes it as a "mass exodus." And it wasn't contained to the visual arts. Writers, poets, musicians, composers, actors, and performers left, too. The arts in Buffalo boomed from 1962 for a little more than a decade; and then, starting around 1975, the tide ebbed, taking with it a generation of singular talent, and leaving behind a rich and complicated legacy.

Andy, Cindy, and John and Lisa Toth were among the last of their generation to leave. They'd known for years that it would come to this. They knew it even at the height of the early Hallwalls scene, which had seemed a world apart from the Albright-Knox and the hustle to impress Buffalo's handful of trust-funded art buyers. And they knew it in the aftermath of that benevolent chaos, a decade when all the young artists, it seemed, worked together, exhibited together, talked and fucked and fought and kept making art through it all. They had real apartments, had kids, and were beginning to enjoy the stability and safety of the teaching gigs they'd earned. They saw ahead of them in Buffalo long decades of tenure and members' shows, comfort bought for the cost of obscurity.

Some, of course, stayed. Don Metz and Brian Duffy were among those who weighed the cost of departure on marriages and kids. They stuck it out in Buffalo and did find success as artists, teachers, curators.

But there wasn't enough room for everyone. Andy and Cindy knew they had to leave, and they managed it in stages.

Starting in 1980 or '81, Andy, John, Brian, Barbara Rowe, and many other friends made frequent trips to New York, often catching $19 same-day round-trip tickets into Newark on PEOPLExpress. Sometimes they brought Andy's brother Tom. They set up gallery visits and scouted studios, always picking their way to University Place for a stop at the Cedar Tavern, a hangout in the 1940s and '50s for the abstract expressionists and members of the New York School. They imagined themselves as permanent residents, earning a spot at its fifty-foot mahogany bar.

For a time in 1983, Andy stayed in New Jersey at an apartment with his brother Thomas, nine years younger and then a master's student at NYU. Andy ran up astronomical telephone bills placing calls to galleries in Europe, which had begun to take an interest in his work; the arrangement with his brother, he later told a reporter, became "untenable," and he moved back to Buffalo.

But Cindy, it seems, knew that Andy wasn't going to stay. By 1983 she was beginning to emerge as a "working" artist, showing beyond Buff State's annual student exhibitions. That July, she and Brian Duffy had a joint show at the Artists Gallery in the Essex Street icehouse compound—he remembers that she was working in oils, doing minimalistic geometric forms, and two of her black-and-white sketches appeared on the promotional flyer. Andy got Nina Freudenheim, who ran the city's only commercial gallery and essentially represented Andy in Buffalo, to come to the opening, and she liked the work. This would have been an enormous boost of confidence for Cindy, still only three years out of Sacred Heart Academy. She was nearing the end of her bachelor's degree—80 credit hours toward a total of 120 for completion, according to records I obtained from Buffalo State's registrar in June 2021.

As I read the transcript, I rescanned my memories for any traces of the information and ideas she would have picked up in these years between 1980 and 1983. She had taken introductory and advanced courses in printmaking, papermaking, painting, pottery, photography, figure modeling, and sculpture; she had taken introductory art history and courses on nineteenth- and twentieth-century art; she had studied jazz and country music, Chinese and Japanese philosophy; she had taken intro to psych, existentialism, astronomy, religion/myth/magic, and exploratory design—even one course called "Stunts and Tumbling." She had loaded up her schedule for three years, even taking summer courses. And then she dropped out. An era was ending, Andy was leaving, and the next time he tried, she was determined to make the jump together.

In 1984, Andy stayed in New York with another artist, Chris Walsh, a New Hampshire expat who had graduated the previous year with an MFA from Pratt and wound up working at the Brooklyn Museum with Charlotta. Walsh had a clean, modern apartment on Fifth Avenue in pre-gentrified Park Slope.[6] Andy needed a studio, and Walsh connected him with another artist, Jim Osman, a lifelong New Yorker from a working-class background who had come up through Queens College and knew several mutual friends among the concentric and intersecting circles of the city's art world: the Pratt contingent, the Parsons scene, the Cal-Arts kids, associates of Artists Space, Mudd Club members-for-life, friends of Mary Boone—and spread throughout, the Buffalo affiliated. Jim and Andy looked at a studio in the Brooklyn Navy Yard—$200 a month—but Andy dropped out at the last minute and returned to Buffalo.

Then, in November 1984, Andy received an offer of three days' work hanging a show at a gallery in Manhattan. This time, he also had a partner. On a wish and a few thin promises—a single cash payment and couches friends had pledged—Cindy and Andy left Buffalo for the final time.

Tangents

ARTISTIC COMMUNITY MEANT little to me when I first started to take writing seriously. This was around 2008, toward the end of my freshman year of high school. I couldn't name a single *New Yorker* staff writer, but the magazine signified everything I thought I wanted, and I sent poems and stories to die in its slush pile every few months. I sent a piece of fiction to the *Atlantic*, a magazine nearly as glamorous and equally abstract, and months later received a square of paper with a rejection from C. Michael Curtis, signed in what I assumed to be his own blue ballpoint pen.

I had only recently graduated from *Nintendo Magazine* to *Rolling Stone*. I had read all of Fitzgerald and most of Vonnegut; if pressed to identify contemporary authors I might, after giving it some thought, have named Salman Rushdie. My friends didn't write and most didn't read beyond the books assigned in school. There weren't poets or novelists on our faculty, and there weren't any writers in my family. I wasn't passing artists in the supermarket. Writing was something I did late at night, alone, after homework and clubs, band practices and parties. I wrote in a folding chair at the family computer beside a second-floor window looking out onto the gutter-yellow lights of Hertel Avenue—which, by no coincidence, provided the setting for nearly all of my stories—and I shared this writing with no one except the anonymous interns of venerable New York magazines. I recognized the incredible distance between me and these editorial desks—I was an insatiable consumer of the earliest literary agent blogs—but I had no way to measure it, and no peers to measure up against.

In June 2009, my mom spots a note in the *Buffalo News* about a new literary arts magazine, *Tangent*, that is launching out of Buff State and accepting submissions. I send a few poems and by July receive an acceptance. For the first time, I feel the rungs of a ladder beneath my hands. I don't know how many intervals stretched between me and those offices high above Broadway and Madison and Hudson (streets and numbers I've memorized from my countless self-addressed, stamped envelopes), but I think, now that I'm in print, that reaching them will just be a matter of persistence, success inevitable so long as I continue to put one hand over the other.

The launch party that fall is at a new art gallery on Amherst Street in the passed-over neighborhood of Black Rock, not far from the college. I borrow my mom's red Mazda sedan and drive west, past the supermarket, into the unfamiliar corner of the city. The sun sets in front of me, an orange flame blanketing the lake and burnishing the faces of the people who stand outside the gallery as I drive by. I park outside a row of buildings typical of Buffalo's commercial streets—hundred-year-old mixed-use doubles, glass storefronts below and apartments above—and walk past the social smokers, in their trilbies and flip-flops and khaki cargo shorts with frayed legs, gesturing with cigarettes clamped to the lips of plastic wine cups. As I reach for the old door's brass handle, I repeat, silently, football's evergreen end zone mantra: *act like you've been here before.*

The art on display ranges widely in sophistication—from mimetic weeaboo cartoons and pop surrealism to bolder mixed-media explorations of queer sexuality—but energy circulates in the room and the atmosphere is collegial, not competitive. People, young people, are talking seriously to each other about art. They aren't looking at the pieces on display—at least not in the manner of patrons in established collections, who circulate clockwise, hands loosely linked behind their backs, pausing at equal intervals—but each artist's selected works, tightly packed and spotlit from above, seem to lean off the walls and into the party like distinct personalities.

The *Tangent* editor, Christina Surdi, spots me, and says a few nice words about the poems I'd shared. I don't realize it now, but this is my first real-life encounter with a person who'd read my work. She introduces me to the gallery owner and arts editor of the magazine, who says something polite before the currents of the room take him back. I swipe a cup of purply Cabernet from a table near the register and focus on dispelling the correct impression that I am alone, sixteen, an interloper.

This was the way I fell into the outer orbit of 464 Gallery and its proprietor, Marcus Wise.

In 2009, shortly after Marcus launched the gallery with Jill Hart, 464 was on its way to becoming one of the brightest cultural loci in Buffalo, anchoring a few blocks of Amherst Street and helping to catalyze a revitalization of the area. While 464's focus was visual art, it also spun off another group, Emerging Leaders in the Arts Buffalo, or ELAB, which drew in a more eclectic membership spanning poetry, architecture, and art history, focused on improving the city and undertaking large-scale events. Like Broadway-Fillmore's J. C. Mazur Gallery more than thirty years before, ELAB and 464 were both exercises in art-led community and economic revitalization: 464 helped bring Black Rock into the twenty-first century, while ELAB looked to the south, and in 2012 it produced an arts festival called "City of Night," which reintroduced the region to the wonder of its greatest relics, the hundred-foot grain silos along the Buffalo River, triggering a cascade of attention and investment.

But it was later in 2009 that Marcus launched his own magazine, *Spark*, a venue for promoting his cohort. Eager for clips,

I got back in touch, and he asked me to write profiles. I spent time in the gallery conducting interviews and getting to know the artists who exhibited at 464, rented studio space above, and gathered nightly for film screenings and cookouts in the yard next door. I was never more than peripheral to the inner circle, but Marcus had offered me my first brush with the idea—and practice—of artistic community.

In July 2016, Marcus left for Milwaukee. I saw the news on Facebook. We had fallen out of touch after I left Buffalo to study in Scotland, and I hadn't gotten around to checking in on 464 since returning the previous September—but I knew what his decision would mean.

Picture a spinning carousel suddenly arrested, all the painted horses flying off in every direction.

Tangent and *Spark*, both hopeless expenses, had stopped printing long before. City of Night had collapsed under its own success, unable to support the requisite insurance policies for ten thousand visitors to wander semipreserved shipping relics. ELAB limped along and then evaporated. And the core artists I had known at 464 had moved on to other rented rooms. Some had given up, surrendered time and space in their lives to other pursuits, marriages, careers, vacations, leaving less for art. But others, like Chuck Tingley, who had debuted at 464, would go on to stand among the most in-demand creators in the region. And new artists, younger artists, hungry artists moved in to take any open space available. For seven years, 464 had continued to draw and foster new talent, attract attention, and expand the production and enjoyment of art, reaching new lives and new areas of the city.

This kind of artistic community requires, as Don Metz might have put it, a catalyst—one or more individuals whose vision and charisma inspire and sustain an atmosphere of collision, collaboration, confrontation, collage.

Marcus didn't invent the role he occupied from 2009 to 2016. He inherited it.

Colin Dabkowski, the great *Buffalo News* arts critic of the first two decades of the twenty-first century, covered the loss of 464, reminding readers that the Western New York arts elite had responded to the gallery's debut less than ten years earlier with a mixture of principled disapproval and less-principled derision. The work, the cognoscenti had concurred, ranged from technically accomplished and conceptually advanced to sophomoric, commercial, cartoonish. They also took issue with the practice of charging artists for shows to pay the gallery's rent.

This is a facile, amnesiac critique coming from the boards and executives of the institutions that decades before had locked up the last of this city's inherited industrial wealth in the form of foundations named for the Bairds, Cullens, Oisheis, and Wendts; who had mastered the politics of steady state funding through SUNY and NYSCA; and who pulled down annual six-figure grants from the city's biggest bank. They forgot that originality has always paid its own way. They forgot that originality keeps paying, doubling down, kiting checks, and calling favors, until it wins big or goes broke.

This has been the story since the mid-'80s, since the great exodus. Probably since before that, too.

Every half decade or so, a new community converges around one or a handful of artists who have more than talent—who have charisma. And with only a few notable exceptions, these communities collapse, suffocate, scatter. This happens quickly, before the broader cultural ecosystem has even recognized the significance of the emergence—and often just at the moment the buzz reaches the general population of Bills ticketholders.

This isn't just a Buffalo phenomenon. Artistic communities don't last anywhere. I'm not talking about museums or magazines or theater companies, though these, too, often disappear or, worse, become desiccated carapaces of habit. I mean the molecular combinations of the creators themselves, drawn together by common preoccupations and held there in a tension of perspectives, ambitions, or media. By "community" I mean when artists congregate, night after night, often in the same basement, bar, garage, loft apartment, or living room, to sharpen one another in conversation or deaden themselves with old jokes and alcohol.

Whether or not they choose to name themselves, like the Inklings or the Factory, Black Mountain College or the East Buffalo Media Association, these groups fall apart—a key member makes it big, another dies, others fight, and still others get the itch for different scenes in different cities. This is true even in Paris and New York and Los Angeles, as we can see in Hemingway's *A Moveable Feast*, Patti Smith's *Just Kids*, Chris Kraus's history of Tiny Creatures,[1] and so many other elegies to those unstable isotopes of the art world, salons and klatches and collectives that flare up for a generation, the better part of a decade, or just a few bright months before burning out.

But this is vividly, tragically true in Buffalo, a city with space and heat and history enough to bring artists together, but without quite enough money or glory to keep most of them from moving on—leaving galleries, reading series, and whole movements to collapse behind them.

These groups, these movements, disappear even before the rising generation can recognize and rebel against them. This means that young artists in Buffalo too often waste time chasing ghosts—or fighting with them. And if you're an artist chasing ghosts in Buffalo, sooner or later you'll end up in New York City.

New Scenery, New Noise

A WHITE LIQUID TWINGE courses Cindy's right arm and she feels a single heartbeat, like something falling off a shelf in another room. She flexes her bicep and shifts her feet. Facing a window that opens to an unobstructed view of water and cloud, she has the naked sensation, for a moment, that she is a bird, never tired in flight. She is weightless, the weight in her hands something she presses against more than holds. The sky rushes soundlessly into the room and laces her hair with particulate ice.

"No...no...not this one," the suit says.

Across from Cindy, Peter Muscato breathes relief through his nose. They lower the framed canvas, a charcoal drawing, and stack it with the others beside the neglected snake plant.

The water outside the window is the Passaic River, and the sky is the sky above Newark, New Jersey's downtown business district. The building is the headquarters of Prudential, and the suit is a mid-thirties executive, an AVP or VP or SVP, tasked with selecting art for the top offices of a division that has just been shuffled to this renovated floor.

He wants to give the impression of having strong opinions but can't quite put them into words. Not Picasso prints but real, contemporary art. Nothing too political, we're in insurance, after all—maybe safer to say nothing, nothing, what's the word, you know—*representational?*—representational. Safer with something... abstract. But it shouldn't *feel* safe, it should feel... well, like this building: concrete, glass, structural steel. Something that signals...power...but not greed. Not the softness of ingots but the iron of the buried vaults that keep them. It has to be...all right, sure, sexy. B-b-but not *porn*, okay?

This is the seventh work of art they've held against the wall for the executive's appraisal. Cindy and Peter look past his padded shoulder to the elevators, where Andy stands by a dolly stacked with a dozen works. He pulls one off the cart and removes its thin foam shroud. Cindy and Peter share a glance. They know the work at once—and it hadn't been on the list to pack this morning.

Andy holds the frame out in front of him like the Gospel in procession at St. Casimir's. Peter and Cindy fall back as Andy steps to the wall, holding the frame there himself and turning to watch the suit's reaction.

A stark hypotenuse bisects the canvas diagonally, finely rendered in graphite dark as jet. The other legs of the triangle swing out, making a perfect shaded gradient that ends in an unmarked point where the triangle's third corner might have been. It pushes off the canvas in three dimensions; it is either an object fallen from space or an invitation into an ageless Cimmerian night.

A certain look passes over the suit, a look Andy knows. It isn't comprehension, but a recognition, a recognition that this—

"*This* is it," the suit says. "This is the one. We'll take it."

Andy lets a faint smile pass in a single pulse between the corners of his mouth, hidden by a bristly black goatee. Cindy and Peter smile, too, trying to tamp amusement down into a more appropriate professional pleasure. They set about shrouding and stacking the other works and wheeling the cart into the elevator.

The suit's head snaps up, as if from a trance, when Andy lifts the chosen work—his own, of course—and wraps it in foam.

"You..."

"We'll be back to hang it on Friday," Andy says, stepping into the elevator. "This one doesn't have its mounting gear."

Cindy hits the button to make the doors shut faster. Only when the compartment starts moving downward do all three of them break into breathless laughter.

The years between arrival and *arrival* in New York City had been a constant hustle for Cindy and Andy. Andy moved first, staying for a few months with Chris Walsh in his Park Slope apartment— Andy's off-book, subleased space was, essentially, a closet—while Cindy secured her own short-term rental in the same neighborhood. Peter Muscato, his wife, Beverly, and their newborn, Pietro, were also living there, on Sixth Avenue. Before the end of '85, though, Andy and Cindy had moved together into #4L at 440 Broadway in Williamsburg.

Their $1,200 a month secured them more living space than they had ever enjoyed, even in Buffalo; access to an unoccupied ground-floor studio that Andy was quick to claim for them both; and an attached grassy yard that they could reach by leaving the building on the first floor and turning the corner at Penn. They set about finishing the raw space, then decorating, homemaking—they stashed tools and supplies in the studio and converted the weedy lot into a garden for themselves and the other artists in the building.

Soon this included the Muscatos, who seized an opportunity in '87 to take another unfinished space, sanding, framing, painting, and arranging it into an apartment. What happened on Broadway is what had happened on Essex Street in Buffalo a decade before, what was happening then all over SoHo and Brooklyn, and what has happened in hundreds of ex-industrial zip codes in large and small cities in every year since. Andy and Cindy made a home, and then with other artists they made a community. Then, of course, they had to start making art, showing art, and selling art.

Andy and Cindy bounced between galleries before finding steady work at C. S. Schulte, a fine art dealership at 317 Valley

Andy and Cindy under the L train near their apartment and
studio space at 440 Broadway in Brooklyn, mid-1980s.

Street in South Orange, New Jersey. This was not an easy commute from Williamsburg—it took over an hour in moderate traffic, and because neither of them owned a car, they had to borrow one from the Schultes. But the work paid well enough—and there was enough of it to go around—that they were able to entice Peter away from his gig at the much closer Brooklyn Museum to join them.

The gallery was attempting a new kind of venture that demonstrated the influence of Wall Street on the art world of the late '80s. Andy, Cindy, and Peter worked in the back framing pieces for exhibition. Cindy also helped out with the books, taking phone calls, a mix of front- and back-office responsibilities. But mostly the three friends drove around the tri-state area in a white panel van visiting corporate high-rises and suburban office parks selling art on the spot. Investment brokerages, insurance companies, law firms, real estate offices—every white-collar outfit in the late '80s and early '90s wanted in on the art boom, saw taste as an investment, part of turning the corner on the sleaze, squalor, and stagflation of the '70s. But bank executives didn't have time to visit galleries, and they didn't want to pay gallery prices. So Schulte put the gallery in a van and brought it to the buyers. Andy, Cindy, and Peter would hold up different pieces on blank walls for the bosses' approval and leave the selections behind them—sometimes handling the hanging—driving away with a lighter van to the next stop.

They sold a lot of art that way—and Andy recognized the opportunity to add some of his own to the mix, playing artist and dealer (a new kind of art dealer, more Willy Loman than Mary Boone) at once.

Cindy's work, at that time, wasn't exactly the sort that corporate types snapped up. She was practicing with sculpture and mixed media using found materials—architectural but messier and more particular than Andy's palatable postminimalist works on paper. But she didn't seem to mind. She gave her work to friends, showed a little of it in group exhibitions in the city, and helped Andy with the business end of his own practice.

Corporate offices started to buy enough of Andy's work that he needed to reduce his hours at Schulte to make more. He dropped down from five days a week to four, then three, then finally cut himself off completely. After a few larger sales he bought himself a boxy Jeep Cherokee so that he could get around town to visit galleries while Cindy kept working at Schulte.

Because she handled front-office work as well as sales, she was able to compile a list of all corporate collectors in Pennsylvania,

New Jersey, and New York. This eventually ran to thirteen pages, with more than 200 entries, like this:

Johnson & Johnson	SOURCE: dealers, consultants
1 Johnson & Johnson Plaza	SELECTED BY: corp. committee &
New Brunswick, NJ 08933	consultants; Art Advisory Svc
201-524-6336	Museum of Modern Art, NY
ATT: Corp. Art Coordinator,	
Michael J. Bzdak	

Over this, Cindy included her own handwritten notes about specialty interests: Steinway & Sons, "collection art related to music"; Deutsche Bank, "collection art work incorporating photographs & photog."; the International Paper Corporation, "collection art work related to paper and wood." She made another list for second-tier purchasers and referrals, mostly interior designers and architects, with shorthand notes on previous and recommended contacts: "sent brochure 12/4," "send info 11/8," "very interested 11/7."

Andy wasn't selling to collectors, and he wasn't pulling in major commissions—Cindy, working at Schulte and taking side gigs from the classifieds, brought the steady income—but the art he made in the first-floor studio on Broadway wasn't staying there. That was the main thing. That, they both knew, was the measure that mattered.

Magic Geometry

The romance of disappearance was arguably one of the great organizing myths of the mid-20th century.

—CHRIS KRAUS, "No More Utopias"

MOM PASSES THE padded mailer to me and I push my empty plate away to clear a space on the white tablecloth. It is February 2020, and my mom's side of the family has gathered in the back room of an Italian restaurant in West Seneca for a surprise party—my cousin Anita's thirtieth birthday. I've angled my chair to keep one eye on the door and watch for Anita's arrival with her husband, Jeff, and their two kids, Anthony and Cecilia—but I've also been watching this envelope make an epicyclical circuit around the dinner tables.

It is addressed, in a large and somewhat wobbly hand, to Uncle Tom. I don't recognize the sender or the address: Eric Siegeltuch, on Cary Street in Yonkers.

I tug out the envelope's contents, a little more than a dozen developed film photographs. They are images of Andy and Cindy—images none of us have ever seen before.

Andy, Cindy, and another man—this Eric, I assume—are pictured in and around Paris. They are strolling through the Luxembourg Gardens, crossing the Pont Neuf, lighting candles inside Notre Dame. The pictures tell a piece of a story already in motion, and well advanced—flipping through them feels like dropping into an episode of a long-running TV series that I hadn't been following. As I shuffle and reshuffle the pictures, I see the trio breeze through Paris's arrondissements under a typically overcast sky—Cindy in a gray wool coat, hiply big and falling to her ankles, and a white silk scarf with flowers; the presumed Eric in a brown trench coat over a suit and tie, smiling through a chestnut goatee; and Andy, the very picture of an artist in the '80s, wearing dark jeans and a black sweater under a matching sport coat, big sunglasses, and a little black-and-red scarf, a cigarette always burning in his right hand.

Applause pops around the room—I turn to the door and stand to greet Anita walking through, Anthony leading, three-year-old CeCe trying to hide behind her legs. Talia takes the pictures as soon as my attention shifts, and they continue their circuit through the family.

Half a decade of knocking on doors during weekend trips to the city hadn't led to any swinging open for Andy, but, by the time he and Cindy made the move in earnest in 1984, it had made him plenty of friends. He owed his first real big city breakthrough to them—and, in a broader sense, to the pattern of seasonal and permanent migrations between New York and the Niagara Frontier.

In late '85, one of those friends, Douglas G. Schultz, walked into a new gallery at 568 Broadway in SoHo and spoke a few words that would have a defining impact on the next few years of Andy's—and Cindy's—life.

Doug had replaced Bob Buck as director at the Albright-Knox two years earlier. His pacific appearance—sleepy eyes beneath owlish spectacles, neat cranial part, and kitchen-whisk mustache—belied a tremendous competence and a vision commensurate to straddle centuries.[1] Building on the model Gordon Smith and Seymour Knox had introduced, Doug balanced the local and the personal aspects of his job with the global and the institutional. The cultural frontiersman regularly took trips to larger cities in the US and abroad, seeking art to acquire for the

Albright-Knox, and in his close confabs with gallerists, he often recommended favored expat artists for acquisition, exhibition, or representation. Doug couldn't do this too frequently—such discussions were too easily misread as quid pro quo, leading to calls months later from gallerists expecting favors, and sometimes such discussions *did* involve a tacit transaction of money, honor, or influence. So Doug was selective. And in 1985, at 568 Broadway, Doug selected Andy.

The gallery—a new one, with paint still fresh on the walls—belongs to Eric Siegeltuch.[2] Doug had called in advance, and Eric is ready to meet him. Doug smiles broadly, eyes pinched behind his glasses, as Eric waves an arm out across the exhibition space and the pair begin to pace the floor. A few shrewd, cursory questions confirm Doug's guess: Eric's gallery caters neither to stars nor to truly unknown young talents, but to the "emerging" bracket and to mid-career artists who deserve more attention than they had received.

And Broadway is the place to get it. In 1985, artists and other gallerists are snapping up the Cast Iron District's airy lofts and ground-floor showrooms at bargain rents. The collectors and the papers are taking notice. SoHo is happening. Into this mix, Doug tactfully promotes Andy.

A new talent has arrived from the Niagara Frontier, he says. Andy Topolski. Prodigiously gifted. Wholly himself. Unrepresented.

Schultz's schedule is busy—the routine scouting tour would be nonstop through Sunday—but Charlotta Kotik, he says, can put Eric in touch with Andy.

Andy couldn't have asked for a better advocate—important, as just *any* advocate wouldn't do. Conceptually complex but assiduously undidactic, Andy's isn't a corpus easily summarized, branded, or pitched. But since the mid-'70s, Charlotta has been both a passionate admirer and keen observer of Andy's practice.

She calls it beautiful, poetic; she praises his selection of shapes and hues. But she is also able to put simply and memorably what makes Andy's work stand out in the landscape of 1980s postminimalism, neoconceptualism, and neo-expressionism: "magic geometry."

Drawn in by Doug's and Charlotta's double recommendation, Eric calls on Andy in his studio. And Eric loves the work immediately.

Eric can remember the feeling today.

We connect on July 30, 2020, six months after the envelope arrived at Uncle Tom's. I worked off the return address and found the website for his business, a solo financial advisory practice catering to high net worth individuals and advertising a focus on artists and art collectors.

He's been in this business since 1992, the website says—likely just after the period in the photos. I can't imagine why a financial advisor would have been lighting votives in Notre Dame with my aunt and uncle, so I dial the number on the contact page.

Andy and Cindy had not been a part of his life for decades, Eric tells me—in fact, when he discovered the copies of his pictures of their trip to Paris, which he eventually sent to Uncle Tom, he had thought Cindy was still alive—but clearly the memory of their personalities and of their work remains vivid.

"Extremely intellectual," he says, remembering his first visit to the studio Andy and Cindy shared on Broadway. He insists on the immediate communication of genius that Andy's work suggested—but then, lacking Charlotta's confidence in simple expressions, drifts into silence.

He remembers Cindy's art, too. It was austere, architectural, mysterious, he says. He knew he was looking at a talent in Cindy, as in Andy. But it was a fuzzier talent, one less attended to. And, more importantly from a gallerist's perspective, Cindy was producing work, but Andy was producing a *body* of work.

Eric knew at once that that body of work would be difficult for many to appreciate, but, for Eric, it was a once-in-a-lifetime opportunity to represent.

For Andy, a big fish not six months removed from Lake Erie—and, to a materially lesser extent, for Cindy—the representation was pivotal, too. The Oscarsson-Siegeltuch Gallery at 568 Broadway was at the very center of the city's art scene in what was called—briefly—LoBro, Lower Broadway, a sub-neighborhood of SoHo. The "hipness and self-consciousness" of New York art, as one *Times* writer described it in 1985, was concentrated among the dozens of galleries in this busy corridor.[3] Now, instead of tipping back fifty-cent Tyskies at the Dom Polski bar with pensioners and postgrads, or huddled in the icehouse listening to a Sun Ra record and talking about Fluxus, Andy and Cindy were attending LoBro openings, fetes, and fundraisers,[4] and bringing new friends they met in Manhattan back to Williamsburg, to a place that every day felt more like home.

Talent, time, and comped gala tickets aren't enough. To navigate a milieu like this, an artist needs a team: someone to talk you up and talk you down, someone to keep you focused and working, someone to bring collectors and curators around to your studio, someone to get you press, someone to steer you into the right conversations at gallery receptions, and someone to hawk your name and work the rooms where you don't yet hope to have an invite.

At the center is often someone like Eric Siegeltuch—a "quarterback," he tells me, reflecting on his own fifty-year career in various positions on and off the field. These quarterbacks, Eric explains, are typically gallery owners who barter with each other, trading their main commodities: an established venue and an uptown mailing list. When Eric began representing Andy, he followed a well-worn playbook. He placed calls to contacts in Los Angeles, San Francisco, Chicago, Houston, Boston, Paris, and Berlin, trying to fit Andy in shows. In turn, Eric would take calls from the same gallery owners in all these cities and agree to show their artists in his space.

The quarterback handles sales, too. They play agent and matchmaker, connecting artists with collectors based on an intimate understanding of the latter's tastes. When an important collector is interested in a piece, the quarterback knows to offer a ten percent discount. The quarterback also takes their own ten percent finder's fee before splitting the proceeds between the artist and the gallery—and the quarterback knows whether the artist they're representing has enough pull to take fifty percent of the net or fifty percent of the gross. (The quarterbacks who do this well are dealers; the quarterbacks who do this intermittently are gallerists.)

And on top of this, the quarterback often manages the artist's emotional needs—the moil of craving and anxiety, of hope compressed into bitter ambition by years or even decades of nurturing unrecognized talents, of experiencing door after door slammed shut.

"Keeping him happy was a full-time job," Eric tells me. He doesn't add much when I press him for details. He gives the impression that Andy needed a lot of talking up and talking down—and that he (Eric) was willing to jaw, pitch, spin, and negotiate as much as Andy needed.

Eric mounted a solo show of Andy's pieces in 1986. That same year, at Peter Muscato's suggestion, Charlotta included some of Andy's work in *Monumental Drawing: Works by 22 Contemporary Americans* at the Brooklyn Museum. Eric booked other shows in New York, at galleries comparable to his own, in a nuanced game of buzz and baiting. By showing Andy, say, at the galleries of Eric Stark at 50 West Ninth Street or Margaret Thatcher (not that Margaret Thatcher) on West Twentieth instead of at his own gallery, Eric would have to split his commission on Andy's sales, but he would increase the hype around Andy, and additionally produce more gallery booklets, brochures, posters, and postcards with high-quality color photos of Andy's work. These he could mail around to galleries in other cities—even in other countries—following up with phone calls to try to get Andy shows in these untouched markets.

"No artist wants to feel obliged to someone—they want to feel the work does it," Elaine de Kooning remarked to Jeffrey Potter. "Well the work doesn't do it. What does it is the PR."[5] A quarterback like Eric has to accomplish effective PR while making the artist feel like the art is the thing all along.

One of Eric's phone calls paid off, and he booked Andy a show in Chicago. Then he booked a show in Paris—the trip that produced the film photographs that I found myself flipping through some thirty-four years later.

This level of support—and strategy—was unlike anything Andy had known in Buffalo. But he was ready to shoulder the new mantle of attention and acclaim. He played the artist. And he kept producing the work.

Underneath Andy's cool was a relentless hustle—one that Cindy shared, possibly as the pacesetter. I only discover this when I visit the Burchfield Penney archives—but there, the material record is clear. In the lead-up to every show, Andy and Cindy spent hours writing notes by hand on the back of promotional postcards and mailing them to friends in New York and other cities. After the shows, they composed polite letters—on a typewriter—to people who stopped by or who had missed the show. And they didn't forget their roots—Andy and Cindy were diligent about writing back to Nancy Weekly, Edna Lindemann, and Anthony Bannon at the Burchfield Art Center (as it was known from 1983 to 1994) in Buffalo.

Just a quick letter to say hello and give you an update on the things in NYC and elsewhere, Andy wrote to Bannon, dated "01 Oct. 89."

> *I recently had a one-person show in Munster and in Berlin (enclosed invites), as well as a group show in Koln (catalog enclosed). I'll will have a one-person show in Koln next May [sic]. The shows went well and I basically enjoyed Germany, though still a racist country.*
>
> *I'm having a one-person show in Paris which will open November 14, with a catalog. I'll send one to you when I get them.*

The tone is close to that of a grown son hoping to impress a distant father. The letters are focused, free from general updates and the drama of daily life. Besides the occasional political color, Andy's missives traffic almost exclusively in the narrow, hieratical language of status in the international art world: group shows are to be endured as a necessary precursor to solo shows; catalogs convey credibility; everything abroad is to be documented and parlayed for greater access in New York.

> *Things are happening here, too, but, still in negotiation. Hope all is going well for you and the B.C. Say hello to Edna and Nancy for me. I should be in Buffalo soon, I'll give you a call.*

He wrote again a year later, October 14, 1990:

> *I really want to thank you for stopping in to the show—especially since you had already had such a big evening! Cindy and I wish that we had more time to talk with you and to see your exhibit . . . I'll be up in Buffalo about the end of October. I hope we can meet for lunch or a drink. I'll phone you a week in advance to see if we can set it up.*

The Andy captured here is the successful Buffalo expat, a darling of the marble capitals of the Old World. But he is also the hustler holding his own works up for the appraisal of South Orange office managers on a decorating budget.

Andy felt his place in the art world was never quite secure, recognition of his next lunge at new expression never guaranteed.

Charlotta likened it to a "mythical gift"—in other words, the kind the gods give to heroes, often with hidden costs, the deferred payment of which illustrates something about the frailty of our human nature. Once an artist has proven an ability to create at this level, she said, there is an enormous pressure to keep it up, to develop the idea, to exceed every success. And it can break people.[6]

There is a grim and practical haste in these letters, a sense that each success is falling back from him the moment he seems to reach it. That each exhibition or commission is a door swinging open onto a receding mirror—a mise en abyme—reflecting his own face in a moment of unguarded need.

Eighty Percent

It is very clear that without your support over all these years, none of this could have happened.

— ERIC SIEGELTUCH, postscript to a letter to Wynn Kramarsky,
December 22, 1989

Dear Wynn. Many <u>Thanks!</u> Article was great. Your support is always a source of inspiration. <u>I mean it.</u>

— ANDY TOPOLSKI, letter to Wynn Kramarsky, September 27, 1990

Dear Wynn, I wish to thank you for buying the two works from Stephen + Fran. It gave me a boost, as the work continues. I do think things will be better this year, different for sure. I push forward. Again, thank you for your understanding support and,… being a wonderful <u>human being</u>!

— ANDY TOPOLSKI, letter to Wynn Kramarsky, February 15, 2000

I WALK EAST down the steeply sloping street, heels starting to ache from the knobby cobbles and uneven bricks I can feel through the gum soles of the Clarks I've been wearing every-where since the weather brightened. It is spring 2015, and the clouds have opened over Edinburgh, making everything golden and precious—all the more so because I can see clearly from High Street that the sky is dark over Leith, where the Firth of Forth opens into the cold North Sea. I am in the center of Scot-land's ancient capital and the heart of its contemporary tourist district, the Royal Mile in Old Town, a place that, after a year in the city, I rarely visit. But a special occasion has brought me here, far from the student cafés and among the Scotch emporia, post-card shops, and kilt purveyors. I have passed up and down the same stretch three times, peering into each establishment: the Real Scot Cashmere Shop, the Nether Bow café and bistro, and a bar called the World's End. I am looking for number 14—home to the UK publisher Canongate Books—and find no mark of either the company or the address.

I had concluded earlier than my uncle that Buffalo was not an appropriate theater for my artistic ambitions. This was perhaps clearer to me because I am a writer, and there is no analogue in writing to galleries like the Albright-Knox and Burchfield Penney, no talent "import-export" shops like Hallwalls, no equivalent to collectors who buy individual pieces to hang in their homes. A stable income as a writer is accessible through full-time employment with a large magazine or a contract with a large commercial publishing house, negotiated by an agent. While some literary agents have come *from* Buffalo, there are no literary agencies *in* Buffalo; there are no large magazines or staffed literary journals in Buffalo; and while there are publishers everywhere, most are niche and under-resourced, many are unscrupulous, and none in Western New York offered a path to a literary career.

I know that I want to be a writer, and I race through my undergraduate degree at Canisius College in Buffalo with no plan other than to succeed as a writer. In three years I finish the degree along with a bloated but workable draft of a novel. I believe I will find an agent to champion this novel. Instead of studying for finals, I send queries and samples. As a backup I apply for a Fulbright to study in India and to the master's programs at Oxford, Cambridge, and Edinburgh, reasoning like so many lost souls before me that travel of any kind is both a marketable life experience and an effective method of forestalling serious commitment.

The Fulbright doesn't pan out and only Edinburgh offers me a place, but one agent bites—before commencement, and a few weeks shy of my twenty-first birthday. He is a figure of uncommon stature in the New York literary scene of the 2010s, and his response alone means so much to me that I barely register the chilly Oxbridge rejections. I send the full manuscript upon his assistant's request and pack my bags, expecting to land a deal by the time I touch down in Europe, and to spend the next few months working on revisions, my postgraduate studies an afterthought.

Nearly a year later, that first agent has passed on the book—more than two dozen other agents have followed suit, a reception as bleak as the weather—and my twenty-one-year-old hope has turned to a twenty-two-year-old fixity: hard, polished, baffled, and cold. I will succeed, I still believe. I just need to meet my advocate.

Arthur's Seat, the volcanic hill in the middle of the Scottish capital, has already erupted in the purple of its springtime mantle. Rude, erumpent crocuses and dew-heavy daffodils now trace the half-hour's walk I take each day from my flat below the Blackford Hills to the campus on George Square. I know my time in Edinburgh is ending, and always panting at my back is the thought of returning to Buffalo—likely to my parents' house—broke, with a crisp new degree but no closer to the very specific standard I'd been seeking since high school. I am unable to speak in plain terms of the shame I feel approaching this crossroads. I do not admit it to myself. But it drives my decisions at every level. I am taking wider and wilder swings at success.

After reading a story online about the antics and unlikely successes of Jamie Byng, Britain's literary bad boy and the owner of the large indie publishing house Canongate, I fantasize that he will see me as a kindred spirit. This is a thin conviction, likely premised on little more than our mutual fondness for

Parliament-Funkadelic and a vague roguishness that I fancy fraternal. I picture the longhaired lord tapping a vial of cocaine out on the table where we sign and countersign the contract that will make me instantly rich and famous. I use up my university printing allowance to produce a hard copy of the manuscript, seal it in an orange envelope, and set out in search of his headquarters.

On my fourth pass over the spot where number 14 High Street ought to have been, I decide to try my luck down a narrow lane that I thought, at first, would lead to residences. Edinburgh's Old Town is honeycombed by "closes," little alleys that open into courtyards or connect the higher and lower terraces that make up this part of the city. Next to the Real Scot Shop is an entryway to one such close, ornate and painted in faded greens, reds, and golds. Below the top of the arch is an escutcheon I hadn't noticed, bearing the Roman numeral XIV, and beneath that a legend that reads "Tweeddale Court." I step into the dark.

After about six yards the close opens up into the court it had advertised, just a hidden vacancy in the stone tenements yellow with the wan spring light. In the far corner, a brass nameplate beside one of the doors suggests an office rather than a residence. I knock and, hearing no answer, push inside.

The scene is of a lukewarm workplace party, complete with paper plates of cubed cheeses and plastic cups for Tesco prosecco. I take a few steps into the room, navigating around stacks of books that reach nearly to the ceiling and making friendly eye contact with the women (no Byng) getting politely buzzed there that afternoon. They all pay me an indirect kind of attention. No eye contact. No "hullo."

Finally I lift my envelope and announce—gently, as if discussing the weather—that I am there "to drop off a manuscript."

Hilarious laughter arcs toward the ceiling, like the jets of the fountain in Princes Street Gardens.

"We were wondering—whose boyfriend is *he*?" one of them says.

I resist reading into this.

They tell me it is a going-away party for an assistant. They take my manuscript and drop it on a desk. A small part of me expects an invitation to share a cup of the bubbly or take a plate of bites for the road. None is forthcoming, and I retreat with an apology.

Weeks later, when it is clear I'm not being offered a publishing deal, I write to the office manager asking instead for a job. *I happen to know you have a vacancy*, I say.

The response is not warmer than before.

Even with talent, a good work ethic, and a support network of friends and family, "making it" as an artist is eighty percent luck, Charlotta Kotik tells me. Like Andy in the '80s, I hadn't looked long for luck in Buffalo—and like Andy I left, I worked and networked, kept knocking on doors, kept putting in my twenty percent.

For Andy, eighty percent stood four foot eleven and blinked at him from beneath eyebrows as heavy as the towers of the Brooklyn Bridge.

Werner Hans Kramarsky, "Wynn" to his many friends, was one of the most influential figures in the world of art in the late twentieth and early twenty-first centuries. Wynn was born in Amsterdam in 1926 and—his family was Jewish—emigrated in 1939, fleeing the Nazis and resurgent antisemitism across the continent. His father, Siegfried, was a banker and art collector—he owned a mix of Old Masters and impressionists—and Wynn had frequently accompanied him on visits to the greatest galleries of Europe. While the adults stood and talked in front of the most celebrated pieces, Wynn would wander off to the empty drawings galleries, where he developed a fascination with the works there—black and white, often charcoal and ink, and typically on paper rather than canvas. Often dismissed as drafts, curiosities of more interest to academics than collectors, the young Wynn felt that "works on paper" allowed him to feel the movement—especially the first movement—of the artist's hand.

Wynn was not an artist, at least not in the typical sense, although as a patron he would rise to the highest level, what the poet Ezra Pound, in flattering the New York lawyer John Quinn, called a cocreator of art, one who "builds art into the world."[1] But Wynn first was known as a public servant and a power broker. Involved in Democratic politics in New York City—he was among the cohort of young idealists who overthrew the last Tammany boss, Carmine DeSapio, in 1961—Wynn dropped out of NYU law school in 1965 to campaign for John V. Lindsay, then a congressman and a fusion candidate for mayor. He served in the Lindsay administration, left for a stint in consulting, and later earned praise for his service as commissioner of the New York State Division of Human Rights under Governor Hugh L. Carey.[2]

Wynn left government for the last time in 1982—but his greatest accomplishments lay ahead. Up until that point, he had lived a double life as an art collector. In 1958, he had purchased a Jasper Johns drawing for $175, which he paid in installments over six months. Over the next half century, until his death in 2019, Wynn and his wife, Sarah-Ann, would amass a collection of more than 4,000 works and rise to the highest places in the art world.

At a time when big money was remaking taste in New York and abroad, and everyone from private equity titans to disco entrepreneurs wanted to add expensive artists to their investment portfolios, Wynn and Sarah-Ann practiced a different kind of collecting. They saw true talent, not trends, and they lifted countless names out of obscurity by insisting that the many galleries where Wynn served as a trustee or lender exhibit works by unknown or emerging artists with their more celebrated showpieces.

Andy and Wynn were a perfect match, and perhaps destined to collide. Andy's work on paper, often characterized by bold black lines and broken circles, nonrepresentational but founded on complex collations of mathematics and music and cartography, clicked with Wynn's taste for minimalist, postminimalist, and conceptual works—typically nonrepresentational, often process-oriented, pieces that "require close study and unfailingly reward a viewer's curiosity," as one curator described Wynn's collecting.[3]

Wynn was more candid and more colorful about his appreciation for art like Andy's. "You could go up, and you could look up close; you could see how it was made," he told an interviewer in the late 2000s.[4] "I'm still doing that. I want to go and look and see: How was this made? The great thrill that I think very few people get, except collectors, is that at a certain point, you have a sheet of paper in your hand. It's not glazed, it's not framed, and there is nothing sexier—well, maybe my wife—but there's nothing sexier than that feeling of being right there, that feeling when you can feel the motion of the hand of the artist making what is there."

A supporter of the Brooklyn Museum, Wynn visited Charlotta's *Monumental Drawings* exhibition in 1986. He bought both of Andy's works included in the show on the spot. Then he wanted to shake the hand that made them.

Andy isn't counting, but the M train has passed three times. Each time his ground-floor studio fills with the noise, a tidepool of sound. And each time it leaves Andy unmoved, slumped in a recovered lawn chair that slants so far back his bent knees are nearly level with his shoulders. Across from Andy, by the door to 440 Broadway's hallway, is a stack of framed works—works returned, unsold, from Eric's gallery.

Eric had left Andy's studio perhaps half an hour before. He

brought bad news, the kind it's best to deliver quickly and then get away from: he was closing the gallery.

The year is 1988. Only three years earlier Eric had hung up a shingle with a partner—it was called the Oscarsson-Siegeltuch Gallery, then—but he was soon on his own and struggling to make rent, keep the lights on, and front the considerable costs of acquiring, moving, storing, and marketing art. He was struggling to manage his business and to manage his artists, too.

In under three years, Eric had arranged for Andy to show in eight cities in three countries. Now, Eric told Andy, he has to hang it up. He doesn't know what he'll do next, yet—but Andy can always count on him as a friend, he said.[5]

He unloaded the last of Andy's unsold works from his car, left them by the door, and got out of Brooklyn.

Andy thinks about going upstairs to the apartment to use the telephone, but he doesn't know whom he would call. Cindy is at work in Manhattan—editing copy at an advertising agency, her new gig since giving up the commute to Schulte. Peter is out meeting a client. For just a second—absurdly—he thinks of calling Eric.

Then another name appears to him—a friend, a lifeline; someone who would want to know, someone who could tell him what to do next. He would call Wynn.

By 1988, Andy was a card-carrying member of the "Wynn Crowd"—a group of collectors and artists including Sol LeWitt, Eva Hesse, Brice Marden, Agnes Martin, and Richard Serra, along with dozens of lesser-known talents whom Wynn championed with a particular passion. The loose group centered on Kramarsky's office on the sixth floor at 560 Broadway in SoHo and extended into numerous galleries and collections around the country where Wynn had either donated work or served on a board. With help from Wynn—and Cindy—and others in Wynn's orbit, Andy was able to keep up the momentum he had built in the mid-'80s and carry on to the next decade without Eric's quarterbacking.

In 1990, Wynn auctioned a piece of his inheritance, Vincent van Gogh's *Portrait of Dr. Gachet*. Depicting in muted blues and loud yellows the doctor who treated van Gogh after his breakdown in 1888, the portrait captures at once the lucid melancholy of the subject and the emotional intensity of the period of its composition—just six weeks before the artist's suicide. It went to Ryoei Saito for $82.5 million, making *Gachet*, at the time, the world's most expensive painting.[6]

It also made Kramarsky fabulously rich and known to a new echelon of the art world. With the sale of *Gachet*, Wynn had enough money and influence to open a wing in his own name at any major gallery in the country. But instead, he chose to wield that money and influence in ways that would maximally benefit the unrecognized talents he championed. With the help of his assistants Michael Randazzo and Leslie Spectre, Wynn maintained a mastery of everything going on in the New York art world, and his influence reached much further.

"If we can't make the world beautiful ourselves, we should help the people who can make the world more beautiful," Wynn once said—and he meant the *living* people who might make the world more beautiful *today*. When Wynn lent work to galleries for shows, he extracted promises from the curators to show his works by celebrity artists alongside the works of artists like Andy and other Wynn favorites. And instead of donating large bodies of work to single galleries—which would have earned him more recognition, heartier thanks, all manner of embarrassments—he spread works by his favorites around to scores of galleries across the country.

There were other benefits to finding welcome with the Wynn

Crowd: Wynn helped the artists, and the artists helped each other.

Ann Ledy was another member of the Wynn Crowd, and in the late '80s she also happened to be employing Peter Muscato to take photographs for slides of her work.

Like Andy and Cindy, Ann had moved to New York for opportunity. She came from the Twin Cities, Minnesota, with $200, a sleeping bag, and a single suitcase. She stepped off the Greyhound at the Midtown Terminal, pushed her glasses up into her hair, stiff from sleeping, and looked up once at the mirrored towers all around her. Then she dropped her eyes, fixed her glasses back over the bridge of her nose, recinched her sleeping bag over the top of her suitcase, and walked out into the city. In 1979, Ann earned a spot on the Parsons faculty, and by 1991 she was chair of the Foundations program serving first-year students.

By then, Ann was familiar with Andy's practice. They had shown together at Eric Stark's gallery and elsewhere in SoHo, and exhibited at the same time at different galleries in Germany. Andy was at Dortmund's Museum Ostwall, under the auspices of the Dortmunder Kunstverein, and Ann was at Andrea Bergmann's gallery, Art & Language, in Drensteinfurt; Wynn visited them both, and all four—Andy, Ann, Cindy, and Wynn—made a party of it, hilarious and intimate, with nothing behind them and everything, the whole world, just on the other side of sleeping.

Impressed by the breadth and depth of Andy's technical background, Ann hired him to put together and oversee Parsons's first woodworking shop. This quickly led Andy to a position on the Foundations faculty. The steady gig provided Andy with space and materials, the inspiration of working weekly with eager students, and the productive pressure of collegial competition with the other practicing artists on the faculty. He would meet lifelong friends there—like Raymond Saá, a younger artist who looked up to Andy, and who, with his wife Catherine, would number among Andy and Cindy's closest companions in Brooklyn. The stability of a regular paycheck was a relief for Cindy, too, who had been (and who would remain) the partner responsible both for income and budgeting. By the early '90s, partly through the gravity of Wynn Kramarsky, Cindy and Andy had "their people" in New York—and anyone who's moved to New York in any decade knows that this makes all the difference.

Andy and Wynn became close—not just as artist and patron (a word Wynn hated), but as friends. Wynn took over the fifth floor at 560 Broadway and opened a noncommercial gallery space there. Frequently Andy's latest work was on display. Wynn also kept close to Andy through Michael Randazzo, who as a Columbia grad student had answered Wynn's classified ad seeking help with data entry. Michael, a fast-talking local with a background in computers and no training in art, helped Wynn catalog his growing collection with the ArtStacks software that had just rolled out. He also developed personal relationships with artists.

I find Mike in September 2020, tracking him down through a series of tips from former colleagues. His memories of Andy and Cindy—and of Andy's relationship with Wynn—are, like van Gogh's *Gachet*, frank, plain, and emotionally charged.

"I didn't know what I was talking about, but I knew what I liked," Mike tells me. And he liked Andy's work immediately.

Accompanying Wynn on trips to Andy's studio and gallery exhibitions, Mike bonded with Andy over typography and the influence of the Russian constructivists. Sometimes he helped Andy in the emerging field of computer-assisted graphic design. And he became known as a champion of Andy's among the Wynn Crowd, always reporting back to Wynn on Andy's latest projects.

But just as he had discovered as a child wandering the wood-paneled drawings gallery of the Rijksmuseum, Wynn preferred his relationship with an artist to be intimate, unmediated.

Friends recalled Andy as sometimes impatient or reluctant to explain his work in the studio—preferring "you wouldn't understand it" to an effort to translate the language of his practice into English. But on afternoons or weeknights, following the hum, flash, and drone of an opening reception, you would find Andy pacing his own shows, alone in the gallery except for Wynn—in shirtsleeves, suspenders, horsebit loafers—bobbing somewhere below the artist's shoulders.

Wynn understood this about Andy and his work; he embraced its resistance to description. In 1991, Wynn sponsored a solo exhibition of Andy's work at the Galerie von der Tann in Berlin. He prepared remarks for the opening and had them translated into German weeks in advance so that he could practice his delivery. The speech—which is preserved in English and German in Kramarsky's MoMA papers—is a remarkable snapshot of Wynn's mind, of Andy's work, and of the two men's connection.

> The first Topolski work I saw was at the Brooklyn Museum['s] *Monumental Drawings* exhibit in 1986. I was immediately struck by the musicality of the work, the spatial rhythm and the energetic thrust. It was only somewhat later that I became aware of and involved with the more direct abstract content. It may not have been Topolski's intention to seduce his viewer with his music but in my case it was most effective. Since then I have become increasingly challenged by many other aspects of the art of Andrew Topolski.
>
> Topolski makes his art to translate very complex thoughts into simple expressions. His gesture is disciplined by the choice of essentially mechanical and architectural draftsmanship, a narrow range of primary colors and simple everyday devices and materials. The "found object" is here refined to the "fitting object" and the mystery of the surreal is replaced by the transparent and direct quotation from a mathematical formula.
>
> This description is, as it should be, totally inadequate to

describe the art; if it could be described, Topolski would not need to make it. Topolski's work does not mirror the condition of the nuclear threatened world; rather it draws attention to opportunities for a more rational society. Clearly, Topolski warns us of the hazards of global catastrophe; clearly he also recalls for us Pascal's statement that, "Nature is an infinite sphere whose center is everywhere and whose circumference is nowhere."[7]

Between 1987 and 1999, Wynn purchased twenty-nine of Andy's works.[8] At the time of Wynn's death in 2019, he had gifted or donated all but one, an untitled study of graphite and collage on tracing paper. And Wynn's acquisitions and attention prompted other acquisitions from friends, collectors, fellow artists, and institutions that moved in his wake.

The impact of this friendship both in terms of Andy's finances and his legacy is beyond quantification. If you look at where Andy's work has ended up today, it's easy to see Wynn's guiding hand: the Brooklyn Museum, the National Gallery of Art in DC, the Seattle Art Museum, the Columbus Museum, the Boise Art Museum, the Columbus Museum in Georgia, the San Diego Museum of Art, the Krannert in Urbana-Champaign, the Weatherspoon in Greensboro, the Menil Collection in Houston, the Contemporary Museum in Honolulu—as well as the galleries at Harvard, Dartmouth, Yale, the University of Richmond, and Southern Methodist University, and of course the Burchfield Penney in Buffalo—all places where Wynn wielded influence. Kramarksy's collection at MoMA Archives, which I finally access in June 2021, reveals even more. In letters spanning more than two decades, I find Wynn purchasing works from galleries, arranging exhibitions, funding gallery catalogs, advising on contracts and other business matters, recommending Andy for a Guggenheim award, and making gifts and introductions to his moneyed friends.[9]

. . .

In the archives of the Burchfield Penney—masked, alone, handling the papers with thin gloves—I saw successive iterations of Andy's résumé. As I spoke with Eric Seigeltuch, Michael Randazzo, Laura Kramarsky, and others, I pieced together a much fuller picture of my uncle's career than I had ever before apprehended. His output was prolific; his reach was global; his worth was permanently established in more than two dozen institutional collections.

I asked Michael, Did I misunderstand my uncle's success? Was this man—the one who took me to Woodstock, bought me a toy spear at Fort Delaware, spent hours with me shooting pellet guns off the back deck on Seminary Road—some unknown titan of art in the late twentieth century?

In an email, Michael talks around the question—but the answer is enough to deflate, a little, this evolving impression of Andy.

> *Success in the art world is fleeting (we could talk A LOT about this); it's about being lucky and playing your cards right. Being discovered by Wynn was a major break for Andy BUT one collector was not gonna make the total difference....I would say that b/c he didn't come from $$ (which is hard to do in the art world) he really struggled. That and not being super tolerant (I would say that he had a biting sense of humor, to say the least!) meant that sometimes he wouldn't compromise about stuff that maybe he should have.*

Michael's memories chimed with impressions and bits of information I'd received from Charlotta Kotik, Peter Muscato, Eric Seigeltuch, Bob Gulley, and other sources.

I had the records; I had the résumés. Nearly three months after starting to write about my aunt and uncle, I was beginning to realize that I needed to approach the project from a different angle. I had to ask a different set of questions. I felt a sinking sense of arriving at these questions too late. Wynn, for example, who would have been an irreplaceable resource, had just passed away; others were long gone, or unreachable. But, in late September, Michael Randazzo, at least, was ready to talk.

Let's try to speak at 4pm today, he wrote, *call me when you're available....*

For Rent or for Sale

"ARE YOU HUNGRY?" Peter Muscato asks me.

He walks up to the gate of 207 North Seventh in Williamsburg, crossing a courtyard where he and Cindy and Andy had spent most of their nights for nearly a decade. He points out where they'd built a fishpond and where he'd bricked up a door that once led into Andy's ground-floor studio at Number 211.

"Yes," I say. "Definitely hungry."

Peter and I haven't seen each other since I was six—probably in this same courtyard—but we talk like old friends, walking North Seventh, Driggs, Bedford, Metropolitan. Peter and his son Paolo, who helps run the framing business now, take me to an old Williamsburg bar called Teddy's, with a stamped tin ceiling and stained-glass windows unchanged since the 1880s, they tell me. Peter and the boys came here with Cindy and Andy almost every Friday for all-you-can-eat bite-sized fish fries. The menu is a little more sophisticated now—all three of us order medium-rare burgers topped with astounding portions of lobster mac and cheese—but the decoration is original due to an airtight deed restriction.

"You're sitting at one of the exact same tables your Aunt Cindy sat at," Peter tells me, pointing—not at me but through me, into the past.

Finally, in the summer of 2021, after a year of phone calls and digging through archives, I've traced Cindy and Andy's footsteps to Brooklyn, circa 1995.

. . .

Following steady work, social acceptance, and some artistic acclaim, the next requirement for really putting down *roots* in New York has to do, of course, with rent and real estate.

My memories of visiting Andy and Cindy in New York as a child are dim and figurative—the impression of green against black, for example, stood in for a rooftop garden; or the image of a box of Cookie Crisps under a yellow bulb suggested their kitchen. I have no memory of geography or even detailed interiors.

I thought figuring out where my aunt and uncle had lived would have been easier. I ask my mom and she sends me a picture of her address book, which lists Cindy four times.

440 Broadway
Brooklyn, NY 11211

211 North Seventh Street
Brooklyn, NY 11211

113 Withers
Brooklyn, NY 11211

69 Seminary Rd.
Callicoon, NY 12723

The first two entries are crossed out. It is a progression, clearly, but no one around me can place exact dates.

My mom sends about a dozen pictures —Andy and me on the covered couch, Cindy and Andy standing in the shadows beneath the elevated train, Cindy on a bench in her garden or looking glamorous in profile against a blue-sided building. I want to map these against the addresses; the suggestion of a world that would emerge from them would be fragmented, I think, but at least it would be accurate.

But the pictures are more than thirty years old—when I ask my mom, she can't name the streets, buildings, or even boroughs they depict. But, she says, Peter might.

Peter Muscato—another Buffalo expat, and one of Cindy and Andy's oldest and closest friends—is the easiest source to find. I am immediately relieved when I pull up his simple, business-card-style website, muscatoframes.com. It lists an email, a phone number, and a business address: 207 North Seventh, right next to where I know Cindy and Andy had lived.

I send a message and he immediately agrees to a phone call the next day. While I wait, I click into the Google Maps plugin on his site, cruise North Seventh in street view, and swipe through every picture of the area, cross-referencing all the visuals with the photos my mom had sent me.

When he does call—surprising me with a floorboard-rattling basso even lower than Andy's—I ask him to try to plot my aunt and uncle's movements across a map of the city. He jumps into it, picking up their story in the early '90s, when they were neighbors at 440 Broadway.

440 Broadway was old, cold, unfinished, serviced by a freight elevator. Andy and Cindy moved in first, on the fourth floor, and loved it. When a spot opened on the second floor, they told Peter and Beverly, who were quick to move in and frame out an apartment.

They made a life there, a community. Andy and Peter knocked bricks out of the southeast sides of their apartments to install makeshift chimneys for wood-burning stoves, which they kept full of scraps from pallets they pulled apart on Broadway. Around the corner from the building was a lot where the tenants parked, and Andy, Cindy, Peter, Bev, and another tenant, Anton, cleared brush, installed a pond, and made their own pocket park.

The owner, Izzy, kept an office in the building and was perpetually in straits of one kind or another, Peter told me. (While he talked, I looked up the property tax records and confirmed this.) Izzy, a Hasidic real estate investor who seemed to be at odds with a rival Orthodox group, often offered his tenants a discount to front him the next month's rent—usually on the spot, if he managed to buttonhole them in the stairway. Fifteen-hundred might drop to $1,200 or $1,000. By the early '90s Peter, Beverly, Cindy, and Andy had fronted Izzy so much that they were considerably ahead on rent—Peter and Bev by a year or more.

When Izzy's financial difficulties caught up with him, he sold the building to a group of Orthodox investors—possibly the same ones who had been circling him for the past decade—who shortly called the tenants together and detailed a list of promises about improvements. These never materialized. When the new owners tried to raise the rent, Andy and Cindy and the Muscatos led the other residents in forming a tenants' association, hiring counsel and securing a rent freeze. The ensuing legal battle dragged on until 1994 and spelled the end of the couples' time at 440 Broadway—but when it finally ended, it left them all with an escrow account of saved rent that they hoped to put toward something that had been unimaginable when they first left Buffalo: they wanted to buy their own piece of New York.

Peter swept his eyes from side to side as he drove around Brooklyn in those days—November and December 1994—often taking the long way home from client meetings, tracing the borough's maze of one-ways, looking for sale signs. Cindy and Andy and the Muscatos had made an offer on a multiunit tenement in Williamsburg—asking price $125,000—but the deal fell through. It was a warm December, as high as fifty degrees the first week, but as the midday temperature dropped into the forties, then the high thirties, the friends began to worry. Their tenants' case resolved, they'd have to vacate 440 Broadway soon. And the funds in their escrow account would start to drain away.

Then, just before Christmas, Peter saw it—a "for rent or for sale" sign on North Seventh. He pulled the car over to the side of the road, double parked, and started to hammer on the building's front door.

The owner, Anthony J. Santorelli, had two properties side by side on North Seventh—but he only wanted to sell one of them. A retired engineer and snowbird Brooklynite (seventy-nine years young that October), he wanted to keep his second-floor apartment at 211 North Seventh for the months he wasn't in Florida. He offered to sell Peter the property beside it, at 207, a two-story former factory with a gated courtyard and off-street parking—workshop below and comfortable apartment above— for $225,000.

The space was too small for two families, but Tony offered to rent Cindy and Andy the property next door, a three-story building with a first-floor workshop, with an option to buy it for $400,000 whenever Tony felt the time had come to vacate his second-floor warm-weather apartment and move permanently south.

Though Cindy, Andy, and the Muscatos had planned to buy a building together, both deals were too good to pass up. The Muscatos closed on February 16, 1996, using their escrow funds for the down payment on a mortgage. They moved into the factory at 207 North Seventh that month, and Peter built a frame shop on the first floor. Andy and Cindy moved into the third floor at 211 North Seventh and Andy appropriated the first floor for his studio, pushing Tony's unused engineering equipment into the corners.

Separating home and work completed Cindy and Andy's transition from *living* in New York to *having a life* in New York. The space itself seemed to open up new pockets of time that hadn't been available to them on Broadway. On the weekends, from April to late September, you could find Cindy on 211's asphalt rooftop, with its view out over row upon row of other black tar beaches, and between them the steeples and belfries that made Brooklyn the Borough of Churches. In black thick-soled slip-ons, baggy chino shorts, and a sleeveless blouse or loose camp-collared shirt, she'd move among the two-foot and three-foot and four-foot blooms of zucchini and tomato and bell pepper in pots and snug boxes that Andy, the woodworker, made—along with peonies and zinnias, red chrysanthemums, bright buttercups, and scores of black-eyed Susans and big sunflowers framing the door, with broad-leafed ivy covering the shingled sunroom entering onto Tony's apartment. Below, a door from Andy's studio opened into the Muscatos' yard, where the four Buffalo expats and a cast of friends and children spent countless warm nights in conversation.

Inventing Motion / Moving Targets

All the best to you in 1993—it's going to be the year of the Rooster
(Chinese zodiac), which is apparently kind of tricky, so watch out.

   —JESSICA BERWIND, letter to Wynn Kramarsky, January 5, 1993

IT LANDS WITH a *plunk*, like a fingertip tapping a timpani. At
least that's what it sounds like *inside*, sheet stretched taut as a
drumhead above them. Cindy feels the weight of it on her right
hip. For a moment it just sits—and then its exploration begins.
Little limbs skittering up her side, tickling her elbow—and then
nothing.

"Do you feel it?"

Andy's breath comes warm, rich with Gauloises Bleu and
Kronenbourg.

"I think it's on my wrist," he whispers.

There is no light in the apartment, no light beneath the thin,
rebarbative blankets, but Cindy feels as if she can see Andy's face
just inches from her own. For a moment they lie in silence, staring into the brief but total void between them.

And then they explode into laughter.

"Where else would you rather be than right here, right now?"
the Buffalo Bills coach Marv Levy is fond of saying to his team.
He might have asked Cindy and Andy.

Where, after all, could they possibly rather be than Paris in
1993?

Sure, the apartment is dingy and completely infested—Cindy
had shrieked when she saw antennae emerge from the shower
head, and then spent the next ten minutes swatting at corners

with a quickly weary pair of walking flats—but just about every-thing else in their world is *right*.

Cindy and Andy are here with some of their closest friends—Peter Muscato, their neighbor in Williamsburg, and Jessica Berwind, the Philadelphia gallerist and promoter of Andy's work. She had helped to set up a show the previous weekend at Iris von der Tann's gallery in Berlin—where Andy and his work, geometric figurations on paper and enigmatic sculptural installations of metal, sand, and glass, enjoyed an ecstatic reception. From Berlin they traveled by train to Paris, where Andy had a show at Galerie AB.

Jessica had accompanied them to do a bit of networking, but the group quickly lost faith in her contact, the one who proudly had handed them the keys to the hazardous walk-up. The man was exceptionally short, maybe four foot nine, and had piled the entire quintet into what appeared to be a clown car (Cindy and Jessica managed to squeeze in but Andy had to fold up like an accordion to fit inside the passenger seat, and Peter, in the back, wasn't much better off). The Frenchman's vague promises of con-nections didn't pan out, but the AB show was a success, and the Americans relished the time in the city. They went out eating and drinking—Andy found hamburgers to order, miraculously—and they spent long days walking the streets and bridges, follow-ing a copy of *Connoisseur: An Insider's Guide to the Paris Flea Markets* that was three years out of date. At night they smoked French cigarettes and drank French wine and beers and finally, exhausted from all the talk and all the laughter and all the swat-ting at cockroaches, they took to their berths, Cindy and Andy on the one bed and Peter and Jessica on couches, all wrapped up like mummies so that the bugs couldn't touch them, even as the heavy bodies dropped from the ceiling all night long.

And so Cindy and Andy keep laughing. Their friends are awake, too—they can hear Peter's low chuckle begin, and then behind Jessica's happy, exhausted sigh.

They laugh themselves to sleep that night—like they had the night before—laughing under the covers until the cotton carapace runs low on oxygen, and they drift into blissful, delirious, dreamless slumber.

Cindy and Andy had fallen in love a decade before in a combined working studio and apartment shared with another couple in a cramped, rivalrous, chummy, ecstatic, messy, ambiguous, tempestuous, *happening* complex on the west side of a minor city in major decline in the ashen aftermath of the '70s. The mid-'90s found them in a brick Williamsburg tenement, living in modest comfort under a rooftop garden that would have pleased Queen Amytis. Budgeting was still a high-stakes game, but they ate well and enjoyed excellent conversation, surrounded by friends. And maybe most important, they were recognized as artists in the city where it meant something.

Entering my own adulthood in Buffalo about three decades after Cindy, it seemed everyone I knew was talking about going somewhere else. The writers and artists and actors and musicians, in particular, talked incessantly about moving to New York. Everyone wanted to tell you about why they were going, or why they *weren't* going. Often enough I told myself and others these stories, too.

I carried Cindy and Andy's example, or what I took to be their example, in the early years of my decision to become a writer— well before my impetuous intrusion into the Canongate offices in Edinburgh. In the crisp fall of 2010, my father and I had taken the Amtrak into New York City. I was a high school junior; Andy was two-and-a-half years gone and Cindy was in Callicoon. Instead of family, our guides were freshmen at NYU, Fordham,

Columbia. I toured only the colleges with well-regarded English programs, famous professors, institutional ties to publishing. I wasn't thinking of it consciously, but the influence was clear: my earliest models for a life in the arts had left; naturally, I would follow them.

Except I didn't. At my father's suggestion, I connected with Mick Cochrane, a novelist and a professor at Canisius College in Buffalo, head of the creative writing program. He met me for lunch in the campus cafeteria, less than two miles from where I grew up; he gave me a stack of books (including his own) and invited me to a Colm Tóibín lecture happening the next month. The downstate colleges promised an atmosphere where I might imagine myself a writer. Dr. Cochrane took me seriously as a writer, from the start. So I stayed home.

I know now how I benefited from this, but in the years immediately after graduating I often wondered what the choice to remain in Buffalo—the cultural frontier—had meant for my career, my relationship to the world of the arts that Andy and Cindy had occupied.

I had dealt with these feelings by the time I began this project, but nonetheless I felt the sharp shock of recognition reading Andy and Cindy's letters—the record of their struggles.

Andy was as singularly, anxiously fixated on success as I had been, I saw. And Cindy had been as cool, composed, and persistent in pursuing it, after repeated, draining setbacks.

On balance, I don't regret my choices, but I have in many moments felt the chill of wondering what it would have been like to spend just one year closer to my godmother—my freshman year, 2011–12, what would have been an indelible, formative time for me—and for Cindy, the year she most needed the family that wasn't around her.

Reading their letters and learning their stories I felt at once less and more alone in my pursuit of art than ever before.

By the dawn of the 2020s, I'd seen a dozen friends who left for New York return to Buffalo—they'd hung on for a while, but soon someone moved out and the rent was too high; the trains were always late; a degree didn't lead to the job it had promised; a pandemic obliterated live theater and music, and day jobs walking dogs and waiting tables, too. Sometimes there were no explanations—a New York scene that had welcomed them ten years before just mysteriously, but definitely, evaporated.

But ten years into their move to New York, Andy and Cindy were hanging on. Hearing about their experience of the early '90s from people like Peter, I realized that my aunt and uncle were living *the life* that tens of thousands of artists in places like Buffalo dreamed of—that I had dreamed of—that unnumbered masses to come will dream of, too.

A message in a spiral-bound reporter's notebook from this period turned up nearly three decades later in the posthumous Topolski retrospective show at the Burchfield Penney in Buffalo in 2013. The show's curator—Andy's friend Don Metz—placed it in a glass-top display case with other ephemera. Across two pages, Andy had illustrated a rose growing from a heart pierced with an arrow. Beside the rose is a message in his jagged hand:

> *You are great Cin!*
> *I am so proud of*
> *you and grateful*
> *to be with you!!*
> *I Love You So*
> *Much!!!!*
>
> *p.s. I know I*
> *should have*
> *bought one*
> *but, well…*

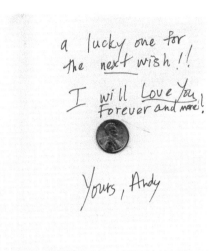

Andy's note to Cindy, undated. Courtesy of Cindy Suffoletto Estate.

> *… a*
> *rose is a*
> *rose is*
> *a rose …*

Beside it in the case was another note. This one was a card Andy had made from folded computer paper; he had taped a penny inside.

> *a lucky one*
> *for the next wish!!*
> *I will Love You*
> *Forever and after!*
> *Yours, Andy*

Seeing the notes again years after the Burchfield Penney show—on Facebook, in blurry pictures a stranger had captured with a digital camera—I gave up the last gasp of a story I had imbibed young and believed for too long. It was the story of the lone genius, an artist who leaves home to make a name in a new city, to struggle and finally prevail against the stacked odds of indifference and disconnection and orthodoxy. I had long ago released this on a rational level. I had experienced too much of the worlds of art and cultural commodification to believe that any talented individual could succeed entirely on their own—I knew well by then the networks of influence, the workings of chance, the nature of artistic alliances. But seeing Andy's naked pen marks, the frank messages in what was never really his first language, I understand a simpler, subrational truth about art and about life. To succeed—in art or anything, really—one needs love. Love—in one of its innumerable forms—always makes the difference.

If this sounds a bit neatly sepia tinted: it is.

Andy's love notes to Cindy are undated and seemingly tied to mysterious, private occasions, but they offer a searing snapshot of the partnership. They capture a sense of two people rooting for one another, two people devoted and in love.

Cindy and Andy's partnership ran deep. Jessica Berwind once remarked to me that "they had a relationship that few of the people closest to them even knew about." In the period from which these letters date, theirs was in part a partnership *of artists*. When Eric or Wynn came around to visit Andy on Broadway, he would always proudly take them over to see whatever Cindy was working on. A large, architectural diptych of Cindy's hung prominently above the couch in their apartment.

Context and commentary from surviving friends complicate this picture. Under glass at the Burchfield Penney, the letters appear as artifacts of an epic artists' love—and they are. But carried back against time's current to their origins, the letters suggest more, the subtle pulse of another narrative. In these letters, too, we have a sense of Andy's haste, his charming cheapness, the tug of his focus elsewhere.

This much I can say with certainty about the author of the artifacts. As to how Cindy received them, I couldn't venture a guess. To say anything about the way Cindy felt between the mid-'80s and the early aughts is to take aim at a moving target.

In the early '80s, Cindy was finding her footing as an artist in Buffalo, showing at Hallwalls and Buffalo State. In the late '80s, Cindy was just beginning to find her footing again as an artist in New York—independent from Andy, but with support from some of the friends she'd made back home. In autumn 1987, Charlotta Kotik and John Toth selected two of Cindy's works for *Painting into Sculpture*, a show the Brooklyn Museum put on in the Rotunda Gallery in the Brooklyn War Memorial. This was not a museum nor a commercial gallery, but the setting in Brooklyn's Cadman Plaza—a long vista ending in the austere granite and limestone memorial building, bookended by the twenty-four-foot statues of Victory and Family—was a suitably grand setting for Cindy's large architectural pieces and her debut outside Buffalo. Her work earned a paragraph in the *Phoenix*, a local paper:

> Cindy Suffoletto's *Arc I* and *Arc V*, for example, are geometrical assemblages that evoke at once the serenity of a sunrise and the majesty of Genesis when God divided heaven from earth and light from dark. In *Arc V*, the gold and white semi-circles rise out of a flat, earth-colored horizon into a grey upper boundary. Through a balance of contrasting colors and a symmetry of shapes, Suffoletto invents motion and, at the same time, a sense of equilibrium.

Motion in equilibrium, or equilibrium in motion—either way, Cindy was moving in those years. Andy was represented, was selling the corporate work and getting the commissions, but the record shows that they were finding traction together—if unevenly—in the New York art scene toward the end of the decade.

No one alive today remembers any sense of competition between them. Cindy was devoted to Andy—and to his career— they say, while Andy showed Cindy's work to collectors and encouraged her into opportunities that were chiefly his. The record bears this out. In 1990, Andy and Cindy appeared together at the Gallery Schüppenhauer in Cologne in *Autour de Kolář-Collage*, a show honoring the great Jiří Kolář, where their collages hung alongside pieces from twentieth-century legends like Max Ernst and Victor Vasarely. (Andy had appeared the year before in the group show *WortLaut*, and Christel Schüppenhauer would give him a solo show in 1991.)

Exhibiting in Germany with Ernst and Vasarely—it's hard to imagine anything further from the teenage Cindy's fashion sketches of mannequins at Hengerer's, or even her undergraduate student shows at Buff State's Upton Hall. But *Autour de Kolář-Collage*—a group show honoring another artist—may have been the last exhibition of Cindy's life. And a grainy scan of the write-up that ran September 3, 1987, on page fourteen of the *Phoenix* might be the only extant critical examination of Cindy's work.[1]

Friends who remember her from Buffalo insist that they knew Cindy as an artist first—not as Andy's partner, manager, or support system. But in the mid-'90s, she underwent—with eyes open, it seems—a transformation of identity.

It was a transformation familiar to many female artists. As Mary Gabriel remarked of Helen Frankenthaler following her marriage to Robert Motherwell, "She had apparently joined that deadly artistic category: 'wife who also paints.'"[2]

Cindy and Andy were not married yet. But the label is eerily apt. When I contact Galerie Schüppenhauer for information about these shows, I receive a wealth of detail about Andy's exhibitions. And in "*Kolář-Collage*," Christel adds, "I included works by his wife."

It was around the time of the *Kolář-Collage* exhibition that Cindy stopped making art entirely.

In Buffalo, any grad student or upstart could find a wall to hang work. For the price of a case of Budweiser, you could probably get a small crowd at the opening reception. In New York, attention was harder to come by. And in New York, it was clear that Andy was the rising star.

Andy understood and resisted the siren song of art-adjacent gig work. He clocked in to his studio as he would any other full-time job. He produced prolifically because of it. Later, teaching part-time at Parsons, Andy still thought about art and talked about art and made art—even focusing on student work he was able to continue testing new processes and materials for his own practice. And while he was a devoted teacher, this was still a side gig.

Cindy, in contrast, had traded spotty and exhausting gallery gigs for a full-time position at the Manhattan architecture firm Furman & Furman. Hired as a bookkeeper and assistant, she excelled there and became a right hand to her boss, Richard Furman, a confidant he turned to for cool counsel on personnel and personality issues or suggestions on clients and collections.

"She worked full time," the friend and gallerist Jessica Berwind remembered and related to me over the phone one day. "She would be up at six o'clock"—no matter how late she had entertained their friends the night before—"and off to work."

In her free time, Cindy cataloged Andy's work and managed his business transactions.

"She would get very serious when you were talking about the work, the exhibition," Jessica said. "She was really involved in all of those processes."

Cindy accompanied Andy to openings and other events important for making connections, for staying connected—and, ever the booster, she brought her boss, Richard, and his wife and work friends like Gene Khananov. At art world events especially, Andy needed Cindy to balance his sometimes slant personality, to quiet his turgid anxieties, which a taste of success had only exacerbated. He worried constantly—about whether he would lose his teaching job, about whether he'd made a bad impression, about where the next acquisition would come from. And on nights when there wasn't an opening to attend, Cindy and Andy's apartment—first at 440 Broadway, then at 211 North Seventh—turned into a meetup for friends, family, and busybodies from the art world.

I call Richard Furman in late September 2020, asking for his impressions as well as his fact checking. He tells me that Cindy worked for him for more than a decade; they had been "couple-friends"; and Richard and his wife were regulars at Andy's shows. Cindy had moved to New York to become a practicing artist, but she had ended up bookkeeping for an architect. I put the question to Richard plainly: "Why?"

"In the entire time that I knew her," Richard tells me, "she never showed me any of her work."

Richard knew Cindy "had been an artist before"—but by the mid-'90s, when they met, this didn't seem to be a part of her life anymore.

Christiane Fischer-Harling, another friend and collector of Andy's work, says almost exactly the same thing when I call her in March 2021.

"I never saw an artwork from Cindy. She never talked about it. There wasn't even anything of hers in the house," Christiane tells me. "I knew she was an artist and I never questioned it. I rationalized it. But I never saw it."

On North Seventh, Cindy didn't have a studio of her own. She didn't have the time. And, according to Peter Muscato's memory, her memorable diptych that had hung above the couch on Broadway disappeared.

"Andy and Cindy were a team," Jessica Berwind tells me. But "she definitely put herself second."

Andy was showing at the Hood and Chelsea's Universal Concepts Unlimited, Frederieke Taylor's TZ'Art and later her eponymous gallery, at the Drawing Center, and the UBS Gallery, and he was welcomed back multiple times to certain houses in Europe—the von der Tann, Schüppenhauer, and von Bartha galleries. In those years, Andy was attaining greater attention overseas than he was at home, with solo shows at Galerie AB and Galerie du Génie in Paris, at Green Collections Multiple in Tokyo, at the Madrid Art Fair, and in a half-dozen cities across Germany, where he was particularly loved—Berlin, Köln, Drensteinfurt, Lünen, Münster, Bochum.

After Eric Siegeltuch closed his gallery in 1988, Andy had found other New York gallerists to favor him, even if he never again found representation. Two in particular were champions: the fierce and savvy SoHo redhead Elga Wimmer, who, like Wynn Kramarsky, had a space at 560 Broadway; and Philadelphia's sui generis Jessica Berwind, who was making a name championing those outside the gallery mainstream.

Back home in Buffalo, Andy still had the affection of the collector class, including the grocery magnate Armand Castellani, who purchased a dozen works for Niagara University's Castellani Art Museum and another twenty for his personal collection.

Of course, Wynn's advocacy was an immeasurable help. After a decade of making connections and placing individual pieces in galleries, Wynn had included Andy in a major internationally traveling exhibition, *Drawing Is Another Kind of Language*, which ran from 1997 to 2001. This brought Andy's work to dozens of major galleries in as many cities, and permanently associated his name with the talents that then defined the world of works on paper.

Christiane Fischer was also a close friend and advocate in those years. A rising star in the finance department at Daimler-Benz and later in the art arm of the international insurer AXA, she was in a position to influence significant corporate acquisitions. A rural German turned global executive, with a blonde bob and a broad, bright, inquisitive demeanor, Christiane cut quite a contrast with Andy, the dark and often reticent American artist, but they were another immediate match: so much that Christiane and her husband, Bernhard, hired Andy directly to teach art to their daughters. Daimler-Benz had commissioned and acquired a few pieces from Andy in the '80s. When Daimler-Benz merged with Chrysler and moved its New York staff to Detroit, Christiane moved to AXA, first as COO and director of communications, then as CEO of its fine art subsidiary. AXA was the outsider in fine art insurance, but under Christiane, the giant bested the old stalwarts in the gallery and private-collection insurance marketplace, becoming a dominant player. And she took Andy on her ride to the top. In Christiane's boardroom—where influential collectors, gallerists, and museum trustees regularly passed—there hung one of Andy's works she had personally selected, a massive piece. She bought a dozen of Andy's works herself and used AXA to acquire even more.

Also in the '90s, Cindy helped Andy annually prepare applications for a dozen-odd awards and fellowships. They went after the New York Foundation for the Arts (NYFA), the NEA, the New Jersey State Council for the Arts, the Mid-Atlantic Arts Foundation, the Guggenheim. They consulted a paperback copy of *Money to Work II: Funding for Visual Artists*. The archives of the Burchfield Penney hold these applications in Cindy's hand, and hint at the incredible labor involved in the process: Cindy would take Andy's dictation, longhand, then type his artist statements and mark up successive drafts.

They were sometimes successful. Andy netted awards and recognition from the Karuizawa Drawing Biennale, the Wakita

Museum of Art, the National Endowment for the Arts, and the Mid-Atlantic Foundation. After applying in 1990 and '91, Andy finally won a needs-based grant from the Pollock-Krasner Foundation, with an application including a letter from Andy and Cindy's dentist, Charles Ptak of Long Island, who happened to be a collector of Andy's work—and a patron of Cindy's bookkeeping services—attesting to Andy's need for $8,000 in emergency oral surgery.

Andy even secured small sums for some of his pieces to appear in films—one on the wall of Harrison Ford's house in *Regarding Henry* and another, *Sea Cliff*, in Susan Sarandon's house in *Igby Goes Down*. The contract for the use of *Sea Cliff*—which earned Andy $150—is marked up in Cindy's hand.

More important than any gallerist's attention, more important than the steady acquisitions of Armand Castellani or Wynn Kramarsky, was Cindy's support. And this support was a full-time job. Into Andy's career she channeled all the artistic ambition that had fired her as a seventeen-year-old art student in the plaid skirt and cardigan uniform of Sacred Heart Academy. And the impulse to express herself redirected into the apartment, into the garden, into uncountable small gestures—homemade gifts, creative thank-you cards—remembered to this day by her friends.

These gestures are, for the most part, lost to time. Lost in another and even more distant sense is a decade of art that, it's clear, Cindy would have produced had she even split her time, space, and attention between herself and her partner.

But as I uncovered this, and inquired with friends from every stage of Andy and Cindy's life together, I kept running up against a wall at *Why?*

Why would this artist stop making art? Why not find even a *little* time for it?

Triangulation only takes me so far. I feel I can conjecture that Cindy felt more than a merely managerial interest in the business side of Andy's career. There seems to have been a sense that she was participating in the art-making itself. This comes from the record, but also hinges on hints from people like Eric, Peter, and Jessica.

But I can't guess what Cindy felt about that participation—or its costs. There are limits to what I can learn without any record in Cindy's own voice.

But every new way I find to ask the question, I end up back at another of Jessica Berwind's observations.

"Cindy always struck me," she said, "as someone who was doing what she wanted to do."

Cindy Suffoletto, untitled oil on canvas.
Copyright Cindy Suffoletto (n.d.). Courtesy of Cindy Suffoletto Estate.

Cindy Suffoletto, untitled mixed media.
Copyright Cindy Suffoletto (n.d.). Courtesy of Cindy Suffoletto Estate.

Cindy Suffoletto, untitled mixed media.
Copyright Cindy Suffoletto (n.d.). Courtesy of Cindy Suffoletto Estate.

Cindy Suffoletto, untitled mixed media.
Copyright Cindy Suffoletto (n.d.). Courtesy of Cindy Suffoletto Estate.

Arrivals

In the dark, I grew up.

—MOLLY BRODAK, *Bandit*

THE PIZZA OVENS radiate heat and invisible particulate grease beats against my back as I stand at the register all afternoon and evening. By the time I clock out at nine or nine-thirty, the atmosphere has baked me into a slick and fragrant second skin—I slip like an amphibian into the cool, pooling night.

I work at Bob and John's La Hacienda, a pizza shop and restaurant across the street from our house, through my junior and senior years of high school, typically weeknights from four to nine and weekend afternoons. Around the holidays I also sell watches inside the Macy's at the mall. But Bob and John's is the regular gig. I work mostly because I need to put gas in my parents' cars to visit my girlfriend, who lives half an hour away in Clarence, a suburb like a monkey's fist of cul-de-sacs, a place without sidewalks. I need money for burgers, beer, dates, movies. I don't think about saving for anything further away than Christmas gifts.

Like other kids who work the register, I am a transient presence in the kitchen. The cooks and managers tolerate me so long as I stay well away from the ovens opening and closing, the long wooden paddles like boom gates swinging, the traffic of boxes and plates among the prep station, the warming shelf, the dining room, and my counter. The other employees at Bob and John's—the waitresses, line cooks, oven masters, sub assemblers, drivers, and dishwashers—are, for the most part, lifers. They've seen changes, seen plenty of kids like me come and go. The way their bodies move in the kitchen gives them away as teammates, like the clips of NBA players with even their tics in mysterious sync. They have long and murky histories with one another. They date and are interrelated—mothers and daughters swapping wait shifts, cousins sharing the cigarettes that always burn like votives in an ashtray by the open back door to the dumpster lot. Most nights they take their pay to the Wellington Pub next door, drink Molsons, play Quick Draw. Typically tightfisted, on second Fridays they become princely, buying rounds, leaving packs of Marlboros open on the bar. And because of this they enjoy an easy if sometimes aggrieved sense of intimacy, a private language of gesture and slang, arcane callbacks, expletives and explosive sighing.

I haven't earned the use of this language in large part because I'm not equipped to test it in the narrow arena of the kitchen's common interests. I don't have bills or kids or health concerns, and the rest of the workers don't have final exams or college applications or girlfriends with hypervigilant mothers—so commiseration, that most powerful binding agent, is not an option. ESPN plays constantly on a small TV near the ceiling, and I like watching sports, but I have no patience for fantasy leagues or commentary, can't follow their granular assessments of players from other cities' teams. I *almost* speak up when the whole kitchen argues over the merits of *Recovery*, the bestselling album of 2010, but my coworkers have Eminem T-shirts, tattoos, and ringtones—as a casual listener, any opinion I can offer is sure to hit a trip wire. So most of the time I work silently.

But one slow summer evening, mid-shift, as the sun pours fiery gold all down Hertel Avenue, I find myself in a conversation with a few of the other workers in the kitchen—something unexpected, collegial. Someone asks me to pick up a weekend shift. "I can't," I say, "I have a gig."

"Music?" says Justin, one of the managers.

We call this "common ground" with good reason—at once I feel more sure-footed in the kitchen. I turn from the register and start to talk with him about my band, a standard basement-rock outfit that occasionally plays block parties, parish lawn fetes, fundraisers at community centers.

When I mention that I play the drums, Steve, a driver, perks up. This is particularly notable because Steve is an astringent, high-strung person. A little older than most of us—he has kids in junior high—Steve is a senior driver, a semi-official position that involves standing at a map tacked to the wall in the stairway that leads from the kitchen to the basement, assigning delivery orders to different drivers on- and off-site, and screaming at anyone whose tardiness throws off his careful campaigning, like Nick Nolte in *The Thin Red Line*.[1]

"I play, too," he says, joining the conversation from his usual post.

Immediately I try to picture him behind a drum set and can only imagine something like the fight scene from *Stepbrothers*.

"No kidding," I say. "How long?"

"Since I was your age, maybe a little younger," he says. "I just sold my kit."

"Oh yeah," I say. "Why'd you sell it?"

The kitchen falls completely silent.

Tiffany, at the sub station, tosses her blonde, permed ponytail to look at me. A perpetually stoned driver whose name I never learned leans out from the back by the fryers to watch. And Steve doesn't answer. He keeps picking up order tickets and impaling them on a tiny metal spear, eyes forward to the corkboard beside the ovens.

I know now what I had done. I know I won't say another word this shift, won't be invited to participate in any more casual conversation. Still Steve will not look at me, though I can see the churning behind his face.

Finally Justin, on the other side of the room, speaks for him. "For money," he says.

A summer morning, 1995—Sixth Avenue is still in shadow. Cindy breezes out of the station at West Fourth Street and Washington Square headed south, like most of the foot traffic at that hour, aiming vaguely for the Twin Towers of the World Trade Center that swing like the doubled southern tip of a compass needle above Lower Manhattan. A neon sign on the building behind her reads TIME and TEMP, but the tubes are dead, have been dead for as long as she's been taking this stop and walking the nine blocks south and west on Sixth and Carmine to Varick Street, stopping at number 180 and taking the elevator up to Suite 910, the offices of architects Furman & Furman where, since May, she has been employed as a bookkeeper and right hand to the principal and reigning Furman, Richard.

It is a little after seven-thirty on a Tuesday, a comfortable seventy-six degrees that feels like sixty in the shade of the buildings on Sixth. Cindy loves this time in the morning in the city. She wakes early in their apartment—she and Andy live on the second floor at 211 North Seventh in Brooklyn now—makes a strong cup of coffee on the stove, cleans yesterday's dishes from the sink, looks with clear eyes out at the rooftop garden, notes what has changed in the night. She glances at a painting or sculpture she's left off working on late yesterday. Cindy leaves the apartment just as it begins to flood with light, fractaled and latticed by the ironwork outside their windows. In the afternoons, Williamsburg smells pleasantly of pot and pastelitos. In the mornings it smells like swept asphalt, sun, East River air, rubber and grease from the auto shops that open earliest. Some days it feels like the train stops right at her doorstep—she's barely set the latch behind her before she's off, moving at a steady clip toward Manhattan. Ten years in and the novelty of New York hasn't worn off.

But in ten years of commuting—to South Orange, SoHo, Green-wich Village—Cindy has found a rhythm in the city, and in that rhythm, confidence.

Maybe it's because of that confidence, her comfort, or maybe it's because she still moves with the momentum of the M train, a kind of light but insistent force in the small of her back, that she doesn't feel the man dart from behind her on Sixth and slip the purse from her shoulder.

And then she is running—a little black-haired bullet aimed at the back of a man doubling the distance between them on much longer legs.

"Hey!" she shouts. "Stop him!"

People moving in the same direction drift to the edges of the sidewalk, barely turning to look at her over their shoulders. The light at Washington Place turns green, sending a feeling of hope-lessness like a big pill down the back of her throat. She thinks the burly man at the Sabrett stand might move to block the robber's path, but instead he steps back off the curb and into the gutter.

And then her assailant flips—his head hits the crosswalk and Cindy's purse flops behind him like a limp fin. A hand on a lean wrist extending from an army surplus coat is wrapped around his ankle.

The robber scrambles up and dashes into traffic, caroming off the hood of yellow cab and disappearing before Cindy can reach the intersection, but he's left behind the bag. The intercessor—a houseless man, back still against the trash bin under the streetlamp where he always sits—waves her gently away when she tries to dig in the purse for money to offer him. He knows her from among the weekday commuters. She's been kind to him in the past—a few dollars, a few words, the occasional coffee. But they don't even know each other's names. Cindy shoulders her bag, thanks him again—breath already caught—and walks on to Varick.

. . .

This is Suffoletto lore, inked shortly after I was born. I don't remember hearing the story for the *first* time; instead, it was something my mom or dad or grandma would reference in passing, typically to underscore a point about Cindy's independence, her fortitude. Later, when she got cancer—and later still, when the cancer came back—it became a story worn smooth. *Cindy's tough*, we'd remind each other. *Remember when....*

Thinking about it now brings to mind Mack Mahoney's article, "Hard Choices," from '85.

Cindy doesn't appear by name with the other boys in the hometown feature, though she and Andy were both Buffalo artists, had moved to New York at the same time, worked in the same galleries, were soon to share a studio at 440 Broadway. And for all the ink and inches Mack gives to the male expats kvetching about rent, gentrification, representation, square footage, the story misses the moment—the precise moment—that an artist from Buffalo really *arrives* in New York.

"The things I thought would happen didn't," Patti Smith wrote of her own attempts to find direction as an artist after moving with Robert Mapplethorpe to the Hotel Chelsea. "Things I never anticipated unfolded."[2] I think it always goes this way, perhaps especially for those, like artists, most assured of their destination.

Now, with thirty-five years hindsight, I submit to Mack that it—the missed moment—happened not to John or Bob or Andy but to Cindy, almost ten years after she and Andy had signed the lease for their first apartment in the city. It happened on this sidewalk in Greenwich Village, with no witnesses but its two mutually anonymous participants. In this moment of arrival, all that Cindy has gained and all that she has paid fall unexpectedly—and briefly—into balance.

Give Us Barabbas!

Art is a private affair, the artist produces it for himself, an intelligible work is the product of a journalist. . . . What we need is works that are strong straight precise and forever beyond understanding.

—TRISTAN TZARA, "Dada Manifesto 1918"

We felt Robert [Calvo]'s design did everything we wanted it to do.

—MARY S. MARTINO, Niagara Frontier Transit Authority art committee chair, Buffalo News, 1996

DON METZ AND I call each other back and forth several times through the summer of 2020, each conversation starting fresh, and maybe meandering back to where the last had left off—before veering again in a new direction. Reading over my longhand notes from these calls months later, I realize that Don had shared two stories that, in parallax, captured a latent tension in Andy's personality—or perhaps his personhood—that no isolated episode had, for me, uncovered. It was a tension that became more pronounced in Andy as the last century drew to its confused and tragic conclusion.

Art, for Andy, had always been like the event horizon of a black hole that he carried under the surface of his mind. Nothing escaped it. This was especially evident as he moved like a human vector through Buffalo's heady 1970s. From the Stones's *Sticky Fingers* and the Tet Offensive through Skylab and Watergate all the way to Margaret Thatcher, the Ixtoc I oil spill, and national "malaise," the events of the decade either charged and informed Andy's art or passed him by completely, too far away to feel the gravitational tug of his attention. Similarly, he took for himself the materials that gave structure and meaning to other people's lives—the language of music, science and math, anthropological research, demographics, national history, poetry, film studies—and pressed these systems into the service of his art.

"He loved the way science looked. He also loved the way music looked," Don had explained to me over the phone. After graduating with Andy from John F. Kennedy High, Don had left the physical education program at Erie Community College to join the music program at UB, and in those years he was constantly composing or transcribing music—often works by faculty like Morton Feldman, Lukas Foss, or John Cage. Andy would come over to Don's house, take a glance at whatever he was working on, and ask, "Can I have that?" Whatever it was had touched the outermost inclination of space toward Andy's ever-collapsing center. He took what he touched and made art with it. Don's transcriptions might end up shredded and interleaved horizontally with vertical columns of letters cut from a text on local topography—an experiment taking two aleatory erasure poems and smashing them together like nuclei in a fusion reactor—or Andy might take the notes from the score and translate them into a mathematical equation, using the factors in the equation to plot the points of a triangle or determine the radians of an arc he would trace in graphite with Mylar cutouts across his canvas.

But Andy was circumspect in the way he *talked* about this compulsion, this orientation of everything in his life toward meaning-making in media.

"We made art. But we didn't call each other artists," Don tells me once. "That was for someone else to say."

"Is that right?" I asked. "You're telling me Andy didn't consider himself an artist?"

"*Call* himself," Don corrected me. "No, we didn't go around doing that."

Hearing this, I noted that Andy, like other contemporaries,

particularly from the Buffalo scene, had often adopted a studious indifference to the *someone elses* of the world, and to their preferences and opinions.

It wasn't exactly arrogance in Andy's case—it was a defense mechanism. Andy didn't just avoid calling himself an artist. He avoided talking about *his own* art at all, Don and others remember.

"He would even be a little uncomfortable if you looked at it," Christiane tells me the following year. "If you were standing there looking at his work he would walk away."

"My work has not been readily accepted," Andy once remarked to an interviewer, "and that is a fact which I find comforting."

But on another call, Don shares a story that his wife, Camille, had related to him over four decades before. Andy had stopped by Don and Camille's house in Buffalo; Don was in the basement working and Camille invited Andy into the kitchen to wait for him. Talk turned, inevitably, to art.

"Why do *you* make art?" Camille asked.

Note that this was in the mid-'70s, long before Parsons, before Europe, before Wynn Kramarsky, before serious talk of New York—before even Cindy.

Andy replied with a single word. "*Fame.*"

I remember at a very young age, recognizing something slippery and ill-fit about my uncle: he was a *real artist*, but he wasn't *famous*.

I walked past Andy's works that hung in my parents' home nearly daily. I knew that when he and Cindy came home to Buffalo any time other than Christmas, it was because he was having a "show." I came to these shows, toddled through the forests of long wool coats, ate cubes of cheese and tiny sugar cookies from the snack tables. Because of Andy, I knew younger than most children that a real-life person might be an artist.

But at the same time, at five or six, even at eleven or twelve years old, I believed that to be an artist *was* to be famous. I knew this because of the way people talked about artists: in terms of reverence and mystery, always with a little hesitation; normal people never had quite the right words. This was also because of museums. Things in museums were famous, and the people who made them must be famous, too, I reasoned. And this was because of the depictions of artists in movies and on TV—caricatures who might have been a little strange, who might not have lived in perfect luxury, but who were always *watched*.

Yet Andy lived in a normal apartment, wore baseball caps, read to me from picture books you could have bought anywhere. He was *special*, I sensed—so was Cindy—but they didn't bring the candescence of celebrity with them when they visited our house each winter. Cameras didn't follow Andy; his time was his own to manage. I don't think I ever asked my parents to explain this— I accepted the contradiction as part of the mystery of my uncle and his place in the family.

As the curtain started to descend over the twentieth century, this contradiction really *was* an increasingly central part of my uncle's character—though of course I didn't know this at the time.

Never was this tension clearer—and fame's absence in Andy's life more obvious—than in 1995, when the Niagara Frontier Transportation Authority (NFTA) chairman Robert D. Gioia announced a national competition for the design of the concourse of the new Buffalo Niagara International Airport, then under construction off Genesee Street in Cheektowaga. The short age of state arts funding was over, but public art was still a popular priority for high-profile projects. The NFTA was offering a $40,000 commission, with $300,000 for materials and construction—a year's teaching salary in those days, plus the chance to leave an enduring thumbprint on the busiest spot in

Western New York, just a few clicks north from where Andy had grown up.

Andy threw himself into his bid, receiving a vision on a grander scale than anything he had yet attempted: a poured concrete canvas 230 feet long, 65 feet high, and 65 feet at its minor semi-axis, an area larger than three basketball courts and designed to withstand the foot traffic of over five million passengers a year. In typical fashion, his concept drew on multiple disciplines and schemes, incorporating the solar system and the geography and topography of Western New York into the concourse's floor tiles. Andy's process had been characteristically labor-intensive: he had collected core samples from each of the Western New York regions he planned to represent in his design and specified that the final installation use only site-matched and locally sourced minerals.

Tony Bannon, director of the Burchfield Penney Art Center at the time and one of Andy's friends and boosters back in Buffalo, was serving on the NFTA committee selecting the art for the concourse. He and Don Metz, who had just taken a position at the Burchfield Penney in '95, made a trip to New York to scout galleries in the spring of '96 and stopped by 211 North Seventh, stepping into the first-floor studio Andy was then sharing with Tomas Kotik, Charlotta and Petr's son. They found Andy engrossed in finalizing his designs for the airport.

As semifinalists selected out of more than 150 applicants, Andy and three other artists—Robert Calvo of Portland, Oregon; William Maxwell of Boulder, Colorado; and Nori Sato of Seattle, Washington—had already submitted sketches, written proposals and other draft material, and had visited Buffalo on an NFTA-sponsored educational tour. Cindy, of course, had helped Andy at every step, copyediting and substantively revising his portfolios, keeping track of deadlines and correspondence, urging him to drop a line now and then to blockers and tacklers in Buffalo.

Now Bannon paid a visit bearing inside info about Andy's chances.

"Andy," Tony said, "it's beautiful—but the Outer Harbor is in the wrong place."

He was referring to 190 acres along the Buffalo waterfront, a man-made landmass formed from break walls and backfill that separated a deep waterway from the worst of Lake Erie's weather and allowed large ships to dock safely year-round. Dating back to 1836, the Outer Harbor had been part of Buffalo Mayor Samuel Wilkeson's bid to position the city as the ideal terminus for the Erie Canal. It was instrumental in bringing a century of wealth to Buffalo, but by the '90s, the Outer Harbor was barren, abused, contaminated, and out of mind for all but frustrated conservationists.

Andy's scheme was far from geographically literal. Prioritizing the interplay of systems of measurement and navigation over the interests of traditional cartography, it would have placed Lake Erie and Lake Ontario at opposite ends of the airport's amygdaliform concourse.

And Andy refused to change it.

"It's wrong," Tony said.

"It's *art*!" Andy said.

Tony shook his head. Andy's wasn't the deciding voice on that point.

The other committee members were "art experts," according to contemporary coverage in the *Buffalo News*: Mary S. Martino, Margot Glick, Stephen Biltikoff, Duncan Reid, Douglas Schultz, Walter Zmuda, James Pappas, and Tony Bannon, along with CannonDesign's Mark Mendell and William Pedersen of Kohn Pedersen Fox.

Tony wasn't Andy's only friend among this number. Doug Schultz had connected Andy with his first and only "quarterback," Eric Siegeltuch, ten years earlier. He was still a fan. Biltikoff, heir to the Bison Foods fortune, was a patron whose collection included Andy's work and other contemporary expats' work such as Nancy Dwyer, John Toth, and Charles Clough. Mark Mendell, CannonDesign president and leader of the Greater Buffalo International Airport Design Group, considered himself Andy's colleague and was married to one of Andy's oldest friends and former studio mates, Marilynn Deane. And James Pappas had ties, too: a fellow member of the Villa Maria faculty, he had first exhibited with Andy in 1978.

But, unbeknownst to Andy, his former advocate Doug Schultz now favored Robert Calvo.

And the chair, Mary Martino—not an art expert at all, but a powerful city politico[1]—was no fan of Andy's. Tony told Andy that the Outer Harbor was a sticking point for her, and she would refuse to vote for his proposal without a correction.

B-but-but—Andy was so incensed, crucified on an axis of anxiety and stubbornness, that he reverted for a moment to his childhood stutter.

Tony and Don left Andy to come to his own decision.

Andy submitted his final designs with the location of the concourse unchanged.

And the $340,000 commission went to Calvo, whose tamer concept plotted different moments in local history on a map of the region—literally, faithfully rendered.

"We felt Robert's design did everything we wanted it to do," Martino told the *Buffalo News*. "With its topographic map and history of the area, it's an entrance to our region."[2]

Andy would never cross the concourse of the new Buffalo Niagara International Airport. From '96 on, every year around the holidays, he chose to drive the eight hours between New York and Buffalo.

The vote had been unanimous.

Americans Abroad

I BREAK INTO movement when the old woman across from me flicks a strong blunted finger in my direction. It is a command, not a suggestion. I help myself to another serving of cavatappi in blush sauce from the bowl at the center of the table.

We sit on the poured concrete balcony of a brutalist apartment complex in the Scharnhorst district of Dortmund, Germany. It is early August 2014, and my best friend, Steve Coffed, and I are visiting Germany for the second time. We don't speak the language and are completely dependent on our host and guide, Matthias Spruch. Dortmund feels to us the way a favorite childhood campground might have felt—like waking into a lucid dream every time we return to it—and the Spruchs and Matthias's best friend, Sebastian Lindecke, are, by now, our extended family.

Steve and I met Matthias in 2010. He had been an exchange student during our senior year of high school and had fallen in quickly with our circle of eccentrics. The night before he left, we all went out for burgers—Matthias and me and Steve, our girlfriends, Neil, Claire, a few others from the orbit—and returned to my house to spend a few hours pulling up Vine compilations and deep-cut skits from the early days of YouTube on the TV in the living room. At the end of the night, Matthias embraced us—smelling of the cigarettes he snuck in the driveway after my parents had retreated upstairs—and insisted that we visit him for his eighteenth birthday the following summer. We had no intention of taking him up on this offer, but after nearly a year had passed, as we approached our first summer as college students, we better appreciated just how rare of an opportunity Matthias had offered us. After a gut check with Steve, I opened the Facebook Messenger chat where we periodically lobbed old jokes across time zones, and we told Matthias we were taking him up on it.

We made our first trip in July 2012—two months after Cindy died and just two weeks after Steve's father had been killed in a shocking accident while biking to work one morning. We were grieving, ragged, on strained terms with family, on worse terms with our girlfriends; we came close to calling it off but instead doubled down. I packed a fresh leather-bound journal for my first trip outside the country; Steve's mother packed him seventy-two protein bars; and Matthias was prepared with Hansa pilsners, pouch tobacco, and patience. The experience proved an emotional vortex for all of three of us, and we emerged from it more like brothers than friends, promising a return as soon as it was possible.

We do, two years later, and the Spruchs—Matthias; his sister, Sarah Maria; his brother, Tobias; his mother and father, Brigitte and Berthold—greet us like family. So much so that our familial obligations include several social visits to Matthias's extended relatives, an honor and a happy requirement.

Eighty-five-year-old Oma Michalski—the woman slowly immobilizing me with pasta on the balcony of her apartment— had, like Matthias's parents, escaped from the Silesian region of Soviet Poland in the '80s and became an adopted grandmother to the family. When she opens the door for us, I see that she resembles her apartment: compact and orderly. She disappears in a kind of camouflage, a floral dress moving against intersecting panes of floral wallpaper. Decorations hang head-high, for her—for me, at about my shoulders—and consist mostly of Polish Catholic iconography and portraits of family members that I gather are no longer with us. Once she's seated us on the balcony outside, tree-shaded and open just enough to the after-noon's warm breezes, she begins a bombardment of questions in German, smiling the whole time at Steve and me, looking not once at Matthias. Our friend sighs, spins his fork in his fingers and rests it on the edge of his dish—he realizes that he'll have to spend the next hour eating with strategic intent and clinical pre-cision, fitting mouthfuls between translations. He takes another breath and then explains to us, in English, that Oma Michal-ski wants us to tell her about our visit the previous day to the Museum Ostwall, the region's premier collection of postmodern and contemporary art.[1]

I can express the simplest sentiments in a plodding German by now, but I decide to spare us all the embarrassment and aim to deliver an abbreviated review in English, which would be easy enough for Matthias to translate.

"I have never seen such a brazen fraud," I say.

Oma Michalski nods, understanding completely even before Matthias begins his loose interpretation.

The largest exhibition space in the Museum Ostwall had fea-tured a floor covered in metal spoons, with two empty suitcases standing on one end and a sad-looking gray couch on the other. A sign on the wall indicated that one was supposed to pick up a suitcase, walk with it across the spoon pool, and then sit on the couch to contemplate the experience. Steve, Matthias, and I hadn't taken more than a few steps into the room. Some tacit understanding passed among us and we moved on without par-ticipating.

Other rooms held a pile of empty potato sacks; a red square can-vas next to a blue square canvas; globes of LED lights reminiscent of a Michaels end-of-season sale; and a video of the artist Freya Hattenberger performing lackluster fellatio on a plastic-wrapped microphone.

Dead-footed and depressed after this parade of smug banality, we turned a corner into a room loud with dream and gesture. All at once and in the same small space we encountered evocative Picassos and brilliant Beckmanns, an onslaught of emotion that coursed us physically. We turned, and turned, and turned, and took in more and more. Best was August Macke's heartbreaking *Great Zoological Garden*, a triptych giving the impression of a hundred bright panes of colored glass falling through the air—arrested at the moment of our noticing to take the shape of the image the title suggests—and threatening to collapse at a blink.

These were works of the highest order—immortal, awesome. We knew immediately and we knew it together, without speaking it, knew it in every organ. We might have lingered half an hour before moving on.

Turning another corner, we found a framed piece of paper reading: *Form is void. Void is form.*

On a nearby wall was a larger canvas with a faded word in black airbrush—*zerstort*, "destroyed"—and superimposed above that, written in a loopy felt-tipped marker, *Alles ist kunst*, "Everything is art."

And so on, and so on.

We would not feel really alive again for the rest of our time in the gallery.

Marketing text on the museum website sought to contextualize the collection: *Anyone can have an idea.* This became a joke, a rejoinder that we kept repeating to each other for the rest of the night, as we tried to purge the experience of the museum with the only medicine for bad art: schnapps and laughter.

"Ideas are not art," I say to Oma Michalski, with earnest conviction at least equal to the museum's web copy. "Ideas are *boring*."

"Ein Gedanke ist keine Kunst," Matthias translates for me. He picks at his cooling plate of pasta, bored in turn with the effort.

"Ideen…Scheiße," he says. Oma slaps his hand and clucks.

But she understands and tells Matthias to start translating

again: she wants to share a story about the Museum Ostwall. All three of us watch her face as she begins speaking in a hushing Schlesisch dialect, warm and crackling like a well-worn record.

Many years ago, she says, the curators had exhibited a canvas unmarked except for a grease stain in a corner. The canvas was not covered by glass, and one night, a custodian noticed the stain, removed the work from the wall, and used an industrial cleaner to lift the grease stain from the canvas. She put it back—as blank as the day it had been stretched. Oma doesn't mention how long it had taken the professional staff to notice and investigate. But eventually they did, identified the well-intentioned culprit, and terminated her.

Fact or apocryphon, the lesson of the story is obvious: since the last war, contemporary art has been a playground for elites, and its products and playacting have been divorced from the root of all true art, which is feeling.

Twenty-one years old, embarking on a new season of life in Europe, and working the American air out of my lungs—often in gusty pronouncements like this—I was perfectly confident passing judgments in a discipline I hadn't studied.

And why not—wasn't the janitor just as sure?

But for whose benefit did I take up these positions? There was an air of performance, a boyish breathiness in my flight to what I mistook for the front lines of the culture wars—like Byron sitting for a portrait in Albanian dress.

I was aware of a sense, even then, that with every gallery I visited in Europe, from Munich's Alte Pinakothek and the London Met to more off-beat collections, like the Ostwall or, later, Edinburgh's Modern One, I wanted to share the experience with Cindy and Andy.

I feel the same today. It's a physical sensation—a projection of something solid and sought-for just over my shoulder. I always want to ask them both, *Is this shit? Or am I ignorant? Is this one of the real ones? Have I judged right?* And, most of all, *Do you feel what I feel?*

As I grew older, learned more, mellowed, this feeling became less about the absence of affirmation and instruction in art from the only two people in my life positioned to provide those things, and more about a dialogue perpetually unborn. Instead of Andy's and Cindy's answers to questions, I started to perceive in flashes a vast, ghostly current—free-flowing conversations, disagreements, even—the sort of dialogue that forms the moving, liquid core of an artistic community.

Instead I flowed alone, too often unfeeling and unfinished, over years of experiences in art.

I didn't know in 2014, for example, that construction of the original Museum Ostwall had begun in 1947, using salvaged materials from a much older art and historical museum that had been destroyed in the war. Ostwall held its first exhibition in 1949, making it one of Germany's first postwar galleries of contemporary art, and it was founded with a focus on *Entartete Kunst*, "degenerate art," modern work that the Nazi regime had deemed unmanly, un-German (and in many cases, simply Jewish). My final assessment of the spoons, the *Alles ist Kunst*, even the fellated microphone might have softened in the light of that historical understanding.

I didn't know that, over a Schlesisch grandmother's spirals, I had passed unsparing judgment on the work of Ben Vautier and Joseph Beuys—artists inspired, like Andy, by Dada, by John Cage, by the politics of their time—artists who were instrumental in shaping Fluxus, a nuclear relative to Andy's intermedia and Cindy's practice of collage—artists who were part of a rich and complicated dialogue with my aunt and uncle—an aunt and uncle who had become a dialogue of echoes and projections within me.

I didn't know this. And it would be several more years before I learned that in touring the Ostwall's exhibits, I was doing more than passing over my aunt and uncle's influences: I was also walking *literally* in Andy's footsteps.

The past year was a very difficult one for us - and I suppose that sometimes we concentrate on our struggles.

The admission—in a typed letter dated April 6, 1999, which I find in box 2, file 47 of the Burchfield Penney's Andrew Topolski Archive—was an unusual one for Cindy, who so rarely asked for help, who was not constitutionally inclined to betray need.

But her correspondents were uncommonly close friends, despite the ocean between them.

She was writing to Daniel and Josée Aulangier, artists living in Paris who had connected with Cindy and Andy when Daniel reached out for help obtaining a teaching visa (and the teaching gig that was a prerequisite). Andy had helped secure Daniel a position as a guest lecturer at Parsons and the couples had stayed close ever since.

I am sorry, we have not been in touch in so long, Cindy had opened the letter. But she was quick to downplay the admission once aired. *Long, sad, difficult artist life stories, blah, blah ...* she wrote.

But we are still here and of course still trying!!

In 1999—still trying.

Perhaps Cindy's admission was not as forthright as, at first, it sounds. The past year had been a difficult one. But so had the past *decade*. As Cindy wrote to the Aulangiers, Andy was working on a submission to an international competition for a work of art to grace the Hochschule für Musik und Theater in Leipzig, Germany. It was a prominent *Kunst am Bau* project—part of a German government mandate to fund public art for public buildings. Several friends recalled to me that this potential commission dominated a period of years during which Andy was even more than typically single-minded. His submission was a complex three-dimensional structure after the fashion of a music box, which could be played; it used motion sensors to move an engraved piece of glass across intricate resonant components. He included a score with the intention that a German conductor might interpret it, as Petr Kotik had at a preliminary exhibition of the work in progress in New York. The submission was extraordinarily complicated, involving logistical questions that were pure pain for Andy to resolve.

Desperately, Andy had turned to the German artist Petr Mayr, a close friend. They had crossed paths at Harvard's Busch-Reisinger Museum in Boston in 1997 at an opening for Kramarsky's traveling exhibition *Drawing Is Another Kind of Language*. Over the phone in October 2020, Petr set the scene of their first encounter. As was typical for artists—as is typical still—they met while smoking outside the doors of the gallery, Andy and Petr and the renowned sculptor Joel Shapiro. Petr was young, younger even than Cindy; he was bare-headed and short, reaching no higher than Andy's armpits; and he wore a simple silver ring in his left ear. His nose, solid like an earth-tilling tool, made a perfect perpendicular with his flat eyebrows, but his face was expressive, full of laughter and conviction. Andy, Petr remembers, mistook him for a collector rather than another struggling artist. (Petr doesn't say it, but the implication is that Andy tried to schmooze him.) The pair met again a few months later, in the new year, when Mayr visited Peter Muscato. Andy, Cindy, Peter, and Petr Mayr sat in the Muscatos' living room for hours, talking as if Petr had always been a member of their ragtag band. (Andy, for example, didn't betray the slightest hesitation in grilling the visiting German on the Holocaust and his impression of *Saving Private Ryan*, which had just hit theaters in July.)

When Andy won the Leipzig competition, Petr served as project manager. Based in Peiting, Bavaria, Petr traveled the nearly five hundred kilometers to Leipzig more than ten times to convey Andy's instructions to the authorities and make sure the complicated proposal would come off as intended. On July 19, 2000, near the end of the process, Andy wrote to Petr with detailed instructions to receive the work via airmail—in a box measuring 77 cm × 100 cm × 46 cm and weighing 58 kilos—swap out the labels to remove any identifying information, and transport it to the university. On top of this, Petr helped arrange a traveling exhibition for the piece, including stops in Schongau, Dusseldorf, Dortmund, and other cities. The reception was enthusiastic.

Andy's gratitude reveals the depth of difficulty the turn of the century had presented—even as he was showing at bigger galleries, earning write-ups in the *Times* and German dailies, and receiving accolades and fellowships unlike any earlier period in his career.

Regarding the show and the money—Bravo, sir!!!!!!!!! You really have quite a way, he wrote. *Thanks for generating the additional funds—I will need it. I am busted now as it is.*

Andy suffered in part because the art market, both in New York and in Europe, was animated by a kind of Wild West mentality, where debts were conditional and alliances ever shifting.

Gallerists, for example, sometimes had a harder time making ends meet than the artists. They put up the cash for so much—SoHo rents, utilities, promotion, food and drink for openings—that when an exhibition flopped, they were sometimes out tens of thousands of dollars. Many resorted to practices that were at best slovenly or at worst unscrupulous. A significant number were shut down for tax evasion or other financial improprieties. In New York, more than a few gallerists made a habit of losing or damaging work in warehouses and submitting insurance claims without telling the artists. In Europe, which fed on American artists but faced the impediment of freight shipping costs, there was an even more powerful mandate to sell. When exhibitions didn't end empty, gallerists often neglected to return the work—and didn't return letters or calls—realizing they had lost out and only had more to lose by putting up the costs to ship unsold work back stateside. That work exhibited in Europe would be lost or damaged was so well known that one American artist, Russell Maltz, purposely made a series of pieces out of scrap from his day job in construction, designing them to deteriorate to nothing over the course of a European tour.

Andy didn't work this way—and Andy got burned.

On May 28, 1993, Andy was writing to the French artist Michèl Blondel, a friend, about five pieces missing from Elga Wimmer's Broadway gallery—and something to do with *the problem of Patrice*, he wrote.[2] *I believe she will locate them or make good somehow*, he said—but the letter was punctuated with uncertainty.

Even worse, Andy lost a significant amount of work in Europe— nearly forty pieces that vanished from Galerie von der Tann in Berlin.

Andy had shown at Iris von der Tann's gallery a few times: solo shows in 1989, 1991, and 1993; in the group show *Zimmer mit Aussicht II* in 1992; and in a joint exhibition with Cristos Gianakos in 1993. For his solo show in '91, the gallery produced an exhibition booklet and (with Wynn's financial backing) commissioned Charlotta to write an introduction and the German art critic Peter Herbstreuth to interview Andy. But by then the relationship with the gallery was already strained. Mysterious production delays nearly caused Wynn to pull funding for the '91 catalog.[3] And Andy and Wynn also corresponded about five works still unaccounted for from the '89 show.[4]

But Iris was a valuable promoter and offered a critical connection to a receptive European market. The relationship continued. Between 1993 and '94, Iris helped Andy to organize a traveling show, starting at Kohn Pedersen Fox in New York, then to the Freedman Gallery at Albright College in Reading, Pennsylvania, and finally to Galerie von der Tann. The exhibition booklet for this project featured short essays by the art critic and publisher Christine Burgin and by Frederieke Sanders Taylor, a celebrated SoHo gallerist and powerhouse arts administrator known for stints as director at the MacDowell Colony and guest curator at MoMA.

Iris gradually accumulated unreturned works over nearly a decade—not just Andy's works on paper but large installations of glass and steel, mechanical components, freestanding machines, disks of heavy metal. Eventually Andy wanted to reclaim the works that hadn't sold.

In separate conversations over six months of research, again and again I heard about the episode of the art lost in Germany. Charlotta, Peter, Michael Randazzo, Ann Ledy, Tom Kotik, and Raymond Saá all referred to it in vague terms as a defining episode in Andy's life. Only Petr remembered the details.

After months of runaround, Andy realized that Iris was either unable or unwilling to ship his works back to him. Petr offered to rent a large van and take it to Berlin to collect the work and arrange for its storage until Andy could muster the funds to transport it back to New York.

Petr used the phone in his apartment to dial Iris at her gallery— (030) 831 30 26. A long, reedy dial tone, sounding at eight-second intervals. After five rings a recording played—the answering machine was full. Petr waited twenty minutes and tried again. Waited an hour and tried for a third time. No answer.

The drive from Peiting to Berlin was 639 kilometers, or six hours and forty-six minutes. Petr didn't know where to find Iris or Andy's works, which wouldn't be at the gallery, but at a warehouse—and that warehouse could have been in any of the city's twenty-three boroughs. Petr didn't want to leave without a destination—but it would cost money to call New York, and Andy wasn't likely to have any more information. He decided to go through with the plan, hoping to buttonhole the suddenly scarce gallerist at her front door.

When Petr reached Berlin, he parked the van near a café he knew in the Friedrichshain district. He ordered an espresso, asked to borrow the phone book, and lit a cigarette at the counter as he paged through it, starting in the Ts. A few entries under "Tann, von der," but none for Iris.

He tried the business section, then went back to the residential pages.

He closed the book, slowly and with a sense of time speeding up—a sense of inevitability, like watching the prestige scene in a heist film.

Iris had no personal address or number listed anywhere.

But Petr did have the address of her gallery, Liebensteinstraße 4, 14195, in the borough of Dahlem, on a historic residential street snugged between the botanical gardens and the Freie Universität (known fondly as "FU Berlin"). Petr ashed his cigarette, took a last wistful look at the wet grounds in the bottom of his cup, and returned to the van.

He wasn't surprised by his discovery on Liebensteinstraße: von der Tann was gone. Petr found only a modest brick-and-iron fence and a path, slightly overgrown, leading to a prewar house, three-and-a-half stories, with tall windows and a pillared balcony where, even now, Petr could picture patrons and artists mingling, drinking, bartering on an opening night. But now the building was unmarked, clearly empty.

The gallery had closed and Iris von der Tann had disappeared.

Even other members of the international art community— including prominent collectors and connectors—hadn't a clue where to find this former fixture of the Berlin gallery scene—or the more than three dozen Topolski drawings and sculptures that had vanished with her.

In a turn that vexed and infuriated Andy, the same art market that had most connected with his work now posed bank-breaking risks. Besides von der Tann, Andy benefited from several European gallerists and collectors passionate about his work. Basel's von Bartha Gallery showed Andy several times, brought him to their booth at Art Basel, and produced a beautiful hardcover exhibition book. Through the von Barthas, Andy met collectors like Pieter and Marina Meijer, who bought dozens of his works and became close friends, commissioning pieces when Andy's sales would slow. Brian Duffy tells me that some years in the early and middle '90s, Andy was making "six figures," a combination of large corporate acquisitions and sales in Europe. One time, Duffy says, Andy and Cindy flew home after a European tour with tens of thousands of dollars strapped to their bodies beneath sweaters and heavy coats to avoid reporting his sales to customs. But his most receptive market became increasingly risky to reach. This wasn't just about the lost opportunity for a sale or an emotional connection to the work, either. Andy incorporated rare and high-priced elements in his work—precious metals, large glass discs, vellum, mechanical components used in creating larger instruments for the United States Department of Defense. He made all of his own frames. And while artists with gallery representation in those years often enjoyed a stipend for materials, Andy only had his own direct sales to sustain his prolific output. The loss of dozens of works overseas meant more than wasted effort and opportunity cost—it was a hit to Andy's bottom line amounting to tens of thousands of dollars.

Andy wasn't alone in this fate, but he had extended himself logistically and financially much further into the European market than most of his contemporaries. And the von der Tann disappearance had grave implications for his access to that market. When the Dortmunder Kunstverein asked Andy if he would show again there in the late '90s, some of his closest friends—Ann and Wynn, Peter and Raymond, and of course Cindy—counseled him against it: Europeans had lost and stolen his work before and would do it again. It was heartbreaking, Ann told me, to watch this struggle—but Andy had no choice.

Out There

...because as every artist knew in his heart of hearts, no matter how many times he tried to close his eyes and pretend otherwise (History! History!—where is thy salve?), Success was real only when it was success within le monde.

—TOM WOLFE, *The Painted Word*

HE SLIPS INTO the freight elevator just before the doors thud shut. Tall—six feet—with a stiff spray of hair adding another five inches, he ducks his head, even though the elevator is eight feet high.

"Sorry," he says. "I forgot I pressed the button. I—I forgot I was going anywhere."

Bob Gulley recognizes him, recognizes the voice, sometimes sure and sometimes hesitant, almost always gentle, curving off the soft palate.

The year is 1982. Jean-Michel Basquiat is twenty-two years old. He'd been watching *M*A*S*H* while Bob was stalking the jungles of Vietnam. By 1979, a high school dropout, Basquiat was a fixture on the underground scene—a mixture of punk, noise, poetry, filmmaking, and visual artists spanning the Pictures Generation, the New Painting, and pop's old guard. Earlier that year, before he moved into the second-floor loft at 101 Crosby Street on the northeastern edge of SoHo, he had his first solo show at the Annina Nosei Gallery. The freight elevator is busier these days—a steady traffic of gallerists, collectors, writers, documentarians, and hangers-on.

"Hey, you're Bob, right?" he asks.

Bob Gulley looks up, gaze breaking from the pane of air before the sliding doors, where he thought he'd rest politely for the duration of the short trip down.

"Yeah, Bob," he says, "that's me."

"I like your work, Bob," Jean-Michel says. "I—I hit the wrong button a few times."

At 101 Crosby, popular with artists, the freight elevator opens directly into the living spaces on each floor. It isn't quite like the heady crush of Essex Street a few years earlier, but still, punch in the wrong floor or stop on your way down to pick up another passenger, and you get a good sense of what your neighbors are up to.

The doors slide open; Bob waits for Jean-Michel to take the first step out, but he doesn't.

Instead he says, "Hey—I like your rifles."

"Uh … thanks," Bob says. "I … I appreciate that."

Seven minutes later the doors slide open again onto the second-floor loft. Bob, carrying a sculpture of a broom turning into a rifle —or a rifle into a broom—takes a long gulp of the scene around him, trying to retain the full sweep of it before he succumbs to the distraction of the details.

There is a TV and a VHS player—videocassettes of TV shows and movies stacked beside it, and a single chair in front of the screen, uncomfortably close. There is a clarinet leaning in a corner; there are piles of crumpled silk and wool—suits, by the looks of it, and expensive. There are cans of spray paint, oil paint sticks, and buckets of bright acrylics. A mattress floats somewhere like a piece of a shipwreck.

Along the wall closest to the elevator are three stretched white canvases—or what appear to be white canvases. A few steps farther into the apartment Bob realizes these are works painted over in thick coats of white. Traces of past lives, discarded ideas, yearn toward the surface of each.

And everywhere—really, *everywhere*—are Basquiat's paintings, finished works and canvases not yet abandoned. Figures regal, threatening, mischievous, and mysterious tumble toward him from every direction. There is a city in primary colors—school buses and skyscrapers—and snakes and guts and swords and bones, cartoon dinosaurs with crowns—and a cacophony of language, words like "head" and "thread" and "stop" and "gold" and "tar" all shouting at once to be heard.

The work is good, Bob can see. Very good. It's energetic, assertive, *new*, and very much of the city just now reclaiming itself from a decade of smoke and slumber—but it is also *technically* good, with an infallible sense of line and a deceptively delicate attention to composition.

"You like it?"

Jean-Michel emerges from the kitchen. Or what might have been his kitchen. The furniture is sparse and the walls are paint-splattered and densely figured, making it hard to tell where the artwork ends and the floor plan begins.

"I love it."

"Thank you. I really appreciate that."

Jean-Michel's eyes drop to the sculpture in Bob's left hand.

"That's it," he says. "That's the one I saw."

"Well," says Bob, "You can have it."

He holds it out diagonally with both hands, just like they taught him in the Army. Jean-Michel accepts it in the same fashion.

"I can give you some work," he says. He frees a hand to gesture to the floor, where studies in oil sticks are spread out like a windswept game of Solitaire.

Then Jean-Michel looks again at his neighbor. He notices the serious boots, steel-toed, and the hammer-loop in his cargo pants. That was sawdust he smelled on Bob, and he remembers the rumble in the elevator that didn't come from the machinery.

"How much would this go for at a gallery, you think?" he asks, holding up the sculpture. "Come on, tell me."

"I guess, uh, if I was lucky, maybe five hundred," Bob says.

Jean-Michel thinks a beat.

"I know a bargain," he says, beaming. "I'll take it."

Six years later, Jean-Michel Basquiat will be dead.

Two years after that, the art market that he ascended, brought to heel, and then helped to inflate beyond recognition will burst, leaving bad debts, regrets, and magazine told-you-sos all over New York City.

It would take the art market only a few years to recover. But tastes—and dealer practices—would never be the same.

Andy was out of step from the start. On his earliest visits to New York, he and John Toth would stop at the Cedar Tavern imagining that the dusky glories of the abstract expressionists and New York School could be theirs. But Franz Kline, Lee Krasner, Jackson Pollock, Willem and Elaine de Kooning, Grace Hartigan, and Frank O'Hara had departed long ago. The action had moved three and a half blocks to One University Place, where at that precise moment Julian Schnabel was working in the kitchen and Mary Boone was holding court.

In the early '80s, Boone would represent Schnabel, Basquiat, Eric Fischl, David Salle, Ross Bleckner—many of the artists who would dominate the market, hold tight to the headlines, and command unheard-of prices for their work.

"Together Boone and her artists redirected the art world's gaze," reads a profile of the dealer published in W in 2008.[1] "Rejecting the Minimalist and conceptual-laden Seventies, they re-energized painting with bold, heavily figurative canvases and made neo-expressionism the dominant aesthetic."

Andy's technical precision, dense intertextualism, and cool, resistant surfaces were essentially the opposite of the style Boone and her stable, overnight, made au courant: the vibrating primary colors and acute political bent of Basquiat; the playful, approachable street art of Keith Haring; Schnabel's broken plates.

Then, in 1990, demand for art lagged in Europe, triggering a gut-plummeting sag in New York. A *New York Times* autopsy in December 1990 explained:

> The growth of the art market through the 1980's reflected a money-obsessed decade when billionaires replaced millionaires in business magazine pantheons. There seemed to be no limits. Prices went ever higher and the boom offered the once-unimaginable prospect of a $100 million painting. It nearly came to pass.
>
> But then the economy slowed. The weak results from the fall auctions at Christie's and Sotheby's in New York and London indicate the once white-hot market for Impressionist, modern and contemporary art has cooled. About 20 percent of the Impressionist and modern works failed to sell in New York, and no more than 50 percent of the contemporary works moved.[2]

This was the same year that Wynn Kramarsky's van Gogh, *Portrait of Dr. Gachet*, fetched a record $82.5 million (a fund that, it's worth repeating, supported Andy and the other artists Wynn preferred). But speculation in contemporary art evaporated.

Boone, Larry Gagosian, and their like took much of the blame. Suddenly the same media that had participated in the hyping of Boone's artists turned on her. Explainers appeared, condemning the commodification of contemporary artists, the waiting lists for work, the shows that would open with every piece already sold. In 1989 it had been common to see collectors pecking at calculators as they moved through galleries; in the '90s, Sotheby's announced it would lay off six percent of its staff worldwide.

The crash made it easier to see all that had permanently changed since Andy entered the art world in the early '70s. Critically, neo-expressionism and the "New Painting" endured, as the rebounding fortunes of Schnabel, Fischl, and others would make clear. Postminimalism, in contrast, had a more limited audience, and even met criticism—with Serra, the movement's surviving head, increasingly written off as derivative and arrogant. Just as important as the nation's altered tastes was the permanent change in the way that one achieved fame (and financial stability). No longer could a singular talent expect a Martha Jackson or a Gordon Smith to set up a meeting with a Seymour Knox, who might buy a dozen works, or a hundred, and reimagine a museum for you.

Money and influence flowed as they always had and always will. There was still a game to be played to control them. But it looked more like chess than checkers, now. And it required attention, ruthlessness, and flexibility.

After twenty years of hustling for recognition, Andy's pace slackened. It wasn't that he stopped working. Multiple friends from every stage of life attested to me, unprompted, that Andy was the hardest-working artist they'd ever known. While he gave his time and attention generously to his students, while he entertained friends many evenings on North Seventh, and while he spent most summer Saturday afternoons with Cindy at the beach, her most beloved indulgence, he continued to "clock in" at his studio from roughly nine to five, creating relentlessly. In his free time he attended lectures, sourced materials, sketched, assembled, and refined. He declined invitations, kept to a schedule, and if he had to socialize he preferred hosting to going out, so he wouldn't waste time in traffic and wouldn't feel trapped. Several friends pointed out that Andy often worked in difficult conditions, as in the winter his unheated studio spaces could dip below fifteen degrees. He could stay microfocused on a task for hours, working with fingers tinted purple.

But the hustle ended. It happened in the late '90s without fanfare and apparently without a single acute cause. It seemed an inner voice told Andy that he had been at it long enough, that he could cash in, let the recognition come to him.

The art world offered models for this, from the studied indifference of Basquiat to the monumental arrogance of Richard Serra to the cut corners of Damien Hirst. Despite the burst of the art market bubble in 1990, money and power again began accruing to American artists in the late twentieth and early twenty-first centuries to a degree unmatched since the Medicis. A handful of minor talents who learned to repeat winning formulas with the consistency of AB InBev benefited from the disappearance of discerning connoisseurs like Peggy Guggenheim, John Bernard Myers, and Martha Jackson and the rise of savvy new executives like Mary Boone and streak-mad megadealers like Larry Gagosian and Matthew Marks, who were then in the process of turning the American art market—and in Gagosian's case, his own business—into a billion-dollar enterprise.

It was against this backdrop and in this context that Andy measured the loss of the Buffalo Niagara International Airport commission, his lack of steady representation by any single New York gallerist, and the plateauing of his prices and interest from collectors.

Charlotta's attention helped Andy's career, but she had to be ethical in her dealings as curator at the Brooklyn Museum and dispense her limited attention widely. Wynn Kramarsky's acquisitions, commissions, and gifts sustained Andy—but he had hundreds of other talents to uplift, too. After a decade climbing to the top in Buffalo, and another decade of hard work and hustle in New York, Andy still hadn't broken into the secondary market—the blue-chip galleries of the Upper East Side, where solo shows at the front of the house were mere distractions from the real trade that went on in the back, where investor-collectors bet against the house. Once an artist becomes a commodity, part of that increasingly attractive asset class, the hustle stops: every new work, almost without exception, will be snapped up for trading on the secondary market; every piece will appreciate; and artists, like their collectors, start to base their decisions on calculations of profit and risk.

Andy lived in the foothills of this world. It was never to be his.

"Why," I asked Tony Bannon over the phone one night, "didn't Andy ever make it into someone's investment portfolio?"

He explained patiently that Andy's work wasn't in line with the prevailing schools of the day—neoconceptualism, neo-expressionism, or new media.

"OK," I said. "But what *was* it?"

"Arcane," Tony said.

I paused, hoping the silence would tug the venerable curator into an explanation worthy of a gallery book.

Sure enough, he went on. Andy's practice was "a cross between John Cage, László Moholy-Nagy, and Joseph Beuys," he said.

But I could tell he wasn't satisfied with his own answer. "Who would dream of sending political messages through a musical score, arranged by letters he selected from the first page of *Das Kapital*?" he said, trying a third time to answer with a question.

"You could play it as music or you could fathom it as design. But except for someone who's hip to design," Bannon explained, "it doesn't *combine*. You need a guide. And Andy's out there by himself."

I knew that some had explicitly called out a failure to "combine" in Andy's work. In March 1992, the *Buffalo News* art critic Richard Huntington reviewed Andy's twelve-year retrospective at Niagara University's Castellani Art Museum, arranged by Andy's friend and biggest booster back on the Niagara Frontier, the local grocery magnate Armand Castellani. Huntington noted Andy's insistence on an absence of didactic political messaging in his work. The ideas clearly present were "merely a contemporary social awareness of existing situations which we confront daily." Huntington found this unsatisfactory. "Clearly Topolski doesn't intend to sever his politics from his art," he wrote.

> Why talk about using glass because in the tremendous heat of a nuclear blast the heat turns sand into glass? Why titles that sometimes read like scientific cryptograms?
>
> I suspect that the work finally rests on a desire that is not only double but contradictory. The appearance of the art suggests that Topolski follows the formalist dictum that sociopolitical concerns and art simply do not mix. But there is no indication that he confronts the constructivist tradition from which he draws all of his visual vocabulary. He simply borrows and elaborates.
>
> The other half of the desire is to produce an activist's art that somehow will make the world a better place in which to live. But this is never articulated in the art, only coyly obscured by a formal game of hide-and-seek.
>
> And, sadly, these beliefs never can be articulated in the form Topolski has chosen. High formalism—especially of this elaborate kind—just doesn't blend that way.

The generosity of the critic rarely extends to the copy desk, where night-shift grammarians pick headlines and seal fates. Consider the headline that ran above a major *Buffalo News* review in 1994:

TOPOLSKI EXHIBIT AT ALBRIGHT
RAISES A BIG QUESTION: "WHY?"[3]

It's worth noting that the critic and the artist are inherently at odds. Every true artist, no matter the discipline, wants to escape definite meaning, to exceed the cold and final embrace of the critic, which is death. I think of the Gerald Stern line that the writer George Saunders loves to quote: "If you start out to write a poem about two dogs fucking, and you write a poem about two dogs fucking—then you wrote a poem about two dogs fucking." The implication here is that bad art or mediocre art ends up doing exactly what the artist intended at the outset. But *great* art does more than the artist intended and likely ever could have imagined—more, the artist hopes, than the critic could ever possibly articulate.

The visual artist–fine art critic relationship looks analogous to the uneasy symbiosis between the writer and the literary critic, but there is an important difference. The writer feels more comfortably outside the critic's reach; they are working in the same medium after all, and the literary artist, uttering first, can swiftly affect indifference. And (in moments of rare desperation) the literary artist always has the option of *responding*. But the visual artist and the fine arts critic never meet in the same medium. The visual artist seeks to escape the stickiness of articulation itself.

I think of Stephen Dedalus, musing on "the ineluctable modality of the visible" on Sandymount Strand: "thought through my eyes," his syntax seeking an immediacy of thought that language inevitably denies. Andy thought through his eyes. He spoke through his hands. Like James Joyce, he knew that "Everything speaks in its own way," that even sand is "language tide and wind have silted here." So too the soft graphite silted across his vellum.[4]

"The limits of my language mean the limits of my world," Wittgenstein observed.[5] The visual artist comes to their medium in the first place because of the limits of verbal language. They seek a vaster and more mysterious world beyond it. In Andy's practice, Huntington called this coyness. But for Andy, I think, it was freedom—it was a way of saying exactly, and only, what he meant.

But *meaning* doesn't sell. Messages do.

This has been particularly true since the '70s, when critics like Hilton Kramer began to argue of art that "to lack a persuasive theory is to lack something crucial."[6] By this measure, Andy's art failed. It had original composition, masterful execution, rich reference and allusion; it had mystery, surprise, a felt sense of the sublime; but never a "theory."

Tony related this difficulty back to Andy's childhood stutter, the struggle with language that drove him to express himself visually in the first place. "When he thought deeply or felt pressure he would go into his stammer, which didn't help when he needed to be his own interpreter," Tony told me.

Alex Topolski, Andy's nephew, agreed with Tony's reading. Alex had grown up in Buffalo and loved spending time with his uncle when he could—loved to visit New York and later Callicoon, and loved to watch Andy crack jokes at his own brothers' expense back home. He related to something in Andy—the irreverence mixed with earnestness—and something, too, in the particular tenor of Andy's struggles, which Alex could perceive with increasing clarity as the years passed.

"I actually grew up with a stutter," Alex told me over the phone, "and I think it stems from anxiety, there's a lot going on in your head and it's not easy to get it out. As a kid, you don't necessarily have the tools to get it out."

This experience influenced Andy toward the visual arts, the story goes, but it came with a permanent cost: with art, he *could* get out everything "going on" in his head; he could put his deepest convictions, fears, anxieties, and wonders into sculpture, works on paper, or mechanical music boxes. But he couldn't then *tell* you how to interpret them. And increasingly he resented being asked.

Stuttering aside, Tony put Andy's situation pointedly: "He didn't have a mouthpiece."

He's right. In all the ink that others spilled in the wake of Andy's art, in English or in German, from *Artforum* or the *New York Times* or the Japanese magazine *Men's Club* to now five decades of scattered gallery books, much of it is nonsense and the rest is hesitant, stopping short of any definitive statement about his intent or accomplishments. Andy never had a person who could not only advocate for but explain his work to collectors, critics, or a general audience. And after Eric Siegeltuch, Andy lacked a quarterback. Both these roles were beyond Cindy's thinned time and capabilities to fill. Despite Andy's talent and energy and Cindy's coordination and persistence, the hustle lacked strategy, the partnership churning forward without clear vision for the next level of success.

This dilemma, even more so than the airport episode or the loss of some dozen pieces in Europe, captures the state of Andy's career as the century drew down: he was recognized but not compensated. And he felt this keenly.

Now, when new collectors and gallerists visited his studio, Andy's former anxiety and eagerness to please were replaced with an air of implicit importance. Old friends, even Wynn, drew back at the uncomfortable touch of this new attitude.

"He spoke hesitantly, he was defensive, he dressed as he pleased, he could be haughty—or pissy," Tony said.

"He felt like he had paid his dues," Peter Muscato remembered. "And the art world has a way of handling that."

I never saw this side of Andy—the entitlement. But thirteen years after his death, in conversations with his surviving friends, not a single one of them failed to mention it—even if only in slightly uncomfortable passing. Most told a similar story: they had been best of friends, then fell out before the end. They cited disagreements but typically couldn't remember the terms. But these arguments must have been serious, for several friends joined in a refrain, a regret that pride and resentment—their own and Andy's—prevented them from ever making amends.

But even as some friends lost touch or turned away, more stuck around, and new ones accumulated. The apartment at North Seventh grew busier and busier.

Cindy and Andy drew people to themselves because they drew energy from people. Socializing was a necessary part of their domestic economy. By the late '90s, you might have thought their place on North Seventh was a gallery and not an apartment, it saw so many visitors some nights—members of the Wynn Crowd, the Parsons scene, the Pratt contingent, the old Buffalo gang, visiting Europeans, and other loose and overlapping groups that made up New York's art world—but also shell-shocked Vietnam vets, friends from upstate, Italian neighbors who liked Cindy's cooking, always new transplants to Brooklyn, political dropouts, misfits with good manners and interesting opinions—Andy's kids, James and Julia, and their friends—family from both sides. Charlotta and Petr were regulars; John and Linda Toth often made the trip; Peter Muscato and his wife lived next door and were often around; Andy's collectors and artist friends from Germany, France, and Switzerland, like the Meijers and Mayrs and Aulangiers, often visited; Bob Gulley, still working construction in Manhattan, was a fixture, and headed to Cindy and Andy's place the way the other men on his crew looked to their corner bars in Queens or Staten Island. Dozens of others knew Cindy and Andy's door would almost always swing open at a knock.

North Seventh was, at least, better suited to this traffic than the studio on Broadway. Andy's brother Thomas and his wife were grounded in New York when a winter storm canceled a flight to Saudi Arabia, and they stayed for three nights at the apartment—no trace of the tensions that propelled the brothers apart after Andy's long-distance calls from New Jersey a decade before. My parents visited in '90, brought me in '95, and brought both me and my sister in '99. Andy and Cindy hosted Christmas parties, New Year's parties, homecoming parties, summer rooftop gatherings, and dinner parties for no other reason than to vent an excess of fellow feeling and to make a sacrament of simple pleasures—wine from the shop around the corner, a little soft cheese from the import mart, a new bit of information from a book or a newspaper that, if introduced at the right moment, could initiate hours of conversation.

And Andy and Cindy could talk with the best of them. After a night on North Seventh you might wake up, eyes fuzzy and head fritzing with nicotine and metabolized alcohol, recalling few details of what you had discussed, but feeling powerfully the sense that "we talked about everything." Andy was fearless and Cindy was gracious, and both were inexhaustibly curious, and this kept the conversations going.

Andy was fearless whether in bull sessions with his oldest friends or just meeting new acquaintances: when he cared about a conversation, he became immediately intense and intimate. There was the time he met Petr Mayr, for example, smoking with Joel Shapiro outside the Busch-Reisinger. They stood in the crisp, ivied courtyard, voices carrying up to the steep angles of the red-shingled roof, alone except for the green copper statue of a lion on a plinth at the center of the square, its head smooth where sockets for eyes should have been. Joel, remember, was a rich and famous artist. And Petr, Andy had mistaken for a wealthy collector. But, despite the obvious risks and tempting rewards of impressing such a captive audience, Andy launched into an earnest interrogation, demanding to know how the young German felt about the role of the Jewish experience—he meant the recent history of the Holocaust—in expressions of contemporary culture. One of his dearest friendships might have ended there, before it even began. But so many, particularly fellow artists like Petr, found this quality of Andy's endearing, even hastening their bonds with him.

On nights like this, Andy put in mind Charles Portis's memorable description of Rooster Cogburn in *True Grit*—taking his mount's reins between his teeth and charging at the Lucky Ned Pepper gang, two pistols wide on either side of the horse's head and firing as he spurred and spurred, guiding the body of the beast with his knees, guiding its head with his head, the bit in the horse's teeth lashed to the slack, horse-tasting reins in his. Andy rode this way into topical byways and detours that would have killed fainter-hearted conversations: the connection of the American space program to the Nazis, Scientology, and Crowley's occult; the point of view of erotic "French" postcards; the influence of the Bilderberg Group on everything from foreign policy to the latest lowbrow blockbuster.

But when he wasn't interested in a conversation, he fell into a silence that some interpreted as sullen, surly, even judgmental.

And when he wasn't talking, Andy drank and Andy smoked.

Everybody smoked, Charlotta remembered—but Andy smoked "like crazy."

"I never saw anybody smoke as much as he did," Eric Siegeltuch told me separately. "It seems like people smoke at that level because they're nervous all the time."

Never a drunk, Andy held booze with a Polish fortitude and modeled his manners in the style of the fourth-shift workers who had peopled the landscape of his childhood. (And again, more like those General Motors pensioners than his contemporaries, he abstained from pot, psychedelics, and hard drugs entirely.) Still, considered by volume alone, his consumption of alcohol and nicotine was Rabelaisian.

All of this, Alex conjectured to me—the smoking, the drinking, the socializing, and constant talk about art and war—was latent in Andy's constitution but exacerbated by the unique wounds that he had carried with him to New York—from the scars of the Vietnam era to his choice to leave family and security behind in Buffalo. "He drank so much and smoked so much to numb that part of himself to let the creative part out, to make the space to keep creating," Alex said.

Charlotta's read is plainer: people exploited Andy and Cindy's hospitality, she says, and they couldn't turn anyone away. Cindy loved playing the host, and she also loved making a space for "stray" people, like Bob, or friends from out of town, or any number of odd artists. Andy, meanwhile, grew less and less inclined to pay social visits, and preferred for friends to come to him.

And so a rhythm set in.

Andy would leave off working in the studio around five sharp, only lacking a punch card. Cindy would make it back from Manhattan a little later. She might have brought home groceries, or she might try to steal a half hour from the steepening evening and work on some of the bookkeeping and copyediting that she did on the side. But eventually the first guests would arrive. It might be Tom Kotik, an art student who was sub-renting space in Andy's studio. He might have been accompanied by friends from the neighborhood, like John Melville, who drummed in a band, or his then-girlfriend, Janine Tramontana. Charlotta might have dropped in closer to seven, after leaving the Brooklyn Museum, about a half-hour's drive away. And depending on where his job site might have been that week, Bob Gulley would have arrived as early as seven or after ten, bringing apologies and a six pack. Peter would have joined, maybe with one of his hired helpers, like Ian Milner, tan and mahogany-haired, a new arrival in New York, and Ian's future wife, Amy Seiden. They would have started in Andy's studio or Peter's yard or the rooftop garden; in worse weather they would have stuck to the apartment. And Cindy would have been sure to put food out, if someone wasn't grilling, shrimp or cheeses or finger sandwiches or even a soup, and to replenish and reposition the platters as the night wore on. She would have welcomed every guest, accepted more or less the same compliments on the garden or the apartment's quirks and comforts, made sure everyone felt attended to, and stepped in to head off any percolating arguments.

And eventually the moon would have ducked behind the

high-rises and the quiet of the night would enter the apartment, the final guest, to find Cindy in the living room straightening cushions and emptying ashtrays, or over the kitchen sink leaving dishes to dry on the rack.

In a few hours the sun would rise and paint Brooklyn a sinister yellow, like a bloody egg yolk, but by seven or eight the morning would have mellowed into something cool and blue. Cindy would have left the apartment—spotless, ordered, and aerated—to catch her train into Manhattan.

A little later, somewhere on the block, Andy's white Jeep would cough to life. He would rattle away, not to the little grocery on Meeker, but across the Brooklyn-Queens Expressway toward East Williamsburg and to the beverage center. And in under twenty minutes the Jeep would return, and Andy would step out, toting a fresh case of Budweiser.

Ian, Peter's assistant at the frame shop in those years, told me this was the scene on North Seventh *every morning*. It became a joke between him and Peter, seeing Andy leave each morning to replenish his fridge. They likened Andy's habit to the Bill Murray movie *Groundhog Day*.

It escaped Ian's attention that the cycle wasn't just about Budweiser, and Andy wasn't the only one trapped.

Crack-Ups

A FIST OF pain appeared inside Cindy's rib cage and tightened around her lung. It felt like a crack had opened inside her, a grinding across some broken place that a moment ago had been whole. She put a hand out and found the cold stone facade of a building. Another crack. A vise tightening. It was her own breathing that caused the pain. She was on the ground, on one knee, her shoulder slumped into the building. Knees and feet brushed around her. She couldn't tell if there was too much air in her lungs or not enough.

Cindy looked up to the sky and pursed her lips once, twice, trying to push a word out, then just a breath. Her throat opened but nothing happened, nothing but the dulled flap of some failed thing inside her. The sky was white and then the sky was all there was.

After two decades of regular smoking, of being around regular smokers, and of living with a world-class smoker, Cindy had developed emphysema. The elastic tissue of her lungs had accumulated damage, making it harder to breathe, and actually overfilling her lungs, her inner wings spasming and pushing up against her ribs and other organs. She ignored the pains in her chest, told no one. And then, heading into work one morning in 2000, on a street in Manhattan—even Cindy couldn't remember which—one of her lungs collapsed.

The doctors told her the chest pains she had been ignoring were from smokers' emphysema, the weakening of her lungs' elastic tissue. This wasn't the cause of her collapse, but it had been an untreated risk. They called what happened to her "pneumothorax."

She shouldn't fly on an airplane, they told her. She should be cautious about strenuous activity, like running or swimming. And, overall, they said, Cindy had to *slow down*.

For fifteen years, Cindy had been breadwinner and homemaker both.

She kept the apartment, cooked and cleaned and maintained the garden. She played the host: feeding, entertaining, comforting, shepherding, politicking, and cleaning up after the hordes of regulars on North Seventh largely fell to Cindy. And she "managed" those relationships with friends. It was Cindy who remembered every birthday, Cindy who plastered over the cracks of slights and disagreements.

She also worked full time, first at C. S. Schulte in New Jersey and then at Furman & Furman's architecture firm in Greenwich Village. And she always had little tributaries of secondary income: she copyedited advertisements for dentists in solo practice and did freelance bookkeeping for small businesses. The Topolski Archive at the Burchfield Penney has some dozen-odd invoices in her name—jobs at $25, $35 a pop.

The archive confirms much more. Cindy "organized Andy's life," Peter Muscato had told me: she took care of his bookkeeping, sales, and registrations, tracking where art was on loan or exhibited, keeping him on schedule, sourcing and organizing potential buyer lists, applying for grants and awards, even writing and answering correspondence. In 11 boxes and 392 individual files, I found Cindy's fingerprints—and her unmistakable handwriting—everywhere.

I remember again that Cindy had come to New York to leave a different kind of mark.

Andy and Cindy had shared a spacious studio on the first floor of 440 Broadway; Charlotta, Peter, Eric, and other witnesses confirmed this and were familiar with the work she had done there over her first nine years in New York.

I asked all three: *Where was Cindy's studio after they moved to North Seventh?*

From what I've been able to discover, Cindy didn't have one.

She still found time to collage or piece together curiosities with domestic detritus; on weekends she might take a little easel and her watercolors to the beach; but she had no time or place dedicated to her art, and nothing like the space or materials she would have needed to work on the kind of sculpture she had been producing on Broadway.

It's likely that Cindy never sought to *rival* Andy's position or recognition. As Lee Krasner had recognized early a world-historical genius in Jackson Pollock, Cindy spotted both Andy's talent and his frailties; she felt called to promote and protect him. As Peter put it, she knew that this was "Andy's show," and she would do anything to keep it going.

But what, exactly, Cindy sought for *herself* in the art world remains a mystery.

She left high school wanting to be an artist, she left Buffalo wanting to be an artist … and then her trajectory was interrupted, permanently redirected. Cindy wasn't reviewed, awarded, represented, or collected. Cindy never developed an equivalent to Andy's body of work or singular, coherent vision. Perhaps most importantly, she didn't have Andy's time—time that she made possible for him.

Cindy was born into a long line of strong women who supported their families. If they felt they played supporting *roles*, I found no evidence that any one of them expressed it. But still, my grandmother, my great-grandmother, and her mother before her—these were women who were most renowned, best loved, not for their hobbies or careers or other individual accomplishments, as the men in their lives might have been, but for the resilience they built into the deep bedrock of their families. Cindy wanted something else. And though Cindy broke from tradition, moved to New York in an unconventional partnership, she slipped almost unnoticed into the space that had been waiting for her from the beginning, a groove in the universe cross-hatched by sex, genetics, and choices—hers and Andy's. She was coming to understand the trade-off bound up in her love: Andy had introduced her to the art world she'd dreamed of entering since high school, but the price for this was her own identity as an artist.

It was past midnight in Williamsburg in the predawn of the new century. Bob Dylan's *Time Out of Mind* had stopped spinning in the CD player in the third-floor apartment at 211 North Seventh, and no one had moved to replace it. Blistering hip-hop floated up to the open windows from passing cars, and a breeze off the East River ruffled the gauzy curtains above the couch, draped in a makeshift pink slipcover, where Cindy and Charlotta sat. Bob Gulley, working a 5:00 a.m. shift, slipped out early; Raymond and Catherine Saá had gone; Peter and Beverly had left half an hour ago. But Charlotta felt something keeping her from letting go of the conversation.

Andy was working his way toward the conclusion of a sentence; whole zip codes of ellipses, semicolons, and parentheticals had passed, and if someone just then entering the apartment had interrupted to ask where the thought began, no one present would have been able to say with certainty.

"Yes, but is that a cause or an effect?" Charlotta offered into one of his pauses.

This set Andy off in a slightly different direction. Cindy watched the cigarette in his left hand jabbing backward in the air, its ember tip pointing toward the kitchen, where the sink and the countertop beside it were full of upturned pounders and stacked plates from the pico and banana pepper dip and fresh bread and sweet meatballs she'd served the carousel of guests that night. When the breeze outside subsided, the room exhaled its warm breath into the night, tugging the smoke from Andy's cigarette across the room, over their heads, and out the window.

Still talking, trying to find his tongue, like a foot, on something solid, Andy gestured with his empty Budweiser to Cindy. It was a simple, easy gesture, like the tolling of a clapper in an invisible bell at the end of his outstretched arm.

Charlotta could feel Cindy coil beside her.

She stood, gathering the room into sudden silence.

"Get it yourself," she snapped.

And Cindy left her friend on the couch beneath the windows, left Andy tongue-tied and guts plummeting, and disappeared into the bedroom.

Seminarians

THE CLERK'S OFFICE in Sullivan County, New York—a wooded, pond-spotted, and river-cut collection of sparsely populated hamlets in the former Borscht Belt of the Catskills, about two hours north of the city—records the transfer of the deed to 69 St. Joseph's Seminary Road on September 20, 2001. Robert and Margaret Stier, who had lived since 1971 in the house on the hill above the town of Callicoon, sold it to Cindy for $86,500. Only Cindy's name appears on the deed, and she relied on a sizeable mortgage—inked just prior to Alan Greenspan's one percent interest rate. Beyond the down payment, the house needed work: new floors, new electrical, the removal of drop ceilings and hideous mid-century paneling. But it was work they wanted, Cindy and Andy. Work and space, far from anyone they'd ever known. The snug 1,340 square feet contained a kitchen, living room, and dining room; three bedrooms; a walk-up attic; one full bath; and beside it a detached garage, with its own wood-burning stove and tin chimney. All of this was nooked into a third of an acre that falls back steeply to a wet, woody gorge etched by the creek that issues from the pond at the top of the hill—a gorge, a creek, a pond, and a hill unnamed on even on the oldest county maps. It was perfect.

Life in New York was becoming harder to bear at the start of the new century. Andy and Cindy had arrived when the city was beginning its upswing; by 2000, New York had experienced two decades of declining crime, rising rents, and gentrification, a process driven by yuppies and speculators, but in which artists like

Cindy and Andy played an important part. The city's population had grown by almost a million people since they had arrived fifteen years before: traffic was worse, even corner-store beers cost more than a dollar a bottle, and Tony Santorelli's promise to sell the building at 211 North Seventh kept receding ahead of them into a more distant future, as the value of all the properties in Williamsburg climbed upward.

Andy in particular started to push for a total break from New York, an escape from the pressures of work and teaching, the attention of friends, the weary circulating through endless openings and receptions. They spent a few weekends touring towns east of the Catskills before their friend Amy Milner pointed out her childhood haunts in the west. One of the winding highways took them into Callicoon, a train-stop town. They loved it instantly—its quietude and coziness, the green undulations in every direction—and they decided to buy there at once.

But on their first trip to their second home, a two-and-a-half-hour drive from Brooklyn, Cindy and Andy brought the city with them. They carried it—its toxic dust and ash—in the folds of their clothes, in their hair, in the beds of their fingernails and the creases of their elbows, in the images that yawned awake behind their eyelids.

Andy and Cindy were both working that Tuesday morning, nine days earlier. At 8:46 a.m., when Mohammed Atta directed American Airlines Flight 11 into the North Tower of the World Trade Center, caving in the ninety-ninth to ninety-third floors and starting an inferno of paper and a countdown—102 minutes—until the tower collapsed, Cindy was seated at her hutch at the Furman & Furman architecture firm on Varick Street, just a mile north of the World Trade Center, beside a window facing west. She couldn't see the impact, but she felt it.

Another mile uptown, Andy was in his Foundations studio on

the ninth floor of the Parsons building on Fifth Avenue between 13th and 14th Streets. Ann Ledy's rigorous syllabus didn't allow for a "soft" start to the semester, and the students were already beginning their first projects, but Andy was patient and accommodating, as a diverse group of learners equalized—lifelong New Yorkers, wide-eyed kids from big towns and small cities, and jet-lagged international students starting only their fourth day in the US. Freshmen in particular loved the Parsons building on Fifth for its inspiring view of Lower Manhattan to the south. From the ninth floor, all of the Foundations faculty and students couldn't miss the collision, couldn't look away from the burning tower.

The dread really dropped on Andy and on Cindy—on everyone in New York—at 9:03, when United Flight 175 slammed into the South Tower, striking the eighty-fifth to seventy-fifth floors. Now they knew—everyone in the world knew—that there hadn't been a tragic accident: the city was under attack. The fact alone was a thing impossibly massive—a physical weight that pressed the air out of their lungs and ground their minds down like glass lenses, to train them only, only on the locus of a horror beyond their comprehension, all of it in hyperreal, skin-pricking, unblinking detail.

Later they would learn that hijacker Marwan al-Shehhi had used the Parsons building, because of its size and location, as a guidepost, flying directly over it, straight down Fifth Avenue and into the South Tower.

Andy's daughter, Julia, who had graduated from Parsons the year before, was working in Midtown and took a train that passed under the towers on her morning commute. Andy wanted to call her, to call Cindy, but Ann quickly summoned all faculty present to aid in an evacuation of the students. His responsibility for the students relieved him, in a way, from the impossible choice of running in search of either Cindy or Julia.

A little higher, a little more strained than usual, Andy's

recognizable bass-baritone directed the students out into the hall and toward a central gathering place. Faculty caught each other's eyes, mouthed to each other noiselessly, *I don't know, I don't know*. There wasn't a protocol for an evacuation in these conditions—in a city under attack, no cell phones, no transit south of Forty-Second—but Ann decided to group students based on residence and send each pod home with a faculty escort.

Cindy, meanwhile, was running—then walking, as the streets thickened—finally letting herself be carried by a momentum that arose from the whole crowd, and not the sum of individually moving bodies. Rich Furman had sent everyone home immediately, but the M train to Brooklyn had stopped. Cindy headed east and crossed the Williamsburg Bridge on foot, by then caked in a gray mixture of sweat and ash, the space in the sky where the towers had stood already looming empty over her shoulders.

The South Tower collapsed at 9:59 and the North Tower followed at 10:28. Andy and the other Parsons faculty had grouped and guided the last of the Foundations students in the building out by noon. By then they had realized, had whispered to each other, that exactly half of the class, two hundred students, were in their dorms at Ground Zero that morning—none accounted for.

After escorting his group back to their residences in Manhattan, Andy tried to reach Julia unsuccessfully. He thought about placing a call at a pay phone to Cindy's office, but he knew the building would have evacuated by then. People were turning back out of the entrances to subway stations, faces pale, as all the trains in Manhattan had been suspended. The only thing left for him to do was walk home. He could taste the smoke in the air, moving outward in all directions and silencing every intersection that it touched. Andy turned east and kept walking.

Families fell inward for support after the horror of the morning—and for a dozen or two dozen people out of the eight million in New York City, Andy and Cindy were family. That evening, 211 North Seventh held a family—a nuclear family, bound by the strong nuclear force of unconditional love and the weak nuclear force of merely having nowhere else to go. In the living room Cindy and Andy sat with Peter and Bev and their boys, Paolo and Pietro; Julia; Raymond and Catherine; John Melville; Ian and Amy Milner; and others—watching the TV, holding one another, crying.

But as we know now, life continued. Traffic followed new patterns, but it still moved in the same directions. Routines reshaped around new habits. And will, like water, found new courses toward the sea of toil.

Cindy and Andy felt closer to their New York family that day, but the urge for distance came back doubled, too. Suddenly, everyone felt the same way. "All of us who lived in New York had the sense that we needed to get out of the city," Andy and Cindy's friend Christiane Fischer-Harling told me over a video call from Germany nearly twenty years later. "Nobody knew... is this the beginning of something? We need a place ... *if need be* ... we need a refuge," she said.[1]

Cindy closed on the house in Callicoon in less than two weeks, and they started packing Andy's Jeep with essentials, warm clothes, the tools they'd need for the winter's work ahead.

A year later, the high-beams of my father's burgundy Buick Rendezvous swept over the banks of the Delaware River and across a two-dimensional screen of trees as we passed from Pennsylvania's Route 1018 across the state line and over the river onto Old Long Eddy Road, New York's Route 97, slowing as we traced the steep incline up Seminary. A Narnian lamppost stood off a flagstone walk midway between the front porch and the road, and lights inside the house were on, yellow and warm, grainy with the bodies of moths and midges. Cindy was waiting for us in the doorway.

Callicoon wasn't exactly the getaway Cindy and Andy had imagined, but they did find comfort in building a life there, away from the heart-wrecked city, and they were eager to share that life with friends and family from both corners of the state and beyond.

In the beginning, friends from Brooklyn made the two-hour drive almost every weekend. Christiane and her family came up for Thanksgiving 2001 and she and her husband decided—on the spot—to drive their own stake in Callicoon, too. They bought a little yellow ranch house at the top of the hill, five minutes' drive from Cindy and Andy, with sliding glass doors opening out onto a view over mountains and fields.

And family visited. On our first visit, in the fall of 2002, we admired the deck Andy had built off the back of the house, the way Cindy had enlivened the kitchen and laid out the comfortable living room. It was there that Andy taught me to shoot a pellet gun at empty Budweisers. We spent hours on that deck, the two of us alone, shooting BBs at cans that I'd stacked around a bird feeder hanging from a tree. I remember running down the steps to collect the fallen cans from the garden, and setting them, sticky and rattling with trapped pellets, back up in a row. We didn't say much of anything to each other, and no one came to bother us (although on the drive back to Buffalo my parents preemptively noted a pellet gun would be a pointless item to add to my Christmas wish list).

We swam in the Delaware, ate Cindy's meals. We played in huge piles of leaves. Andy took us on long walks down into the gorge, where we balanced on fallen trees, pulpy and black, and breathed in the smell of decomposition that precedes the burial of first frost. I got to drive the riding mower up and down the steep lawns, but I had to stay back on the porch and watch Andy, my dad, and a neighbor disappear into the field across the street and come back carrying huge pieces of wood they'd reclaimed from an abandoned convent, raw material that Andy would turn into furniture. My sister and I sat beside each other on the metal bench by the fire in the backyard, where we ended every night. Even before we had left, we were making plans to come back.

Silence, Exile, and Cunning

I SAVED MY progress in *Pokémon Ruby* once, saved again (I had developed a benign compulsive streak by this time), stashed my Gameboy Advance SP back in its black Velcro carrier, and ran from the car down the gravel lot, my ten-year-old body flying like one long, wobbly, white limb until it sliced the surface of the river. My sister, seven, splashed into the water behind me. The sun was a beaten gold and the August air, even over the river, lay like a blanket on our shoulders. It felt like most days did back then. It felt like my first day on earth.

As an older brother I was often a show-off, frequently moody, sometimes cruel. But when I kicked out into the visible current midstream and swam north, it wasn't to prove to Talia that she couldn't follow me. I just wanted to experience the moving river from some vantage that would be mine alone. I was always this way, whenever I climbed a tree, ran ahead, or walked along the tops of benches or retaining walls—everything was a private experiment in parallax, seeking alternatives to compare with the obvious. So I swam awkwardly north until I saw a spit of wet sand spilling out from the tall grass on the bank, and turned to it, and swam until my knees brushed river grass, finally stooping out of the shallows and falling into a squat to watch the water.

At 12:15 that afternoon—August 14, 2003—679 miles away in Carmel, Indiana, at the headquarters of the Midwest Independent Transmission System Operator (MISO), the energy grid that serves communities from the caribou parks of upper Manitoba to the last habitable slip of river silt below Venice, Louisiana, an analyst called IT. The state estimator, a computer program the grid operators used to measure and regulate the flow of power, spit out a wacky reading. Sooner or later someone was bound to ask, *Have you tried a restart?* Sure, that did the trick. But after turning the machine off and back on again, according to a task force's report on the incident published in April the following year, the analyst forgot to turn back on the automatic trigger that runs the state estimator every five minutes. "Thinking the system had been successfully restored," the report notes, "the analyst went to lunch."[1]

Later that day, in events causally disconnected from the lapse in protocol in Carmel, power transmission lines in south-central Indiana, a generating unit in Eastlake, Ohio, and a power line in southern Ohio all tripped (in other words, the lines stopped carrying current between conductor towers). At 2:02, a transmission line in Walton, Ohio, sagged into a tree, causing another trip. Meanwhile in Akron, Ohio, at 2:14, a software bug caused the failure of an alarm system that would have notified certain authorities and professionals about these various and unrelated events—the alarm didn't go off. Then at 3:05 a transmission line in Parma, Ohio, also sagged into a tree and tripped, for reasons unknown but presumably unrelated to the trip in Walton. Unlike the earlier tree-caused trip, the Parma trip had downstream effects: displaced voltage shifted into another transmission line, causing that line to dip into another tree and trip. By 4:13 that afternoon, 256 power plants across an eastern-central slice of North America had gone offline, leaving 50 million people—including the 8 million in New York City—without any power.

The first thought for those millions trapped in darkened subway lines, in skyscrapers with inoperable elevators, was of an attack. Less than two years after the fall of the Twin Towers, New Yorkers lived with a constant embodied tension. They read and authored innumerable op-eds and articles about possible terror targets and doomsday scenarios, their companies paid for active shooter and bomb threat training, they put on their highest high heels and timed themselves running down the stairs from the top floors of their skyscrapers, and they plotted escape routes out of every physical space they passed through. Within minutes of the mass power outage the FBI Cyber Division was investigating a possible act of terrorism.

By half past five I had noticed, with a faint sense of the strangeness of it, the sediment at the bottom of the Delaware River seeming to rise up like a vast animal to sun itself at the surface. The river was running brown.

I'd swum about a half mile from the beach to get a different perspective on the river that day. If I'd had the benefit of more drastic parallax—if I could have swung five thousand feet above the river to scan its length—I might have spotted most of the 250 sewage treatment plants in the Delaware Basin gone dark, throats open, pumping phosphorus and nitrogen—and worse, raw waste—straight into the river, in such quantities that the cloudy water flowed against the current, upstream.

There were no push notifications—we wouldn't know what had happened until much later that night—but the adults in the party recognized the hue of the river as unsafe, and I heard them calling to me from downstream. It was near dinnertime, anyway. I stood, then stepped out, watching the toes on both feet disappear under less than an inch of the dark water. I took another step, and another, until I had to start swimming. On the shore below the parking lot, waiting with a rough beach towel to wrap around my slimed shoulders, was Aunt Cindy.

In retrospect, it strikes me that the details of our odd experience on the river would have made perfect materials for Andy's art.

An abstracted topography of arcs and angles connecting Carmel to Callicoon to New York to Montreal; scrambled acronyms of the agencies involved: NYISO, MISO, ECAR, NERC, FE, MAAC; calculations involving the 3,500 megawatts that caused the worst of the outages and the 345 kilovolts of standard APS lines; even the uranography of the Milky Way that became visible over Manhattan that night, for the first time in nearly a century.

But Andy had other interests in August 2003.

Cindy and Andy had succeeded in starting a new life in Callicoon. That's what we all saw on our first visit, and on our second. But we didn't know at the time—or at least I didn't know—that Andy's work—his art—had been at a total standstill.

In the text for the gallery book for Andy's retrospective with the artist Michael Zwack at the Burchfield Penney in 2005, Don Metz wrote that after 9/11 Andy took two years off from making art. Christiane, then CEO of the insurer AXA's fine art division, also contributed an essay. She was closer to Andy and Cindy, spending weekends at her own Callicoon home just up the hill, and she was a collector of Andy's work. She wrote that Andy had been inactive for at least three years.[2]

Christiane recalled to me later, when we caught up in a video call in March 2021, that Andy lived almost entirely in Callicoon in those years, while Cindy commuted more regularly for work. Andy taught a few classes at Parsons but mostly stayed at the house on the hill, where, she said, he was relieved to be away from the obligations of the art world.

"Andy wanted to make it, but he couldn't be a part of that *making*," she said. "Andy was not social—famously. Andy was wonderful and really social with a very small group of people he knew, but with everyone else he was not. I don't think he *wanted* representation, he didn't want to go to the parties. He didn't want to deal with it. He was deeply distrustful."

After 2001, Andy stopped worrying about lost or stolen art, rigged or wrongheaded contests and public art commissions, the problems of representation, the opinions of critics. He no longer felt the pressure to explain himself and his art. "He seemed really happy in his little bubble," Christiane told me.

Instead of fine art, Andy turned to furniture. Wood, raw and reclaimed, was plentiful in Callicoon. And New Yorkers with disposable income started filling up Callicoon and the little towns around it. There would be no more smuggling bandoliers of cash back from European sales in the new millennium. Usually hard up, Andy would ask friends like Christiane and her husband if there was anything he could do, anything he could make. So he made beautiful tables and chairs, commissioned pieces or sets to sell on consignment at the shop in town, and even worked as a kind of handyman up and down the hill. Later, Christiane paid Andy to give art lessons to her three children, who were close in age to my sister and me. He was wonderful with them, she remembered—they learned the fundamentals, but he also delighted in teaching them how to use all the hundreds of curious tools he kept in his Callicoon studio. The children made art there. Andy only instructed, encouraged, and watched.

Andy wasn't just taking a break. Friends noticed that he had stopped making new work. When they asked him about it, Andy always cited the memory of September 11.

The attack on New York, the uncompassable scale of it, the acute panic of having lost contact with Cindy and even more so with Julia, had left Andy trauma-fogged. He was mentally and emotionally present for his students, but the time he spent in his own studio was unproductive.

Don's essay in the gallery book for a 2005 show at the Burchfield Penney takes a quote from an uncredited source in which Andy talks around the impact of the event and how it intersected with some of the fundamental concerns of his art.

"I have always been influenced by my life experience, beginning with the Bay of Pigs as a child, by Vietnam as a young adult, and constant threat of nuclear (as well as other forms) of destruction," Andy said. "Machines are brilliant and horrible; men are ingenious and destructive.

"To some degree," he went on, "I am studying the struggle of men with powers that shape their world, struggle of men among themselves as well as within themselves, and the repercussions of their actions."

Andy's nephew Alex—who started to collect and study Andy's art only after his passing—said that war and violence were his uncle's "muse." If we can understand making art as an individual's practice of setting up and asking questions—not to be answered definitively, but to be followed as far as one can take them—then war and violence suggested for Andy limitless questions that unspooled for immeasurable distances. For a time at the start of the new century, it seems, Andy stopped making art because he became afraid of the questions, or afraid of what he apprehended on the path.

At sixteen or seventeen years old, the same summer that my family and I first visited the house in Callicoon, Alex and his mother drove down from Buffalo to stay for a long weekend with his uncle and Cindy. They drank, took the Jeep down to Woodstock, smoked cigarettes on the back deck. Alex and Cindy took kayaks down to the Delaware River and smoked a joint that Cindy presented, rabbit-in-hat style, from her life vest. Later Alex and his uncle stalked the fields and woods shooting Andy's .22. With a gleam in his eye, holding the rifle, Andy burst into the kitchen where Cindy and Alex's mother were preparing dinner and shouted, "Diane! There's been an accident! I shot Alex, there's lot of blood!"—a joke, Andy's kind of joke. Later that night, when all had been forgiven, they all got drunk and watched *Platoon*. In other words, Alex found his uncle upbeat and engaged in his usual habits and preoccupations—which were morbid. The four of them finished two thirty-racks of Budweiser that weekend. Alex had so much fun that he returned the next summer with a carload of his high school buddies.

Alex didn't recognize then what would have registered as a total aberration to any of Andy's friends: during both trips, Andy didn't spend any time in his studio.

Petr Mayr frequently visited New York in those years—he estimated that he came to the city at least forty times between 1998 and 2003, usually exhibiting with private collections, and on most trips he stayed with Cindy and Andy in Brooklyn, often using the snowbird Santorelli's apartment without permission, sometimes for one or two months at a stretch. Calling me long-distance from Peiting, Germany, where he stills keeps his studio, Petr recalled visiting the city in September 2001, delivering a large acquisition of his work to AXA. He chartered a helicopter flight over lower Manhattan on September 10. The next day the world changed. Petr had been staying at a hotel in Manhattan, but two weeks after 9/11 he arrived on North Seventh to finish out his stay in the States with Cindy and Andy. He remembered that they were still outwardly shaken, like everyone else in the city, but already going through the motions of life as they had lived it before. Andy had booked Petr two lectures at Parsons and accompanied him there; visiting his classroom studio, Andy pointed out the emptiness in the sky and spoke about what he had seen. He was depressive, distracted, and definitely not working.

Andy was arguably approaching the height of his career. He was slated to appear in DC in October 2001 for an exhibition at the National Gallery titled *A Century of Drawing: Works on Paper from Degas to LeWitt*. Wynn Kramarsky had donated Andy's *Overground II*, a work in graphite and pigment on architects' vellum, one of only 140 works that curator Judith Brodie, head of American and modern prints and drawings, selected. Brodie had interviewed

Andy in February 2001 and produced a short essay on his practice and career for the beautiful gallery book, where Andy appeared alongside Degas, LeWitt, Picasso, Braque, Dix, Agnes Martin, and Charles Sheeler; Andy was to appear in person at the opening along with most of the other living representatives of a century of works on paper. But the event was downsized drastically because of an anthrax scare. As Cindy's lungs were still too weak for the flight, Andy went with his old friend Marilynn Mendell as his plus-one.

In November, Andy flew to Prague for a show that Charlotta and Petr Kotik had helped arrange. Marilynn's son Michael Tunkey accompanied Andy, and Petr Mayr and other German friends met them there. Instead of enjoying a victory lap through Europe—recently lauded as among the greatest living artists in the States, even if he had been denied his spotlight—Andy was still withdrawn, morose, and uncomfortable, Petr and Michael separately remembered. He drank and smoked with his friends and they talked intimately, as they always did: about the still-present horror of the morning, about the precipitous decline of American politics, the parameters of acceptable debate and acceptable policy changing faster than anyone could apprehend.

In essence, since the early '70s, Andy had been striving to bring his artistic sensibility and attention closer and closer to the very forces that would be unleashed so nakedly and massively on September 11, 2001, and in its aftermath.

In three decades as a working artist, Andy had been both prolific and extraordinarily varied, but the trajectory of his development until 2001 was an ever-greater refinement of form toward pure expression—work that expressed the "first movement" of the artist's hand, which Wynn found so compelling, so "sexy," so essential.

It's a similar inclination to what Alex identified in Andy's proclivity for pranks (particularly pranks that jeopardized his relationships). "Those are moments when you get to see other people's real emotion," Alex suggested. So too with the aim of artistic expression refined down to convey a "first movement"—so too with an intimation of mankind's most terrible and inarticulate impulses.

"The struggle of men with powers" might bring to mind something fleshy and horrible, like Picasso's *Guernica*—but for Andy, it might be a broken rhombus in black that little light escapes, a cascade of charcoal arcs, measurements set down in the same Prussian blue of "the gas flame that always accompanies the firing of missiles," as Charlotta noted in the catalog copy for a 1987 show at the Brooklyn Museum.

Philadelphia Inquirer art critic Edward J. Sozanski noted this on April 4, 1991, in a review of a show at Jessica Berwind's gallery.

> On one level, Andrew Topolski's drawings and constructions...
> exhibit an overly rational, austere quality. They incorporate a
> strong sense of mathematical progression, of mechanics and of
> precision, especially involving measurement and the location
> of specific points in space.
>
> On the other hand, Topolski ameliorates this dryness with a
> luscious hand-wrought quality in the drawings and touches of
> romanticism in the constructions, like arcs roughly scratched
> on a piece of green synthetic stone.
>
> ... one is inclined to describe it as the "music of the spheres."

The search for pure geometry—geometry as an expression of philosophy, as the love of pure knowledge—continued. And critics everywhere recognized it.

"'Euclid alone looked on beauty bare,'" begins a two-inch note in the Memphis *Commercial Appeal* dated October 25, 1992, quoting the poet Edna St. Vincent Millay—"and one receives that impression of precision and passion from New York artist Topolski's work." It goes on: "One of a pair of monumental drawings on vellum, *B./B.S. II* conceals its references and inspirations beneath a geometrical world of subtle and sumptuous color and form. The elegance is tempered by the smudges and powdery haze left by the artist's hand."

In November 1996, Marek Bartelik covered Andy's show *North, South, East, West* at Elga Wimmer's gallery with a full-page write-up in *Artforum*. He pauses over *Dead Weight, Five Balls*, which "consisted of a cane- or umbrella-like construction that pierces a polished steel cylinder, itself supported by a metal pedestal that stands on a high, narrow table on which eighteen small balls were arranged to resemble a control panel."

"Menacing as it is," the critic writes, "this piece is so immediately enchanting that it could be nothing other than the handiwork of an insatiable dreamer."

Finally, on Friday, June 15, 2001, Andy made the *New York Times* Art Guide.

"Mr. Topolski draws like a 21st-century Neo-Platonist," the critic, Ken Johnson, begins. "Circles, spirals, geometric figures and curious, quasi-scientific symbols, all made with exquisite precision, create the enigmatic impression of some cosmic theory of universal being."

Reading these reviews, spaced out over nearly fifteen years, some of which I found online and some of which I found in scans or original clips in his archives, I get the sense of Andy's artistic practice as an experiment in knowing, conducted with ever-more sensitive instruments, and trained at once on notions of beauty, on theories of order, but also on chance and chaos, and on the destructive impulses in history and human nature—an epistemology of paradoxes.

And this practice, these instruments, were smashed against the incomprehensibility of September 11.

"Recent events are too much for me to bear," he said for the Burchfield catalog. "I can't yet reflect or respond."

Silence into Symbols

CHRISTIANE CLOSED HER car door and raised a hand toward Andy's garage, which was open, like the mouth of a cave. Inside Andy was hunched at a stool, his back to the door, and in front of him Christiane's three children stood working with fishtail chisels in pieces of soft wood from the gorge. The oldest, ten, caught her mother out of the corner of her eye and returned the wave, and Andy, noticing, pivoted on his seat.

Stay, Christiane mouthed, flapping both open hands at Andy. *Finish.*

Cindy was already on the porch, waiting for her. In a white tank, stone chino shorts, and a faded navy baseball cap, she leaned against the porch post as Christiane ascended the short slope of lawn that led from the garage. They talked, Cindy on the porch and Christiane standing on the flagstones, of the weather, of happenings in Brooklyn, of the State Power Authority that was marching new transmission towers through the Catskills, mowing fields that looked like landing strips all around them. Christiane could watch the progress from her house at the top of the hill. They didn't talk about the election, which was in full swing. John Kerry was running to unseat George Bush. They'd already told each other everything they could imagine saying on that subject. They talked but mostly they listened—listened to the drone of insects all around them. It was another year of the Great Brood, the black-bodied, red-eyed cicadas that live for seventeen years at a stretch underground as white nymphs, feeding on sap from tree roots, and then shoot upward all at once in their millions after their seventeen cycles of freezes and thaws. Tens of thousands were mating, or seeking mates, chirring in the canopy above them.

"Mom!"

Christiane turned. It was her youngest, holding a little wooden figurine, the crude but expressive shape of a human, limbs splayed as if from the crush of the tiny hand that held it.

The other two raced out behind her.

"Do you mind?" Christiane asked, turning again to Cindy. "For a minute? I need to talk to Andy about something."

Of course, Cindy nodded. "Hey!" she shouted down the lawn, "come show me what you made!"

The children flashed past their mother and huddled around Cindy.

In the garage Andy was putting away the tools from the day's lesson. A song on the radio ended and a commercial began, life insurance.

"Andy," Christiane said. "What are you doing?"

"We—we—woodworking," he said, "I thought we—"

"*No.* I mean what are *you* doing?"

Christiane threw an arm out across the studio. A set of chairs, an end table, and an ornate door laid flat on two sawhorses dominated the space. There wasn't a canvas in sight, no paper except the children's scraps, nothing that you might call a "sculpture."

"What are you doing?" she said again. "You are a carpenter? Andy, you are an *artist.*"

Andy groaned, turned from her. The argument was an old one by now.

"It's—" he said, "I—"

"Oh yes, the world, it's so bad, of course," Christiane said, losing the softness of her transatlantic corporate accent and slipping closer to her native German. "You've been saying for years. You cannot sit here like a, like a, like some mountain man, Andy.

You sit here, no one comes here. No one sees your work. You aren't making any work."

"I need money," Andy said, finding a strength in his voice, in this fact. "People aren't buying art. Aren't buying my art. I can sell tables. I can fix things. And besides, I don't—"

"Enough," Christiane said. "I know you. I know who you are. Get back to work."

She slotted the dark sunglasses that she had been wearing over her knuckles back onto the bridge of her nose and stepped into her car without another word. The children came running down the hill and she pulled out of the driveway, the sound of her engine, the sound of her thoughts, erased under the torrent of the cicadas.

It's spring 2021. The ground will thaw soon. The seventeen-year sleep of the Great Brood is coming to an end. A pandemic is ending, too—at least our patience has run out. Soon the outdoors will explode with life, bodies pale, sun-shocked, and high on root-sap.

"No," Christiane tells me, shaking her head in my monitor. She didn't knock Andy out of his three-year funk. She wouldn't say that. But later he did thank her for taking such a stern tone with him. For caring.

It's likely that an engine inside Andy had turned over much earlier, even a year earlier: Don, Christiane, and others point to the invasion of Iraq by the "Coalition of the Willing" in March 2003 as the proximate cause behind Andy's reawakening.

When we arrived for our second visit to Callicoon that August, only Cindy took us to the river to swim. Andy was sequestered in the garage shop and we wouldn't see him until dinner that evening. He wasn't making art—he was still making furniture then—but he was *feeling* again, feeling something other than shock and despair. He was feeling angry. And soon he'd realize that he couldn't keep expressing that anger in Mission-style nightstands.

Andy's approach to making art is best understood as blue-collar, working class—a temperament stamped by his upbringing in Cheektowaga. He had a lifelong habit of occupying unheated studios, for example. In the first-floor spaces on Broadway and North Seventh, he worked through the winters in subfreezing conditions, as low as fifteen degrees Fahrenheit, holding his instruments in fingerless gloves. He heated the garage at Callicoon with a wood-burning stove, and went there for the greater measure of every day—as if he were punching in. It didn't matter what time an expected guest arrived at the house—whether they were in-laws, old high school buddies like Don Metz, or neighbors from up the road: Andy wouldn't leave the garage until five o'clock. He didn't drift back into work once he'd left, either: he'd offer you a Budweiser and a seat in the living room, and you'd start talking art.

Though he had the temperament and habits of a machinist, one of Andy's core beliefs was in never repeating himself. He brought to this conviction an obsessive tendency and a technical felicity that allowed him to master new modes of expression in twenty-four- or forty-eight-hour bursts of undivided attention, and then deepen his understanding of the new mode or method over years of incorporation into his art practice. He learned everywhere, from other artists, from students, and even from regular trips to MoMA, where he spent hours, never looking at a work straight on, but examining it from sharp angles, pressing his face close to the wall to see how it hung, how the gestalt of its composition and presentation accomplished its final effect.

Raymond Saá, his friend and colleague at Parsons, was a close observer of Andy's thirst and capacity for new techniques, approaches, and materials. Once, Raymond told me, Andy found a piece of glass on the beach in Brooklyn that, for a period of years in the mid-'90s, he and Cindy would visit nearly every summer weekend with Raymond and his wife, Catherine. He wanted to talk about the piece of glass—and nothing else—for the rest of the night. "Do you know anything about sandblasting? Who etches glass in Brooklyn?" he asked everyone who entered his orbit that night. Raymond doesn't believe Andy slept for the next forty-eight hours—because the next time he passed the open garage door to Andy's studio on North Seventh, he had built a full sandblasting station, with air compressors, fine instruments, and a Plexiglas booth, black rubber gloves affixed through two holes cut into the side. He broke scores of expensive glass plates teaching himself this process, but he was enamored, and etched glass would feature in his work for the rest of the decade.

Another time, Raymond said, Andy attended a Parsons seminar on papermaking that the artist Robert Skolnik was giving to Foundations students. Andy sat through the whole thing, taking notes just like the students, thirty-five years his junior. The next day he had blenders and buckets of pulp all over his studio. He started making his own pulp-based canvases and experimented with placing massive circular weights onto his own uncured pulp, making permanent impressions as the paper set—something that appears in many of his large-scale pieces.

In the media environment of the Iraq invasion, which coincided with the mainstreaming of the internet and the mass production of increasingly high-tech consumer goods, Andy was catapulted back to his experimentation with collage and intermedia, which had characterized some of the work that came out of his Essex studio in the '70s. In those days, Andy, Cindy, John Toth, Bill Maecker, and others who rotated through the studio constantly papered the walls in eclectic scraps of inspiration. The art they made then reflected that.

Between 2003 and 2005, Andy produced a huge volume of

work—characteristic of his output overall, which was extraordinarily prolific, excepting the approximately twenty-four months after 9/11. His time away from art-making—and the reasons, whatever exactly they were, that drove him back to it—resulted in a radical departure in Andy's style, not comparable to any of the changes he had undergone before. Unlike his earlier works, which had attempted to harmonize elements of nuclear science, musical notation, geography, mathematics, and other influences, no one would have called his new pieces Neoplatonic.

"His earlier work, even if it had darkness, was very melodic, flowing," Christiane told me. "The mysterious part of his early work was the fascinating part."

Andy's new work, his twenty-first-century work, was jagged, rebarbative, and overtly political.

"The messaging was changed," Christiane said. "It was symbolic."

When I reached the final boxes of Andy's Burchfield Penney archive, I was stunned to discover just how right Christiane had been. Shocked out of the production of art by 9/11, less than three years later Andy was directly confronting that trauma, drafting a vast and detailed proposal for the 9/11 memorial site, and finding solace and structure in an ancient and elemental symbolism finally consistent with his postminimalist and constructivist roots. The plan would have originated at a pile of rubble surviving on the site, with an explosion of four interlocking "ramps"—slender steel trusses to be clad in glass and internally illuminated at night, and each bearing the date and time of a different horrific occurrence (the three plane hijackings in 2001 and the 1993 World Trade Center bombing). A memorial of glass and stone (suggesting strength and fragility, Andy's proposal noted) would be inscribed with messages from the families of the dead and glazed in "tears" continuously cascading from above. He designed several elements to give the impression of "floating"—the surrounding granite wall, grounded in a fine crush of concrete rubble suggesting ash. Part of the wall would feature a collage of granite tiles, recalling one of the images burned most deeply into Andy's mind: the city filled with leaflets looking for lost loved ones in the immediate days following the attack, a sign, to Andy, of a "Last Hope." At the center of the site was to be a "Tomb of the Unknown Remains," a thirty-foot black cylinder holding an eternal flame and leaking water from a crack in its side into channels cut through the entire memorial. Radially positioned from the tomb would have been four black granite "Cubes of Emptiness" floating above the "Pool of Tears"— water from the central tomb. He meant for these to be "empty but geometrically solid," their pure geometry broken by small piles of soil from each of the sites of the attacks, corresponding to the illuminated ramps. The entire circular plaza that the cubes marked out, Andy wrote, would recall the "final circular walk of the victims' families when the last steel beam was removed from the 'Ground Zero' site."

This sort of rich symbolism had never appeared in any of Andy's artwork prior to 2003—but his switch from signs to symbols was not the only change under way. Andy's color palette and the scope of his intertextual practice exploded simultaneously. Now he used sensuous color photographs clipped from consumer magazines, ink illustrations and woodcuts from nineteenth-century science texts, blown-up and closely cropped photographs of historic figures, grids and targets, cave paintings and cartoons, truncated quotes from politicians and generals—all interpolated among the letters, numbers, bisected arcs, and black-and-white angles of nuclear science that had long distinguished his original practice. One work featured bits of wire twisted into the shape of a Havasu man; another pair featured plaster metatarsals, possibly taken from a classroom skeleton. Pulling through the earlier influence of Joseph Beuys, here one senses Robert

Rauschenberg—both his *Combines*, incorporating the detritus of life in New York, and his later prints and collages using clippings from newspapers and magazines.

The titles of Andy's new works, like *You Can't Handle the Truth*, *One Step for Mankind?*, *God Said to Abraham*, and *Highway 61 Revisited*, pulled from pop culture (frequently from the work of his lifelong lodestar, Bob Dylan), in a manner without precedent in his earlier periods.

And he also returned to sculpture. Instead of working with expensive mechanical widgets, sandblasted plates of glass, he used materials only available to him in Callicoon: a stone plinth, the skull of a deer, books from a library fire sale, cross sections of tree trunks—and one that everyone who saw it remembers: a glowering, petrified crow, its silent beak pointed, talons at the ready, and wings fully spread in flight.

Andy and Cindy had always enjoyed a close relationship—friends described them as inseparable, doting, totally in love. While their relationship had, in Brooklyn, evidently reached a point of acute strain, there was something, either in Callicoon or in the tumult of the new century outside it, that drew them closer together. On March 2, 2002, they were finally married—after two decades together—in a small ceremony at the town hall, with only two witnesses: Peter Muscato and Janine Tramontana. In a microcassette video Peter sends me, I watch them bashfully kiss before the town clerk, mug for photos by a stone bridge, and return with their friends to 69 Seminary Road for cake, champagne, and cigars.

Cindy had always "propped Andy up," many friends recall: she soothed his anxieties and encouraged him through his many lows. Certainly he needed this daily support after 9/11. But now, as Andy began working again, Cindy returned to an earlier role: critic, confidant, partner in dialogue. For twenty years Cindy had lived alongside and inside Andy's art—and the art existed first in the context of their relationship.

"Andy was always seeking Cindy's approval in some way about the artwork," Raymond recalls. Cindy advised on sketches and works in progress, and it was usually Cindy who encouraged Andy to connect the finished works with the right opportunities—always providing gentle reminders to send slides to this gallery, apply for that grant, return another phone call. Though she spent her part of their time in Callicoon differently—fishing, lying out by the water, maintaining the house, gardening and canning fruits and vegetables—Cindy was, as before, aware of everything that started happening in Andy's studio, the garage, around 2004. Doubtless, it received her encouragement and her stamp of approval.

As with so many other periods in Andy's career, a network of close, loyal friends and loved ones proved pivotal. Christiane had helped jar Andy out of his funk of inaction. Cindy had supported him as he started his difficult return to the studio. Likely the next person Andy let in on his new direction was Don Metz.

Don was by this time an associate director at the Burchfield Penney, and as an integral member of a generation in Buffalo who had lost significant talent to New York, he had formed certain opinions on the way the city lionized some of its expat artists and passed over others. In early 2005, he pitched and obtained approval to put on a joint show of work by Andy and Michael Zwack, a Hallwalls founder who had left, like the others, for the city. Don could have secured more funding to present "Longo, Sherman, Zwack, and Topolski," but instead he opted to make a bold if implicit statement about the mission of the Burchfield Penney and about an overdue correction to the way Western New York thought about what it had lost in the late '70s and '80s.

Local art politics aside, the juxtaposition was inspired: Zwack, an ordained vodou priest, had found god and presented work in oils and pigments depicting organic patterns and natural imagery; Andy, who had considered pursuing a PhD in anthropology in the '90s, was interested in—anguished by—man playing god, and presented work in the vernacular of hard and social sciences and mass media.

Don visited Zwack in New York and Andy in Callicoon to discuss the exhibit and begin transporting some of the work, and he took a young Buffalo artist and art handler, Tom Holt, to assist. Like Don, Tom didn't buy into the reigning orthodoxy in the Western New York art scene. Longo, Tom said, was trying to master modes that had already existed; Sherman was not inventive. Both were among the most celebrated and comfortably compensated artists of their generation. Andy, though, was a true original, always playing with the boundary between two-dimensional and three-dimensional art, always pushing at the limits of his audience's interpretive energies with the cryptic combinations of his influences and media. Even the smudges— adumbrations of dissonance, dirt, interference, suggestions, and erasures in his work—masterfully apply the maximum of strain that each piece can take.

The show, Andy's first in over four years, was to be held December 3, 2005 to February 26, 2006, in the Burchfield Penney space in Rockwell Hall. Planning to include several sculptures, Andy entrusted the completion of one of his works to Tom. The piece, *Highway 61 Revisited*, is a wooden tower sixty inches high, ending in a movable arm suspending his petrified crow, looking like a weapon of war, an anachronism, perhaps a sentient drone. The bottom of the arm is attached with a rough rope to a golden slug in the shape of a huge bullet or some kind of ordnance, lending the whole piece a potential energy, a sense of movement about to begin—and a suggestion that the bird is meant to be thrown. Tom fondly called it "the Trebuchet." He sketched notes in pencil, like a carpenter, as Andy described the effect he hoped to achieve in displaying the work. Tom was to position the piece ten feet from a wall, with a black-and-white spiral, three feet in diameter, painted opposite—a psychedelic bull's-eye. The bird was to be a projectile, and visitors passing between the piece and the painted bull's-eye were to feel themselves suddenly a target.

I met Tom in person at the Burchfield Penney in September 2020. Sitting opposite each other in the archive room, masked—and later outside, as Tom smoked beside the loading doors—I heard Tom's recollections of the trip to Callicoon. He still remembered his one evening in the garage at 69 Seminary Road as a pivotal moment with one of the living greats—the memory of canned Budweiser, Bob Dylan on cassette, and crickets chirring outside the open door still vivid more than a decade later.

The music played—

> While them that defend what they cannot see
> With a killer's pride, security
> It blows the minds most bitterly
> For them that think death's honesty
> Won't fall upon them naturally
> Life sometimes must get lonely

—and Andy grew quiet on and off, listening to the lyrics or the night noises, or to something else.

Dylan snarled—

> Say okay, I have had enough
> what else can you show me?

—and the cassette player whirred, clicked.

Don and Tom sat up with Andy and Cindy and talked art, talked politics, late into the night.

Just like the old days on North Seventh, on Broadway in Brooklyn and Broadway in Buffalo, on Essex Street.

The music, Budweiser, cigarettes, and conversation lapped like the river in Tom's head as he sank into a deep-country sleep that night. Dylan cooed:

> The handmade blade, the child's balloon
> Eclipses both the sun and moon
> To understand you know too soon
> There is no sense in trying

Tom's mind muddled the rest in tiredness and beer-murk.

> he not busy being born is busy dying
> not busy being born is
> busy being born is busy
> busy being
> not busy is
> is busy dying

Kill Me a Son

CINDY'S CANCER CAME first, in October 2007. The news spread through the family phone tree, following a well-worn route: first to my grandmother Annette, and from her to everybody else. I remember *knowing* about Aunt Cindy's cancer, but I don't remember *hearing* about it. This was typical: Talia and I, the youngest members of the youngest generation in the House of Suffoletto, as a rule lacked a party line into the phone calls that transmitted family news of any import. But it was more than that—the fact of her illness was tacitly but palpably muted among the family, and this had less to do with our group dynamics than it had to do with Cindy and the characteristic way she chose to handle the cancer: with deflecting fortitude, focusing outwardly on everything and everyone else.

How much she hid her sickness from the family and how much she hid it from herself is an insoluble question. Perhaps it was similar to the emphysema seven years before: a total disregard of her condition until it brought her to her knees on a busy pavement in Manhattan. Then again, it was not widely known in the family that Cindy had smoked regularly prior to the emphysema, nor that following her diagnosis, she abandoned her attempts to quit. (Andy couldn't—or wouldn't—join her in the effort, friends remember.) At any rate, the news of her cancer did not dominate the discourse the way one might have expected of a family as close as ours.

Cindy and I had been emailing back and forth sporadically since 2004, when I was in sixth grade. My dad had helped me open a

Hotmail account and encouraged me to keep in touch with out-of-town relatives. I asked my aunt simple questions about life in Callicoon; she asked me about school, music, and girls. And at Christmases I received Cindy's "Elf Yourself" e-greetings—videos of dancing cartoon elves with the faces of everyone in the family.

On November 17, 2007—I was then a high school freshman—she sent me a typical update. The original message is lost, but it's clear from the context that I had asked about her health[1].

> How are you? Your mom tells me you are crazy busy and involved in so many things! That's really great. What electives are you taking? Do you have any ideas for Christmas? Do you want anything special for your drums or fencing or anything else? Drop me an email if you can think of anything.
> I'm feeling a little better. I feel tired a lot and that's the worst part because I like to keep busy...
> I'm looking forward to seeing you.
> Love Aunt Cindy

When she visited a month later, Cindy seemed in subtle but unmistakable ways to have increased the stretch of time that separated her from my mother, her younger sister by one year, so close in appearance that in their childhood they had passed for twins. Radiation had turned the soft waves in Cindy's dark hair tight and wiry. Her face was paler, pressed with new faint lines. Only the smile that she took from my grandfather Hank was unchanged: straight, double-wide, and flashing, stretching her high cheeks taut as trysails.

Time was accelerating in Cindy's body. Time had been accelerating in Brooklyn, too.

Andy and Cindy's relationship with Tony, their landlord, had steadily deteriorated, and had reached a breaking point in 2002. It became obvious to them that Tony had gone back on his promise to sell them the building after watching a decade of construction in the rapidly gentrifying Williamsburg. Physical upkeep of the property had fallen to Andy, who went uncompensated. And Andy, increasingly stressed by the situation with Tony, by the demands of the art world—and obsessively depressive following 9/11—grew short with old friends. And old friends grew less patient. Several friendships fell apart or were transformed in this period. Most notable was Andy's friendship with Peter Muscato, one of Cindy and Andy's oldest companions and allies—and, of course, their neighbor. The "compound" comprising 207 and 211 North Seventh, which once had seemed like an expression and extension of Cindy and Andy's very being into their adopted city, started to feel less and less like home. Less than a year after closing on the house in Callicoon, they abandoned it.

Money in Brooklyn could buy a lot less in '02 than it had in '96. Their new apartment at 113 Withers Street was a tighter two-bedroom on the second floor. They rented it from Robert and Phyllis Paciullo, who lived up the street at 108, for $1,700 a month. They signed the lease July 25, 2002, putting up the first month's rent and another $1,700 as a security deposit.

It was only a ten-minute walk from their old street and the yard where they'd spent countless summer evenings, but the move was more symbolic than physical. When they left North Seventh for Withers, they lost the yard, the rooftop garden, and Andy's ground-floor studio, with its garage door open to the sidewalk, and subtenants and friends always passing through. The change in their physical environment, combined with a complicated network of minor disagreements,[2] created a vicious cycle that led Cindy and Andy to shift the balance of their lives away from Brooklyn, upstate. The wild, vibrant, artistically and politically charged gatherings that had filled every living room and studio they'd ever occupied—from Essex Art House 30F to Sixth Ave in Park Slope to 440 Broadway to 211 North Seventh—shifted finally up to 69 Seminary Road in Callicoon, leaving 113 Withers typically dark.

We didn't expect Andy's cancer, either. In retrospect it would seem incredible for someone who smoked that much to make it out of their fifties without serious incident, but at Christmas in 2007 Andy had presented a hearty figure—maybe a little thinner, but in a way we would have chalked up to fresh food and daily exercise in Callicoon.

The talk, in fact, was of Cindy's recovery. She was feeling good, she said. Tired, but good. Her doctors were hopeful. When she returned to New York she was to begin her second round of chemo.

In reality, Andy was ill that Christmas, and he knew it.

After supper—our usual spread of manicotti, meatballs, and braciola, ham and pickled peppers, vegetables that I never ate and can't remember—Andy pushed his chair out and strained his head back so that he could see into the hall. The door to the bathroom was closed, a light shining out beneath it onto a strip of the pink carpet. My grandmother, at the head of the table, noticed.

"There's a bathroom upstairs if you want to use that one," she said, quietly.

Andy drew in a short breath.

"I don't think I can make it," he said, his voice low.

She thought he was being a bit "dramatic," she remembered, the episode coming back to her, unexpected, as she spoke to me over the phone one afternoon—November 18, 2020, a Wednesday.

She didn't realize at the time that Andy meant he couldn't make it up the stairs.

A few weeks later, early in the new year, Ian Milner was out getting coffee in Williamsburg and ran into Andy on the street—and the apparition shocked him. Andy was gaunt, totally transformed. Though they had grown more distant from Andy over the course of episodic fallings-out, Ian and Amy had kept in regular touch with Cindy—and even she hadn't let on about Andy's illness. Ian stepped right to block Andy's path and asked, "How are you?"—and not in the automatic way one usually delivers those three words.

Andy muttered something unintelligible. His meaning was clear.

Ian reported back to Peter and to Amy, who reached out to Cindy. "What can we do?" they asked. The old fights seemed suddenly hazier, disappearing in a shift of perspective that happened, like so much in those days, with vertiginous swiftness.

Late at night on January 26, 2008, a Saturday, back at their apartment on Withers, Cindy sat down to her computer. Flo Rida's "Low" was playing loud enough in the apartment next door that the melody concatenated with the dial-up tone of AOL. She let her eyes fall from the screen to the keyboard and ran the tips of her fingers through the new hair at her temples, then repeated the motion, pressing harder.

Andy had been teaching at Parsons earlier that month, putting in his obligatory time in the city. He was sick, clearly, but well enough to work. The next day he was in a hospital bed. Andy received a diagnosis—lung and kidney cancer—and immediately began an inpatient regimen of radiation and chemotherapy. Cindy hadn't left the hospital in over thirty hours. Finally one of the nurses told her—firmly—to rest and reset at home.

Her inbox was full. It was the high-water mark of spam and mail forwards, but between these were messages from friends all over the world asking after her health and Andy's.

And at the same time there was a sense in the air—and certainly on the internet—of some kind of imminent change. On the

TV in Andy's hospital room they had watched the nightly news. The spacecraft *Messenger* had reached Mercury, but its images wouldn't return to earth for three years. The business reporters talked about a "Black Monday," the stock market's worst January since the dot-com bubble had burst in 2000. Barack Obama, the senator from Illinois, had won the Democratic presidential primary in Iowa but lost to Hillary Clinton in New Hampshire and Nevada; now the pundits were talking about the Black vote and how a win in South Carolina on Sunday could change Super Tuesday's simple math and give us something still almost unthinkable: the first African American presidential candidate from a major party.

Instead of scrolling the news, reading a book, or watching a favorite old movie, Cindy wrote to me.

> *Your father sent me pictures of your dance night.*
> *They reminded me of when I was in high school ... took the same*
> *pictures. haha You are going to love seeing them many years from*
> *now. Your date is so cute! Was she nice?*

I wrote back the next day, asking after Andy.

His first roommate in the hospital was insane, she answered, at 7:40 that Sunday evening.

> *The man thought he was in Korea and kept yelling and demanding*
> *he wanted to get the bus. He had nothing on but a hospital gown*
> *and a bolo tie (like cowboys wear). and he snuck up behind me and*
> *shouted "Got any GUM??!!!" haha Fortunately, they moved him.*
> *Talk to you soon*
> *Love, Aunt Cindy*

On February 13, Andy called Don Metz from his hospital bed. This was typical—the old friends had been checking in on each other at least once a day.

At the start of the month, Andy had returned to Parsons to teach his spring semester classes. He had told his friend Brian Duffy, in Buffalo, that he was optimistic and "determined to fight." Cindy, meanwhile, had learned in the second week of February, and in the middle of her second round of chemo, that she was "cancer free."

But that morning Andy had felt a terrible pain and weakness—he entered the ER with internal bleeding. Later he was feeling well enough to update Don over the phone.

"I think the only way that I can live now is to become president," Andy said, his low voice an even lower croak, permanently changed by the tumor in his chest, but still strong.

He laughed.

"See ya," Andy said, and hung up the phone.

He died the next day.

He died with Cindy and Julia at his side, old friends like Peter and Wynn nearby—loved ones, some even recently distant, pulled back across time and space toward a collapsing center, a final breath.

I don't remember hearing the news of Andy's death. This is the beginning of a mental pattern: for the rest of my life, cratered with losses, I won't be able to recall the exact moment I learned of anyone's death. I do remember the long drive out to the Pacer Funeral Home, 2275 George Urban Boulevard in Depew, between two apparently symbiotic brake-and-muffler shops, like a blown-up version of the low-slung ranch homes all around it. I remember the smokers outside. I remember what rumbled above—airplanes in crisscrossing flight paths on their descent into the Buffalo Niagara International Airport, just a mile due north.

I remember Andy in the casket, the man in black.

Someone spoke, choking up, working in a few gentle laughs at Andy's expense. The man gestured to Cindy and called her "the person he chose to spend his life with." I remember my father, paragon of Irish propriety, stiffening at my side. A small thing to notice, but true: it was indelicate phrasing to use with Andy's first wife, Pat, in the room.

Later, when we could speak, we wondered aloud if death had been planted in him by the toxic dust that billowed out from the collapse of the Twin Towers only a few years before. The news was filled in those days with stories of young and sudden deaths, strange cancers, all tied to the World Trade Center. But it could have been cigarettes, or it could have been the fumes of paints, primers, and stove smoke stewing in the workshop in Callicoon.

I never did hear a definitive answer.

The closest I came was in the Burchfield Penney archives, when I found a printout of an email that Brian Duffy, Andy and Cindy's friend and colleague from the Essex and Villa days, sent to an undisclosed list of recipients the night Andy died, February 14, 7:14 p.m. Katerina Syntelis, a Burchfield staffer, forwarded it to the rest of the community, and Nancy Weekly, one of Andy's oldest advocates, thought to print it out.

According to Brian, the doctors said Andy had suffered "heart episodes," fallen unconscious in the ICU, and "expired" in the afternoon.

This, of course, brings me no closer to an answer—or to Andy—than we were twelve years ago.

Minds of My Generation

HE HAS NEVER seen the Met quite like this. No one has.

Dressed in black, clutching a gallery book and a copy of the *Times* and other odds and ends smiling people have handed to him, Charlie Clough crosses the huge white rooms of the building's lower levels like a soul in the Asphodel Meadows. He is headed for Elysium but taking his time. He doubles back, gets turned around, traces perimeters and sidesteps sharply dressed art students, somehow always in the way, moving as one does in a dream: trusting his feet to take him where he needs to be. In one room the old artist stops and gazes up into his own eyes, huge and unblinking, in a nebula of red and black acrylic paint.

It is April 21, 2009, night of the opening reception for *The Pictures Generation*, a show so big and bold that it's shaken up the Met's reputation for fustiness and scattershot nostalgia. Douglas Eklund, an associate curator in the Met's photography department, has moved in a grand, swift, and decisive way to identify a generation of American artists who emerged between 1974 and 1984—and whose emergence, works, and practices had permanently altered the course of American art through the turn of the century and into the present era.

By coincidence, the New Museum is putting on another "generation" show, too: *The Generational: Younger Than Jesus*. It escapes no one that these new, mostly Gen X and millennial artists, appropriating and challenging digital imagery, are just aping the actions of the boomers, who were first to explore these ideas—just in different media. The artists in the Met show stand all the taller for the comparison.

Some are already famous; many are not. All, even the best-known names, have been lost in one sense or another—lost between the wars, between economic booms or political epochs, between pop and the new expressionism. Here they are redis-covered, submitted to the appetites of critics and historians. Individually they could only ever mean so much. Together they *have influenced*, together they *represent*, together they *challenge*. They belong here, around the corner from Caravaggio, up the hall from Benin ivories. This is what it feels like to be canonized.

Charlie keeps moving. The work is eerily, transcendently familiar. Much of it he can trace back to 1974—to shows that *he* curated, that the artists on display here *hung themselves*, on freshly installed drywall in the brick halls of the icehouse on Essex Street in Buffalo.

He passes the huge photorealistic charcoals of Robert Longo, dapper men writhing and falling backward in space, looming in the Met's Great Hall[1]—Cindy Sherman's crisp, commercial, and disturbed self-portraits—along with the dioramas of Laurie Sim-mons, the cutouts of Richard Prince. He's reacquainted, too, with Buffalo friends who'd fallen out of touch—like the commercial commissioned posters for rock bands by Michael Zwack, the *fifth* Hallwalls founder among the thirty artists collected here.

Back in the great hall, Charlie catches Bob Longo's eyes, winces from the temples—a smile of private amazement. Bob, talking to a Met board member, returns the smile from one corner of his moving mouth.

Charlie has harbored jealousies toward some here tonight; he's pitied others. Some from the California crowd are com-plete strangers to him. But everything is changed, now. He feels himself newly oriented to all the others, the cords of feeling snipped—some memories spotlit and others suddenly dimmed.

His head is cool, his chest full and warmed as if by wine. The feeling is one familiar to all artists who wake up one day to a new name, a strong and strange name, one they didn't choose and that they have to share with others.

We've made it, is the feeling. Charlie doesn't say it, doesn't even think it—would doubt it if someone else suggested it. But the feeling is unmistakable. *We've made it.*

On Friday, August 28, 2020, an overcast afternoon, in a brief valley between the acclivitous peaks of the coronavirus pandemic in the United States, I sit in the Burchfield Penney Art Center archivist's room across a desk from Tom Holt. Both of us masked, Tom tells me about visiting my aunt and uncle in Callicoon fifteen years earlier, while I turn over the contents of Andy's artist file, a pale folder stuffed beyond any usability, separate from the ordered boxes of his archive. I page through decades of ephemera—exhibition cards, résumés, newspaper clippings, letters to Tony Bannon, and a secretary's notes: *Return call to Andrew Topolski*, and then, three days later, *ANDY CALLED AGAIN VERY IMPORTANT HE SPEAK TO YOU.*

My fingers pass over a smooth tumulus among the papers. I sift out a sealed envelope with a small, rectangular bulge— a microcassette. The label indicates it was a recording of Tony interviewing Andy. There isn't a microcassette player at the gallery and I don't have one at home. I don't know the length of the recording or what subjects are covered, but my pulse picks up. The tape is undated but likely from the mid to late '80s. I am holding the only recording of Andy speaking about his art that would likely ever be available to me. I arrange with the archivist Heather Gring to send it away to be digitized.

Nearly three months later, on the morning of November 22, a Sunday, as I watch the season's first snowfall—the first snowfall that sticks—I get the vendor's email, an .mp3 attached. The recording, only a minute and twenty-five seconds, is brittle and muffled, like voices coming across a cup-and-string telephone, but it isn't difficult to transcribe.

> TOPOLSKI.   There's a lot of work that I've seen that's so overly scientific and overly embellished with things that really …
> may have relevance to our civilization and our time but are
> so overburdened that they cancel themselves out. So it is an equation and if you don't understand that equation, you are lost.
>
> Because it doesn't offer someone, you know, the chance to try to figure it out in their own way, you know, and if they do figure it out …
>
> … in other words, what I'm saying is if you figure something out about my work it may not necessarily be right or wrong …
>
> I mean I'm frankly flattered when people do try to figure out and come up with a solution because that really, you know, to me it is the greatest compliment, or, you know, I mean that's the real pleasure in having someone do that because that's, that's, you know, a lot of what it's about …
>
> BANNON.   [inaudible—then deliberate] … that's exactly my question: Will the work yield a solution?
>
> TOPOLSKI.   [with upward inflection] No.
>
> BANNON.   Um—do you—
>
> TOPOLSKI.   And it isn't meant to.
> You know—
>
> BANNON.   —have … and … ah … uhm … you … may … therefore … trust—

Here the tape cuts out, closing with three seconds of complete silence.

Why didn't Douglas Eklund include Andy in the *Pictures Generation* show? I still don't have a good answer.

Reading contemporary reviews, I find challenges to the notion that Eklund's chosen thirty represented a "generation."[2] But they certainly shared a set of formative experiences that set them—and their art—apart from what came before, and positioned them to influence what came after. "They were born in the mid-1940s to early '50s, in a prosperous but paranoia-prone cold war era," the *New York Times* critic Holland Cotter wrote. "They were the first kids to be raised with television, fast food and disposable everything. As teenagers they were soaked in Pop Art, rock and rebel politics. As art students, even in traditionalist programs, they felt the effects of Conceptualism. Ideas replaced objects and images. Painting was pushed to the side. The movement questioned what art was for and redefined what could be art."

The Met show focused on three communities that had incubated the concepts that came to define the Pictures Generation: the group of artists studying under Conceptualist guru John Baldessari at the California Institute of the Arts, including Jack Goldstein, Barbara Bloom, Matt Mullican, David Salle, and James Welling; a group associated with Artists Space in New York City, including Barbara Kruger, Sherrie Levine, Louise Lawler, Richard Prince, and Laurie Simmons; and founders and associates of Hallwalls in Buffalo—here limited to Charles Clough, Cindy Sherman, Robert Longo, Michael Zwack, and Nancy Dwyer.[3]

At first I wonder if Andy's work simply didn't include enough photography—enough recognizable "pictures." Then I learn my first, literalist perception of the show was mistaken. "All [were] making art that combined elements of Pop and Conceptualism with social concerns about consumerism, political power and gender," Cotter explained. "Their work kept ideas to the fore and rematerialized them as images. Many of those images were photographic, extracted from everyday life, a life that was increasingly a creation of media culture, as Andy Warhol well knew."

If Sherman stood at the top of the pop-influenced side of the

Pictures Generation, then surely Andy occupied the top of the conceptual pillar. His work reified ideas; and he, too, addressed political power; but instead of consumerism and gender he explored architecture, new science, world-historical currents, and humankind's gravitational tendency to ever-refined forms of mass destruction. Andy was less interested in the individual's consumption, more interested in the increasingly complex (and increasingly violent) systems that shaped and guided individual lives.

Perhaps, I wonder, Andy simply wasn't sufficiently visible in the right places and at the right times.

"Reductive accounts of the period pinpoint these trends as coalescing in a 1977 group exhibition called *Pictures* at Artists' Space in SoHo," Cotter explained. "In reality, this was a small-ish affair, mostly of brand-new work, with only five artists—Mr. Goldstein, Ms. Levine and Mr. Longo, along with Troy Brauntuch and Philip Smith—with works by Ms. Sherman installed else-where in the gallery. The show's real influence probably derived from a related essay written by its curator, Douglas Crimp."

"Smallish" events can act like butterflies' wings in the art world. Perhaps Andy's failure to follow his Hallwalls contemporaries out of Buffalo in time for opportunities like the *Pictures* show or asso-ciation with the Metro Pictures Gallery left him out of step with his "generation," at least as far as the critics were concerned.

And that matters. After all, even *I* didn't realize just how much Andy's work aligned with the concepts, methods, and preoccupa-tions Eklund highlighted in the Met show.

Through my interviews I discover that Andy really always was a Pictures artist. His earliest mature work was in photography; in his prolific middle years he took his intermedia practice argu-ably further than any others among the generation celebrated for their "appropriation."

Eventually I come to understand that the intellectual coolness that had endeared Andy's work to certain discerning collectors had also limited his appeal to a wider audience. But looking chronologically at all of his surviving works, a radical shift is obvious. Near the end of his life, without compromising his intellectual rigor and resistance to didacticism, Andy was drawing on more immediately recognizable sources and media, leveraging symbolism to "cut through" the visual noise of an image-saturated culture, and confronting head-on the current events that captured an increasingly news-addicted public.

"The new works... continue the artist's creative and visual language that we know from his previous compositions, but it seems as if we are suddenly allowed a closer glimpse into his anxious soul," Christiane Fischer-Harling wrote on the occasion of a small showing of these new works in 2005—the first exhibited since the "paralysis" of 9/11 and his retreat to Callicoon.

> No doubt, Andrew has raised his voice by a notch or two in
> this new body of work. There seems to be noise instead of
> the comforting harmony of the musical language found in
> the earlier works. A more direct confrontation with instantly
> recognizable imagery has replaced the delicate and atmospheric
> quality of his past compositions. What we see here is
> unquestionably the creative evolution of an artist who seems
> to be growing increasingly restless, as if running out of time.
> The viewer is immediately engaged by a sense of urgency that
> shouts out from each of the pieces.

Christiane's prescience pointed to what even Andy didn't know: he really was running out of time. In his last weeks—for the first time since his MFA show in 1977—he returned to the direct use of photography, capturing images of his own cancer-ravaged body in a project that, in retrospect, charges and challenges Cindy Sherman's earlier innovations in self-portraiture to reach powerful new registers.

Many of the same characteristics of Bush-era America that had caused Andy intense distress were also repositioning both his practice and the mainstream audience for contemporary art, such that the two might finally fit. Tragically, it appears to me now as if Andy was cut down on the cusp of a new reckoning, another shot at the sustained success, even celebrity, that had remained out of reach for his entire career.

I can't help but wonder: What if those final images hadn't remained in a shoebox under the couch in the second-floor apartment at 113 Withers? What if, two years later, they had appeared at the Met?

On one of our calls, Tony Bannon pointedly tells me: "Robert Longo never hesitated to say Andy was 'the smartest of us.'"

On this breadcrumb, I track down Longo's email and reach out to him. I don't confront him with the quote—I just explain the project and ask to interview him about Hallwalls and Buffalo.

Dear Aidan, he replies a day later,

> *I'm sorry I can't help you.*
> *I didn't really know Andy.*
> *I thought he was an interesting artist, but we didn't really run*
> *together at all.*
> *Regards,*
> *Robert*

I write him back the same day, June 2, explaining that I'm not just interested in my aunt and uncle.

> *Hi, Robert, and thanks for getting back to me. I understand you*
> *weren't close with Andy—to clarify, I thought you might give me your*
> *perspective on the founding of Hallwalls, the economic and cultural*
> *dynamic between Buffalo and New York, and whether you feel*
> *you and your contemporaries who left Buffalo brought some of the*
> *collaborative and interdisciplinary energies of the city at that time*
> *into your careers in New York.*

He doesn't respond. I wait three weeks and try a third time, June 22:

> *Hi, Robert. I hope you've been well. I have a very narrow and specific inquiry you may be able to address. I'd love to hear anything that you can remember about your show Spatial Survey at UB's Gallery 219 Jan–Feb 1975. The show included sculptural and situational work by you, Andy, Joe Panone, and Roger Rapp.*
>
> *Do you remember what pieces you included? The others?*
> *Was Gallery 219 in Norton Hall on the North (Amherst) campus? If not, can you clarify the location?*
> *What did the gallery look like? How was it arranged?*
> *Who came and how was the show received? Did people like Charlotta Kotik and Linda Cathcart come? Did other Essex Art Center tenants like Larry Griffis and Duayne Hatchett show up and support? What about the media studies people, the writers around Bob Creely, and local electeds, etc?*
> *I appreciate any color you can provide.*
> *Thanks, Robert—*
> *Aidan*

He answers on the 26th:

> *a*
> *like i said before i really didnt know Andy—he seemed to be on the other side....*

I decide not to push it. This leaves me with conflicting accounts—Bannon's and Longo's. Andy was either "the smartest of us," or he was "on the other side."

If I accept both as true, Andy becomes harder to locate. Like a quantum particle, he remains in both places until observed. And where you stand makes all the difference.

What does Longo's forgotten "us" mean nearly fifty years later? And ... the other side *of what?*

Whatever Longo meant, it reminds me of something he said to Mary Haus for an interview in *Artforum* in 2003. The focus was the New York art world of the '80s.

"When Metro Pictures first opened, the atmosphere in SoHo was almost like a street fight," he said. "Artists should have been wearing leather jackets with the name of their gallery on the back and walking around with baseball bats."

> But the early to mid-'80s was an extraordinary time: the art-music scene, the clubs, the drugs, the camaraderie of artists, the night....
>
> One thing that became difficult in the '80s was that we went into Metro Pictures as a group, but once the gallery opened and shows started to happen, it became clear who was going to get more attention and the group started to disintegrate. Friendships were strained. There was an excitement, even if it was a competitive excitement. Unfortunately the greed-is-good mentality overrode it, but it was a blossoming moment—so much about art had been taken apart and rearranged and given back to us with new parts to work with. It was our time to shine; little did I know burnout would be the next stage.

Yes, Andy could fit into this picture. An explosion onto the scene; camaraderie and experimentation; manic work—then politics, division, burnout. I can see him stalking SoHo in a black leather jacket, a gash on the back where a patch reading SIEGEL TUCH used to be.

But this is an act of imagination. I have to stick to the following facts.

No matter where you pin the birth of Hallwalls—January 22, 1975, or February 22, 1975—Andy was a part of it. With Longo, he was one of four artists in *Spatial Survey*, the Hallwalls debut. And he was back at the icehouse space-warmer the following month.

Similarly, no matter how you tend to define the Pictures

Generation, Andy was not only a coeval, but a recognized leader. Not socially, perhaps—the Mudd Club was a long way from the Essex Street Pub or Teddy's in Williamsburg—but certainly in his art practice, which for his entire career remained far out in advance of the frequently crude experimentations and, later, tired repetitions of many of his contemporaries.

This is what the record shows, for those who know where to look.

Some would rather not.

It's impossible to say and probably facile to speculate whether Andy would have broken through—into bigger exhibitions, into breathless profiles in the *Times*, into the blue-chip galleries of the secondary market—but certainly, because of the shrewdness and timing of Don's Topolski–Zwack show in 2005, Andy and the Niagara Frontier were ready for a reconciliation.

Before his illness, Andy had been working on new pieces for a solo exhibition at Villa Maria College, his first home as an art teacher, organized by his old friend Brian Duffy, who had joined the faculty with Andy in 1979 and was then director of the Paul William Beltz Gallery. Brian was among the friends most viscerally impacted by Andy's sudden passing. And, just months after the fact, he wasn't at all prepared to mount a posthumous show. Brian expanded the concept and invited John Toth, Lisa Toth, Robert Gulley, and Cindy to exhibit. It would be a celebrated return of some of the artists who had left Buffalo together in the '80s. Cindy declined. Brian assumed she was preoccupied, still in shock from losing Andy and struggling to manage both their diminished household and his sprawling artistic estate. I wonder, if after so long without a studio practice, she just lacked confidence in the work she could muster on short notice. Regardless, fifteen years after her last group exhibition at Galerie Schüppenhauer, she decided she wasn't ready.

They call it *Homecoming*. To Andy's friends and fellow artists, many who had shared gallery walls and studio space with him decades before, it felt like a reunion. To me, at fifteen, it feels like a second wake.

I'm disappointed to find only three of Andy's works on the small dark gallery walls. Inscrutable to me, two of them comprise ink arcs that appear first solid, like cascades of cantilevered beams or piano keys, then disappear into fainter pencil sketches winking at the fact of their composition, or into two-dimensional quadrilaterals casting shadows, reminiscent, to my teenage eyes, of Escher. The third is a dark, linear collage: hands in different positions terminating in a slice of a Martian landscape.

I feel a familiar electrical twinge—the body's reaction to beauty. This had been my earliest reaction to Andy's work, the pieces in our house that I saw from different vantages every year, growing closer inch by inch, until I could look at them straight on. I recognized this beauty—immediate as fresh snow on black branches—as something that distinguished Andy's work from other contemporary art, at least the sort exhibited at the Albright-Knox.

Years later, reading every one of Andy's saved reviews, I find that the *Buffalo News* critic Richard Huntington had noted the same in 1992: "The luminosity of vellum paper, the subtle blendings of dry pigment and graphite, the delicate pilings of diagrams, the astutely balanced overall composition itself," he rhapsodized.

This remained the essential characteristic of Andy's work in 2008, nine months after his passing.

"I found his entry point to be elegance," Tony Bannon would tell me years later. Speaking over the phone close to midnight, I write down every word that he utters.

> *The unstated balance, the harmony of parts, that you recognize when it exists....You recognize it as being right. Just goddamn right. And if*

you've got the chops, you might take on the challenge of figuring out why it's right.

But in early 2008, like so many who encountered Andy's work with a mind unprepared, perhaps even misprepared, I want more than beauty—and, chopless or not, I don't care for the challenge.

Does it yield a solution?

No.

All that remains is the work—and the "trust" that Bannon found implicit in the work—and Andy's silence, awaiting our response—that "greatest compliment."

A sophomore in comfortable stride, reading *Candide*, listening to *Autumn Leaves*, making index cards on things like Lend-Lease and the National Bank Act, I had finally arrived at an age where I might have asked Andy to explain his work. And he would have done it—likely in unpretentious, unpretending language, even if stilted, searching, incomplete. I don't much care for the gallery notes, which mention machines, politics, and conflict, and say little to nothing about the works themselves. And I feel it would be too painful to ask Cindy to talk about the work—although of course she would have loved nothing more than to bring her husband, my uncle, closer to me.

I find cheese and crackers, sneak a little plastic cup of red wine out of the gallery and into a long hallway of cinder blocks painted municipal beige, and wait for the end.

Self-Portraits and Sandwiches

Maybe private worlds are all there are. Talking about them is a
way of conjuring gravity between them, a way to pull them near
and make them matter to each other. I mean, to make any one
of them matter at all. Certainly the force of describing them also
changes them....

But it can't be better to say nothing....

Everyone lives alone in families. Everyone goes alone into
action, love, and work. Sometimes, it's why we work. Everyone
goes alone into sickness, too.

—MOLLY BRODAK, *Bandit*

THE YEARS PASSED QUICKLY: garage bands, basement binges,
elaborate courtships, and endless conversations fueled the furnace of the incredible solipsism that dominates the second
decade of most lives—and that certainly dominated mine. Cindy
and I kept up an email correspondence that reads as painfully
one-sided today. I rattled off the subjects I studied and the trips
I took, wrote about having to choose between the jazz band and
the football team. Mostly we talked about music—how we hated
ska and emo most of all, how we loved bebop and fusion and
classic rock bands like Pink Floyd and the Rolling Stones. Cindy
mailed me burned copies of CDs, bands like Creedence Clearwater Revival that she'd discovered when she was my age.

In August 2011, as I was starting orientation at Canisius College—moving into a dorm room even though the campus was less
than two miles from my parents' home, which underscored my
ambivalence about the decision to stay—she sent me Al Jarreau's

Look to the Rainbow, the singer's live album from 1977. I thanked her in an email, wrote about how I'd "jammed out" to the CD with the windows down, driving over the Buffalo Skyway at sunset in the '99 Mazda sedan I'd commandeered from my parents.

I can't believe you are out of the house and in a dorm! she wrote back.

> *It's so exciting.... All I can say is, those years for me will never be matched. I had so much fun "choosing" classes and meeting new people from different places. I loved the energy and probably moreso, the new influences and freedom to express and be creative. Make the best of it!! As Warren Zevon said, "enjoy every sandwich."*

The long grass was cold around Cindy's ankles and rough like a cat's tongue. It was early May, just past seven in the morning, but the sun was already up and intended to stay there for a long while. The air would be warm soon. It would feel like afternoon all day.

"Hey."

Ian Milner navigated the patio steps behind her. He'd rubbed the sleep from his eyes, but it was still evident in his dark, curly hair. Amy followed through the sliding glass deck door, carrying two coffees.

"Perfect day," she said.

And then Bob Gulley rounded the corner of the house, a flat-bladed spade and mean-looking wood-handled cultivator over his left shoulder.

Andy had been gone less than three months. At first it seemed to Cindy she couldn't get away—from family, friends, art-world grifters, woodwork-born acquaintances. Until she could. A few weeks after the funeral she was, for the most part, alone.

But she was in touch with her closest friends and had mentioned on the phone with Amy that she'd been thinking about a patch of wild earth behind the garage that had been Andy's studio, a plot that belonged to the government but that she'd never seen used or surveyed. She wanted to turn it into a garden. She didn't have to say that she couldn't do it alone—it was settled in the hour: Amy and Ian would scoop Bob from Greenwich Village, then swing north for a long weekend in the Catskills. They used the heavy tools in Cindy's shed to cut trees, pull brush, rake, and turn the earth up black. By the midafternoon they were building wooden beds, and on Sunday they planted—then kayaked, had a cookout, ended the night at the fire pit. By summer's end Cindy had raised a huge garden on the land she'd claimed.

I could find no record of the emotional impact of Andy's death on Cindy. I could find no friend who felt they could speak to it. Most accounts confirmed my own hazy recollections: we remember her sadness in 2008, but we remember her resilience more. We remember stories like the one Amy told me about Cindy's garden.

Whether in contrast or merely as context, I found that Andy's passing had devastated friends and relatives in ways that remain legible today. His nephew Alex, for example, has never celebrated Valentine's Day, the anniversary of Andy's death. And Alex told me that his grandparents "essentially died as well; they didn't know how to go on"—he remembers going to his grandmother's house and finding the fridge completely bare. Other living relatives declined, when I contacted them, to answer any questions whatsoever about Andy or their relationships with him—a psychic third rail over a decade later. But more than a dozen friends, initially hesitant to reach back into murky memories, ended up speaking with me for hours, the phone a conduit for powerful reminiscences that ushered out of them almost without their conscious control.

By all accounts, though, Cindy—who had spent her entire adult life with Andy—spoke little about how his loss affected her. Increasingly spending her time in Callicoon, Cindy was kayaking, gardening, making new friends—enjoying every sandwich. By 2011, when she repeated it to me, it was clear Cindy was living Zevon's mantra.

Furman & Furman had downsized after 2000, so while Cindy kept commuting into the city to work a few days a week in the office, collecting a part-time salary, she opened an independent bookkeeping practice that she could operate from Callicoon, where she spent most of her time.

Cindy was still the nucleus of a group of girlfriends in New York: Amy Milner, Janine Tramontana, Catherine Saá, and sometimes Julia, Andy's daughter. Cindy kept in touch with everyone and never forgot a birthday—but increasingly she adopted a measure of Andy's old homebody habits, and home for her was Callicoon.

Keeping the apartment on Withers ($1,700 a month) and the mortgaged house on Seminary Road was difficult on a single income. But Cindy never let on to friends or relatives that her position in the Catskills was precarious. I remember being surprised, after Cindy died, to learn that my grandmother had let the bank take back the Callicoon house. Not even twenty, with no income and no savings, I was nonetheless heartsick, even angry, over it—that we had let slip away not only a place that we all loved, but a place that felt, to me at least, like a kind of portal where we might still have met some part of Cindy.

It took me another eight years to investigate the issue. Looking up the property records for Sullivan County, I found that in 2010, nine years after Cindy had closed on the house, her consolidated mortgage was $120,190—actually bigger than when she had started out.

But she had none of Andy's anxiety, and the financial situation didn't lessen her enjoyment of her Catskills paradise.

Cindy became an even more eccentric collector, as she had been with Andy—not of valuables or even curios, but of odd things that brought joy to her: metal and ceramic dragonfly figurines to hang around the kitchen and the garden; small representations of roosters; several whisk brooms, decorated and woven from sorghum and abaca; scores of heart-shaped stones. These she arranged in a bright and airy house that somehow seemed free of any clutter.

She tended to her requisitioned garden, which grew to tremendous proportions. The harvest each year was too big even to give away, so Cindy bought glass jars and learned to make pickles and jams, giving them to friends who stayed the weekend and shipping some around the state and across the country.

Callicoon and other hamlets in Sullivan County were growing then, as more weekenders from the city sought homes in the southwestern Catskills. Friends from Brooklyn moved in, Jennifer Lopez bought an estate overlooking the Delaware, and every few weeks Mark and Sunrise Ruffalo's Volvo station wagon would pass the lamp at the end of Cindy's driveway. In the summers she went swimming, rafting, and fishing; she fed the deer that visited her porch all through the winter.

Cindy had been with Andy almost since leaving Sacred Heart Academy at eighteen, but in Callicoon she started to see a friend, Keith Manzolillo, divorced with two boys, who split his time between his childhood home of Callicoon and his cattle ranch in Missouri—the last in a line of men who fell for Cindy and never quite got back up.

And for the first time since leaving 440 Broadway in the early '90s, Cindy was making art. The third floor was her studio—a bright finished space with a polished floor and slanting white plaster walls, flooded with sun from skylights. She kept her music and books up there, scraps from magazines (just as she had on Essex), along with reference points for the natural imagery that inspired an outpouring of pent-up creativity—feathers and twigs, delicate moths and dragonflies, birds' nests.

Cindy had always expressed herself inventively, even in the years when she didn't keep a studio. (Ian and Amy, for example, told me that once after they had given her a small gift of a gourmet chocolate bar, she sent them back a thank-you note made from the wrapper—this was a typical Cindy gesture.) But now her mind exploded in a half-dozen directions, as she worked across several media and genres at once. She produced wild, evocative oil paintings of nestlings yearning upward for food. She took photographs. She made startling and intimate self-portraits in collage. In one, she appears many-limbed like a Hindu god, mouth covered in a black bar, embracing a dragonfly impressed upon her torso, feet disappearing into Andy's old brown leather loafers. In another she appears looking downward, apparently naked and holding her knees; the same image floats in miniature above, forming a ghostly crown; and a pair of crossed houseflies rest on her forehead like a maang tikka or Frida Kahlo's wreath of flowers.

Again, a comparison to Lee Krasner is obvious: Cindy managed her husband's career for more than a quarter century, during which time her own artistic practice shrank to the point of invisibility. Cindy didn't move into the garage after Andy passed, as Lee had moved into Jackson Pollock's barn behind their house on Fireplace Road. She stayed in her well-lit attic studio. But both women were essentially reborn as artists after their husbands' deaths, producing an extraordinary amount of new work compared to the years before. Even in content their work from these periods is similar: like Lee's *Embrace*, *Birth*, *Listen*, *Three in Two*, and *The Seasons*, Cindy's oil paintings and collages were explosively colorful, teeming with natural imagery, and steeped in suggestions of death and rebirth. Agony threatens to break the surface tension of these works, Lee's and Cindy's—but they are also roaring with life itself, deeper than any concept of good or bad, terrible in its neutrality, simply continuing.

Critics and collectors were ready for Lee Krasner. Not for Cindy. She wasn't, as far as I know, taking these pieces to galleries. She didn't have a website (in fact, she was busy perfecting a website for Andy, complete with memorials, critical reviews, and a comprehensive catalog). Her Facebook featured only deer, hikes, harvests, a trip to Tulum—likely her first time on a plane after her lung had collapsed a decade before.

Cindy gave so much of herself away; what she kept back, I can only conclude, she did so with intention.

Eternal Recurrence

WE WERE IN the Detroit airport early on Friday, April 20, 2012, waiting for a connecting flight to Minneapolis for the wedding of my cousin Katie, on my dad's side of the family, when Mom got up from our seats at the gate and walked off into the concourse. My laptop was open on my knees and I was outlining a paper due the next week for "Religions of the East." The second-to-last book of the semester was *American Born Chinese*, a young adult graphic novel of the contemporary second-generation American's experience. I was critiquing the book's compatibilist view of divine fate and free will, using Calvin, Lucretius, and the anthropologist Judith Farquhar. The paper was due on May 1, in less than two weeks. I switched between Word and Google Docs, where I was outlining a column for the student paper, a predictable collegiate argument to elevate the issue of drug policy in the 2012 election. My headphones were in and I was listening to the Meters.

"Wait here," my dad said. I looked up—it was only then that I realized Mom had left. I spotted her cutting a path through the concourse, walking with purpose but without any apparent direction, head down, elbows in, one hand holding the phone to her ear and the other pressing white fingers to her temple. Dad had risen and was following her.

Cindy kept the recurrence of her cancer from the family until very near the end. She took to wearing scarves to cover the swelling of a tumor in her neck. At the time my grandpa Hank and Cindy's oldest sibling, Dave, were also sick with cancer. She knew that Dave's was fairly advanced, that Grandpa's health hung in the balance, and that everyone bearing the weight of the situation leaned, at last, on my grandmother Annette. Cindy didn't want to add to the burden.

In retrospect, there were hints. When she shared the advice to "Enjoy every sandwich," I didn't know that Warren Zevon had delivered this remark in an interview on *David Letterman* following his own diagnosis with terminal mesothelioma.

Now, scrolling Cindy's Facebook page, full of Jon Stewart clips, artist profiles, and investigative reports on fracking, pharma, and agricultural chemicals, I spot this, from October 9, 2011:

> *When you're drowning, you don't say 'I would be incredibly pleased if someone would have the foresight to notice me drowning and come and help me,' you just scream.*
> John Lennon (happy birthday)

Given the posts surrounding it, this could have been a comment on the Occupy Wall Street movement. It might just have been a piece of wisdom that resonated on the Beatle's birthday. But now I hear my aunt, a forty-nine-year-old widow, struggling, alone. The post itself is a scream in disguise.

Cindy avoided burdening her friends, too. Peter Muscato told me that he found out by accident that Cindy had been taking taxis or the subway to her treatments at the hospital, making the trip back to Brooklyn alone, dizzy, faint, and sometimes nauseous from the chemo. Finally, he and Amy Milner pressured Cindy to let them help a bit—getting groceries, driving her to appointments, little things. Rich Furman pitched in, too, and Keith tried to dote on her as much as she'd let him, though they'd drifted that year after it became clear she didn't intend to leave Callicoon.

As her condition worsened in the winter, Cindy insisted on driving up to the house to spend long weekends, no matter the weather. "Are you *kidding?*" Amy asked her. "Is anyone going with you?"

"I need to be there," she said.

All this time only her closest friends knew, and only because Cindy couldn't physically keep in her secret.

Finally, in the spring, Peter called Uncle Tom.

My grandparents drove to New York to be with Cindy while she underwent inpatient treatment at New York Presbyterian. They stayed for a week in the accommodations at the Helmsley Medical Tower across the street. Though they had visited several times since the '80s, Cindy had always entertained her family "without necessarily exposing them to her New York friends," as Janine Tramontana diplomatically put it to me. This was the first occasion that my grandparents met some of Cindy's closest friends, people like Janine or Ian and Amy Milner, Raymond and Catherine Saá. Her worlds were converging, merging. Her fight was ending.

She passed on the first of May, four years and three months after Andy.

I wrote a eulogy on the first floor in the library at Canisius, in between finishing final papers and studying for exams, powering through it on a sour cream glazed donut and a tall double-double I'd ordered just before Tim Hortons disappeared behind a metal gate at 10 p.m.

I remember—painfully still—that Cindy was unrecognizable in her casket, wizened with formaldehyde, wiry-haired, frumped up in serious clothes, and finished in makeup that she never would have worn. Seeing her this way was the hardest thing that iteration of my family had ever experienced.

I remember ascending the carpeted steps to the altar at St. Martin's Church in South Buffalo, where Cindy and her siblings had attended Mass and gone to school. I remember unfolding my printed pages at the lectern, looking out at our family and Cindy's friends, black suits washed in gray light, and making a single noise into the microphone. I remember nothing else.

Close friends from every era have said that something changed in their lives after Cindy left. For us, her death was just the beginning of a brutal summer crucible. Uncle Dave followed Cindy on June 26—once a quick-witted, confident joker, finally withered and oxygen-ridden with an unrelenting cancer. On October 1, my grandpa Hank succumbed—less to his own cancer than to the loss of his oldest son and daughter.

We would never be as close, as free and sure with each other, as we had appeared in all those annual Christmas pictures: Cindy and Dave and Papa Hank all smiling, my great-grandma Anita seated at the center, cousins appended at random, and Andy's dark beard bristling over the last row of heads. After 2012 we stopped taking the group Christmas pictures, certainly because we didn't want to be reminded of the absences. Eventually we settled into a more subdued, sometimes even stilted arrangement—still warm, still together, but ever-conscious of the missing seats at the table, of gaps in conversation where an unforgettable laugh ought to have issued. Even today I still catch myself waiting.

The Human Chain, the Human Hand

TALIA LEANS AGAINST a concrete loading dock and waits for me to park. It is a little after four, November 20, 2020. The sun is almost below the top of the two-story building to my left, which casts an outsize shadow over the pocked expanse of asphalt between us.

We're at the Niagara Frontier Food Terminal, a sixty-acre complex of ten brick-and-concrete buildings dating back to the 1930s.[1] Off the great spoke of Clinton Street—only two miles west of Andy's childhood home on Claude—the NFFT was once one of the busiest commercial hubs in the city.

Tonight only a few panel vans, pickups, and SUVs dot the parking lot, and the terminal's ten separate hubs seem shuttered, facing the faded white teeth of delivery-bay doors toward the sunset. From a peak of sixty-two tenants, the complex now houses just over twenty. There is still a produce co-op, and the largest farmers' market in the region blooms here weekly; there's a winery and a kombucha producer, a sausage maker and a wholesale florist. But most of the space sits unused. Down the halls of each of the buildings, under frosted-glass doors with black block lettering, you can poke a finger through the painted mail slots and take in pill-shaped pictures of the past. Cheap wood paneling glows like white gold in the last of the sun. Metal tanker desks manufactured at federal prisons long ago, now too heavy to cart off, hunker unloved like the sad, patchy bison in the zoo. Fax machines sit at odd angles in the middle of the carpeted floors, unplugged, the less-faded slices of low-pile long protected beneath them finally starting to lose their color.

Our grandmother worked here as a secretary in the 1970s for Louis J. DeCarlo and Son, the region's largest wholesale distributor. She hadn't worked since high school decades before and only took the job after all four of her kids were grown-up enough to walk themselves home and make their own lunches. She once told me that when she and the other women asked for a raise, Jack DeCarlo laughed. "Aren't your husbands making enough to feed you?" he'd asked them.

Down the hall and around the corner from the empty DeCarlo office, Talia unlocks a key to a corner studio. Four hundred square feet with a ten-foot ceiling, light pours in through wide slatted windows facing north and east, a tanker desk between them illuminated by a swing-arm lamp and covered in shavings from an unfinished woodcut. I drop a four-pack of canned margaritas on the desk and take in the rest—a wall covered in Talia's prints, figures reminiscent of Pre-Raphaelite women but scored starkly, somewhere between the style of *The Wind Waker* and a Leyendecker advertisement.

Walmart and Wegmans and their vertical monopolies, the disappearance of neighborhood grocers, the draining of two hundred thousand souls from Buffalo—these forces spelled the end of the NFFT's central role in the region's commerce. Space opened up and rents held steady, or dropped. The grocers left behind their freight lifts, walk-in refrigeration units, truckloads of scrap and spare construction materials, and decades of accumulated artifacts.

And then the artists started moving in.

A better researcher could probably connect a human chain, tracing a continuous movement of Buffalo artists either priced out of a neighborhood they helped to gentrify or escaping a scene that had soured. Buff State students seeking cheap studio space founded Hallwalls. Some of the original Hallwalls crowd from the Essex Art Center founded the East Buffalo Media Association loosely based out of the Dom Polski; some in EBMA and adjacent scenes, like John Toth, Mike Basinski, Brian Duffy, and Andy, landed academic gigs; some of their students opened up new spaces in the city, like the Buff State gang that founded 464 in Black Rock in the 2010s. And so on and so on. Chuck Tingley, from the original 464 contingent, brought one of the first art studios to Larkinville when developers refurbished the former factory at 500 Seneca. At the same time, and just a few blocks north from 464, the late Jonathan Casey brought his studio to the forgotten industrial corridor of Chandler Street just east of Black Rock. Other artists followed (as they always do) and made a community there—long before restaurateur and developer Rocco Termini noticed, bought up all the buildings from end to end, and built "Chandlerville," now an upscale district of brick, with a brewery and pizza spot, a pickling business, a farmers' market, expensive offices, a white napkin restaurant, even a members' only pool.

Now the center of art-making in Buffalo has shifted yet again—seeking always cheaper rents, cheaper beer. It's here, in the NFFT.

Matthew Wattles, descendant of some of the original founders and tenants and part heir to the massive complex, saw a chance to bring new life to Clinton Street without the heavy stepping of conventional redevelopment. Hence the tiny winery and kombuchery—along with the artists.

Casey was one of the first to move his practice here and he was quick to bring others. Wattles and his team started fielding calls and emails, lightly fixing up old offices and storerooms as each new artist committed. Brian Wilcox soon became an evangelist, along with his childhood friend and business partner Jim Sikorski. They started to envision filling the whole place up with dreamers and makers—they talked about holding classes and workshops, hosting cookouts, turning the straight brick walls that line the overgrown freight tracks into an open-air gallery. They started to think about festivals. And they started to make more calls.

Ian de Beer, artist and legendary Buffalo tagger of the aughts, came following Casey. His friend Nick Delfino was next. Then Tingley moved here from Seneca. Then Max Collins, the celebrated wheatpaster, whose work seemed to be everywhere in Buffalo in the 2010s. And the sculptor Rich Tomasello and the oil painter Karen Tashjian.

And, of course, Talia, a printmaker.

We chat until after the sun has set—about her work, about my work, about getting to know her neighbors in the massive complex. The pandemic has prevented large-scale events and tamped down casual socializing, but Wattles, she tells me, wants to host an artists' holiday party anyway. Because, as he knows, as all the tenant-artists know by now, the real work hasn't even started yet. The canvas is the space itself—huge empty marketplaces perfect for collaborations across disciplines. Just like at the icehouse, the Dom Polski, the steel mills and grain silos and barrel factories. It's all happening again, right here. Because the draw, for artists, isn't just cheap rents, cheap beer. It's community.

Artistic communities are simply this: the people whose ideas—and whose love—contextualize your work, your identity, the innumerable futures that radiate ahead of you. I've been lucky to collide with a few people very dear to me who, individually, have always been ready with a candle and a little conversation when I needed it—but I have never experienced the sort of artistic communities that Andy and Cindy created and fostered, repeatedly, in Buffalo, in Brooklyn, and in Callicoon. Deciding shortly after Andy's death that I would be a writer, I passed through my teens and twenties seeking the comfort of a context. Growing up in Buffalo, this has meant a tendency to reach for an idealized past.

"Every generation feels like it just missed something wonderful," Bob Gulley, then seventy-three, whispered to me over the phone. I had been asking him about his decision to leave Buffalo for Greenwich Village. "For me it was the Hallwalls scene," he said. "Cindy Sherman and Robert Longo had just left by the time I got there."

I understood that. I caught the tail end of the 464 crowd, missed the City of Night era at the silos, and lasted through a few sun flares in the Buffalo poetry scene. In 2015 and 2016, after I returned to Buffalo from a year in Europe, a few friends and I even decided to assert our own vision of artistic practice and community in Buffalo with a little magazine we called *Foundlings*, which interspersed approachable poetry and cheekily collaged text and images we found and fancied. But still, like so many others, I couldn't help reaching further back—back to when Robert Creeley read poetry at the Essex St. Pub or Charlie Parker played the Colored Musicians Club.

For my entire adult life, though, that searching nostalgia has been layered with the keener ache of Cindy and Andy's absence.

One of my favorite undergraduate professors, Chris Lee, once told me that my writing is syllogistic and syncretic. I was visiting him during office hours to discuss the latest paper I had handed in, a freewheeling and thin-ice comparison of the poetry of the North Indian mystic saints Kabir and Ravidas with the rappers Q-Tip and Black Thought, a premise I needlessly carpet-bombed with references and bypaths into the tonality of Dorothy Parker vis-à-vis Zack de la Rocha, Rabindranath Tagore as conduit of Kabir's influence on W. B. Yeats, Nirguna and Saguna paradigms of the divine, and Simon and Garfunkel dissing Bob Dylan. Chris loved the paper, not necessarily because of its thesis (which was specious), but because of the harmonies and dissonances of its composition. Chris said that instead of prosecuting a linear argument, I arrange numerous disparate assertions or fields of interest into an idiosyncratic system. Sometimes these systems produce conclusions, sometimes questions.

This was perhaps his gentle way of saying that a conventional path in academia was not open to me. But regardless, the way he characterized my writing—really my mind—felt immediately, luminously true. It's strange to put this into words even now, but when Chris explained myself to me, I felt less alone. This was in part because Chris made me feel known, understood. But it was also because of something Chris couldn't have known he was doing. He had reminded me—powerfully—of Uncle Andy.

That same year—2013—the Burchfield Penney would hold its retrospective exhibition on Andy. In a remembrance on the BP website that year Tony Bannon wrote that Andy "made pictures and performances out of other people's words and numbers."

> Topolski anchored his art in texts as another artist might draw upon the landscape, or the figure, or an apple. The texts that he pictured included the Periodic Table and scientific and political tracts on nuclear energy, armaments, space exploration, and the latitude and longitude of personally and politically important places....
>
> Topolski's works teased out grand notions of organization ... the system bestows upon the letters and numbers that generate the work an inference of vast possibilities, almost a transcendence.

Brian Duffy also contributed an essay for the exhibition. He wrote that Andy's art started to come together conceptually—as a singular, apprehensible style—in 1981 at his exhibit *Neologisms* at the Alamo Gallery at UB. There "he began in earnest to combine graphic images from scientific data and musical notations as well as personal imagery to create work with complex meanings usually based on the potentially destructive nature of man. His inventive nature allowed him to explore and combine seemingly impossible materials and constructions in his work."

Aidan and Andy, early 1990s.

And in 1992 (the year before I was born), Andy himself had explained in an interview: "I use and reuse systems, plotting them on a graph in a progression similar to the way musical notes are plotted. The graph will take an angular or circular shape, and the drawings will evolve from there. There is a translation from text to graph to drawing."

I left Churchill Tower after speaking with Chris, walking across the Canisius quad. The air was clear and occasionally loud with the shouts of day-drinkers on the porches along Glendale and Hughes. We had buried Cindy the previous spring, and now were preparing for Andy's retrospective that the Burchfield Penney would open that summer. Memories of his work flooded into my mind.

Could this context be *mine*? I wondered. Was there some correspondence between my syllogisms and Andy's systems?

The question recurred to me often in the years that followed. When I was a senior, I had a short story accepted in the *Rectangle*, the literary journal of Sigma Tau Delta. In a comment, one of the faculty reviewers from another university wrote that "the writing is beautiful but if the story had a meaning, I missed it." I thought again of Andy. By that point, I knew enough about the art world to think as well of Andy's career.

Then again, years later, after I had returned from Scotland and launched *Foundlings* with my friends, I asked myself the old question another way: Was there some echo of Andy's transcendence via bric-a-brac in the text and visual collages of our little zines?

I think now that it's unlikely: I didn't understand Andy's work as a child and I had not engaged with it deeply enough by the time that, as a teenager and then as an adult, I began to think of writing as a way of living. I think now that it's vain and stupid of me even to keep posing the question. It may have become self-fulfilling, I realize—I may be reaching unconsciously *toward* Andy's style in my writing as a way of fulfilling what this lonely undergraduate once thought was a prophecy. But I have no way of knowing this. The suggestion, never to be resolved, is stuck.

It's easier to see Cindy's guiding hand. In long-ago arguments over the Christmas table I can see, through Cindy, models for both my dogged prosecution of conclusions and my dispassionate willingness to entertain any new idea. And I can see my preferences and imitations among the music that she gave to me or that I took from her—my desire for reinvention in the style of her favorites, Bowie and Dylan; the unapologetic excess of André 3000, fellow Gemini; the stylistic arrangement of my writing in a cross-media lineage with the modal and constant structure compositions of Miles Davis, John Coltrane, and even Radiohead.

Her emails and unexpected packages scored direct hits on my wobbly orbit through adolescence. In fourth grade, I think, Cindy sent me a magnetic poetry kit for my birthday. I had never expressed an interest in poetry. At one point, I remember actually *hating* the gift, which sat unused on a shelf, and later in the back of my closet—a symbol, I thought, of being *unknown* to

Aidan and Cindy, early 1990s.

my aunt. I shiver now at the thought of *how much* she knew—
how much more she would have known.

Then again, I think of a few lines in a note by Christine Burgin,
which appears in a pamphlet on Andy's work produced by the
Galerie von der Tann in Berlin in 1993. Looking at Andy's work,
she says,

> there comes that moment when you want to understand more.
> You want to be able to see more, to be better at looking, but
> you do not know. You know that you will not have to build
> from these plans, that you will not have to find your way with
> these maps, yet you are brought up to know that the kind
> of information given to you … is information given to be
> deciphered: coordinates mark a spot, equations add up and
> arrows indicate a path. So one looks in order to arrive at an
> answer.
>
> But what if there is no answer? What if all this information
> that appears to be so useful is not useful at all?

Judith Brodie, curator at the National Gallery, recognized this, too, and went further. In her note on Andy's *Overground II*, included in the *Century of Drawing* exhibition book, she ventures that Andy's work was actually self-aware of its refusal to render definite answers:

> Andrew Topolski's drawing, which reads like an arcane plan for some mysterious device or project, is executed with a polished precision that implies utter feasibility. The interlocking rings on the left seem charged with energy and radiate a metallic glow, but whether they relate to something material or hypothetical is a question that goes unanswered....
>
> When pressed to explain the work's title and significance (does it relate to "ground zero" or "groundwater," or is it meant paradoxically to call attention to "underground"?), the artist states that his titles and imagery are not meant to be decoded.

Strikingly, Brodie closes on a hallmark of Topolski's work on paper, the "smudges" that complicate the piece's inorganic and otherworldly precision. This, she says, "introduces the element of time, as if the drawing had been handled and scrutinized repeatedly. The smudges are the telltale marks of a human hand, perhaps seeking to sort out the drawing's intention or unscramble its mystery."

I think there is a silent corollary folded into this analysis: for Andy's work, further handling can only yield more smudges. Marks he has invited us to make.

All of This and Nothing

I BUILT AND LIT the fire the last time we visited the house on Seminary Road, July 31, 2012. I built it in the morning, a mug of black coffee waiting on a stump behind me. On the weekend that we would have been celebrating Cindy's fiftieth birthday—three months after we had buried her and only one month after we had interred her brother Dave—my parents, my grandparents, and Uncle Tom and Aunt Barbie worked in the house, dismantling every room, loading furniture into Tom's pickup truck and my dad's black Toyota Highlander, putting pictures and knickknacks into boxes. We took Cindy's oil paintings, or what we recognized, but left Andy's works—sculptures like medieval siege weapons and mixed-media creations that took up whole walls of the house, rippling with mathematical symbols and musical notation, fractured arcs, and deracinated text—for his children, James and Julia, and for old friends with small collections who'd already claimed many of the pieces. Julia, Janine, Ray, and Catherine would follow us the next weekend, closing the house and taking Andy's work to the barn at Janine's place in Ulster County on the other side of the mountains. For two days I fed the fire with paper: junk mail, magazines, empty notebooks, and boxes and boxes of tax returns and documents from Cindy's work as an accountant and bookkeeper.

As we divvied up the furniture and decorations—including dozens of those roosters, for which Cindy had an unexplained affection—I took things, too. Things a nineteen-year-old might take. I snuck into the basement at night and removed a bottle of

Veuve Cliquot, which I saved for a two-day Dave Matthews Band concert I attended in Saratoga with the girl I'd dated for most of my freshman year of college, just a few weeks before we'd break up for the final time. Other selections suggested more foresight. In the attic I went through Cindy's CDs, finding artists and bands I was just then discovering: Bob Dylan's *Bringing It All Back Home*, Graham Nash's *Songs for Beginners*, and David Bowie's *Low*, and things I didn't even recognize, like the Psychedelic Furs's *All of This and Nothing*. I found OutKast's double-album *Speakerboxxx / The Love Below*, which Cindy had brought to play for the adults at Christmas in 2003, mailing me a burned copy a few weeks later. I took DVDs like *The Last Waltz* and *Paris, Texas*. I took books from Cindy and Andy's library that I didn't want, need, or even understand yet, but that I sensed would suggest themselves from my own bookshelf years later, when the time was right: *Wim Wenders on Wim Wenders, Architecture in Switzerland*, and William Shirer's *Rise and Fall of the Third Reich*, two volumes in a weathered black box emblazoned with swastikas and a note in from Cindy in silver Sharpie—*To Andy, Christmas 1980*.

The dead leave to us what they will and we try to make something of it. Sense, and if not sense, something practical. And when we can't make sense or use of what the dead leave to us, sometimes we hang on to their artifacts anyway. We can't help it.

Anyone who has work by Andy or Cindy is proud of it, quick to point it out—like Laura Kramarsky, who told me that she kept and treasured one of Andy's mechanical pieces that she remembered hanging in her father's office; or Eric Siegeltuch, who sent me a picture of one of Cindy's sculptures he'd kept for thirty-five years; or Peter Muscato, who gave me some of Cindy's large architectural drawings that he'd kept in a flat file since the '80s.

Cleaning out the house in Callicoon, Julia invited Amy and Janine to take some of the mixed-media self-portraits Cindy had been working on in her final years—something I didn't know until I reached out to these women, strangers to me, to ask them for their memories. Amy sent pictures over Facebook Messenger, Cindy's pieces not brought out from storage, but shown where they had hung, for almost a decade, on the walls of her apartment.

In 2019, I bought out the Burchfield Penney's entire stock of catalogs from the Zwack–Topolski show when I spotted the orange covers standing out from a clearance rack. In 2017, when I was moving into my first apartment in the States, I visited my grandma's attic and claimed the oil paintings and mixed-media works we had taken from Cindy's studio, planning to hang them in my living room.

Ann Ledy—who is exceptionally circumspect about showing favoritism for any of the faculty she hired—also collected Andy's art, and proudly said to me, "I live with one of Andy's works"— her voice tremulous and impassioned as it passed over "live."

In their art, Andy and Cindy left a lasting communication with the world. I understand why we've tried to gather and protect all that we can. But we treasure and reverence stranger things, too.

My mother wears Cindy's thick silver ring. My aunt Barbie took heart-shaped stones that Cindy collected for her own garden.

Amy and Ian also adopted some of Andy and Cindy's odd collections: four cast-metal dragonflies, three sorghum brooms, two framed pornographic postcards, and a plastic model of Popeye and Olive Oyl.

I still have not read *Wim Wenders on Wim Wenders*. But I will not give it away. Someday, I think, it might give back to me a piece of Cindy and Andy that even today I don't realize I'm missing.

Even Cindy's Facebook, which Uncle Tom managed to memorialize, has become something like a physical artifact, or a gathering place. Friends still wish Cindy a happy birthday there. They like one another's comments. On her birthday the summer that I started this project, July 30, 2020, a man named Antoni writes on one of her profile pictures: *We went out for her 18th birthday & I have loved her all these years.*

In a comment on Andy's online obituary, a former biology teacher at John F. Kennedy in Cheektowaga recalled art projects he made for her classroom and claimed still to possess an ink sketch he'd left to her as a student some forty years before. My father, similarly, saved Andy's *Win, Lose, or Draw* and *Pictionary* sketches from early '90s family game nights—excellently rendered, though he says Andy was a tough pick for a teammate, rarely completing his work before the sands in the little plastic timer ran out.

Julia turned over a banker's box of miscellaneous papers to the Burchfield Penney, which the archivist released to me after I started my research for this book. It was startling to see Cindy's driver's license, Social Security card, and scans of her cancerous thyroid; strange and a little funny to page through manuals for twenty-year-old Nokia phones. Talia took a page of pale pink paper, where either Cindy or Andy left a faint pencil note. Talia put it in a glass and metal frame and hung this by a chain when she moved into her studio at the NFFT. Mysterious, incomplete, inaccessible, it seems to speak past the reader, and trails off into a scribble, not even language. It says:

> I am here
> > you are not—
> > *beautiful*
> > Dreams
> > I Love You—

From artwork to knick-knacks to fifty-year-old scraps—like Ann, we've chosen *to live with it all.*

. . .

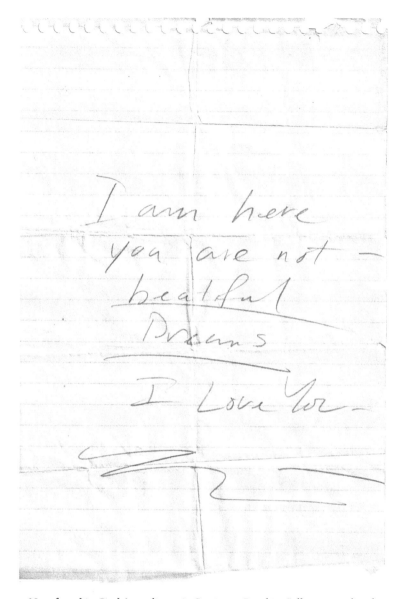

Note found in Cindy's studio at 69 Seminary Road in Callicoon, undated.
Courtesy of Cindy Suffoletto Estate.

My Grandpa Hank had been an unrepentant smoker from before the Korean War until 1998. I helped him quit, unwittingly. I was five years old, the story goes, and had somehow learned about the dangers of tobacco. He was smoking one day inside the house—his own house—when I told him, "You know, you really shouldn't smoke around me."

After that my grandfather, our patriarch, took his cigarettes into the den or outside, and within two years—facing a heart surgery—he quit entirely. I was so young then that I don't really have memories of my grandfather smoking—except for one, not in 1998, but fourteen years later.

That summer afternoon in late July 2012, as we cleaned Cindy's house, I came out onto the porch, maybe carrying some unimportant message, or maybe just to get away from the weight and tension inside. My grandfather was sitting with Keith Manzolillo on the wooden Adirondack chairs that faced the street. I walked out just as Keith, who rolled his own cigarettes from a pale blue tin of American Spirits Original Blend, gestured with his papers at my grandfather and offered to roll one.

"Sure," Hank said.

I knew then that we would lose a third life that summer.

In the back, the fire had swollen into an enormous tumulus of black and gray ash three feet high, which belied an inner furnace that burned through the weekend. Elsewhere in the house, my family was beginning to unravel. And in the attic, stuffing books and CDs into a duffel, I was beginning to perceive the terrifying dimensions of a too-early end. With Andy's passing in 2008 and Cindy's death four years later, I hadn't just lost a beloved aunt and uncle, two people who'd always doted on and taken an interest in me, even from a distance. They had loved me as a nephew and a godson—a child. But I was beginning to become something like a real human being—one really engaging with art for the first time, encountering politics that happened at home and not just on *Meet the Press*, committing to using writing as way not only of expressing myself in the world, but of keeping alive an internal revolution of new ideas displacing old. At the close of the last long weekend at the house on Seminary Road, as I used a shovel to spread the warm ashes of a lifetime of incident over the fire pit, I felt something that I couldn't then articulate. It was this: that the intractable difficulty of loss doesn't lie in retrospect, in remembering the departed, but in a perpetual and evolving present—not in remembering but in imagining each new iteration of a relationship that will never materialize, a relationship arrested in the receding past. At nineteen, at twenty-one, at thirty, what matters most isn't that I lost an aunt and uncle—it's that I lost two people who could have become some of my closest friends.

Something of me ended there in that *could have become*—a place totally frozen, at a distance clouded over but close-up cross-hatched with bonded hexagons in an infinite, static lattice.

Something of me ended there, with them, but did not die.

Epilogue

IN THE SPRING OF 2023, after I have completed most of the research for this book, Keith Manzolillo mentions to me that he has held onto a box of Cindy's artwork in one of his cattle barns in Missouri. He offers to move it to Callicoon, where he still has family; if I want, I can pick it up.

I rent a car in Manhattan and drive northwest, headed for the second time in less than a year to a place that, before all this, I hadn't seen in a decade. I don't know what Keith has kept; I imagine a few oil paintings and collages on paper.

Across from the Callicoon train depot Keith's sister Debbie, a lifer, hands over two cardboard boxes. Inside I find nearly forty works preserved between wax paper. They are collages using photography—in many cases self-portraits of Cindy in various positions—along with found imagery and found items from her environment in Callicoon: preserved bugs, bone, stone, twine, fish scales. I realize that Cindy had produced this series—visually provoking, conceptually mature, referentially diverse, and unnervingly unguarded—in the four years after Andy's death, and following a nearly fifteen-year break without her own active studio practice of any kind. I found no evidence that she had exhibited or even told anyone about this work.

In this moment, I also think of Andy's enormous artistic output. Though I had begun informally to catalog Andy's and Cindy's works as part of my research, it was clear—and remains clear—that scores if not hundreds of pieces are unaccounted for: in private collections, in unknown museums, in storage.

I began this project because I loved two people whom I had lost, and who continue to exert a gravitational influence on my thinking and writing. But as I let go of this book, increasingly I think of them impersonally, as the artists they were and chose to be.

Andrew Topolski was one of the most original minds and exceptional talents of his generation. Today, his output is underappreciated and his influence largely unrecognized. His proper place is not in a nephew's searching memoir, but in exhibitions, in reviews, in art history books. (And perhaps also in an airport concourse.)

Cindy Suffoletto deserves recognition not only as Andy's rock and confidant—though this is important—but as an artist herself, with far more talent than time, whose works, distributed unevenly over the less than five decades of her life, and likely less than two decades of active practice, will yield delights and insights once touched by the critical attention that for so long passed her over.

If nothing else, my hope is that this book offers a lighted signpost toward their work, which for almost half a century has at turns transfixed, charged, troubled, and comforted those lucky few who've known where to find it.

Acknowledgments

THIS PROJECT REINFORCED the lesson that any endeavor in the arts eventually requires the support of friends, family, and an expanding community of shared interest in the work. I saw this play out again and again in Andy and Cindy's lives while, in parallel, I was benefiting from the same kind of support—sometimes even from the same individuals.

I am particularly grateful to the many members of my family who contributed to this project, and especially to my grandmother Annette and my mom, Sandy, my father, Dan, and my sister Talia—and to the broader family who have supported me as they supported Andy and Cindy. I am grateful to this book's many living sources, including Anthony Bannon, Stefan von Bartha, Diane Bertolo, Jessica Berwind, Judith Brodie, Charlie Clough, Brian Duffy, Douglas Eklund, Christiane Fischer-Harling, Richard Furman, Bob Gulley, Charlotta Kotik, Petr Kotik, Tom Kotik, Laura Kramarsky, Ann Ledy, Robert Longo (in his way), Petr Mayr, Pieter and Marina Meijer, Don Metz, Marilynn Mendell, Amy Milner, Ian Milner, Peter Muscato, Michael Randazzo, Raymond Saá, Christel Schüppenhauer, Eric Siegeltuch, Eric Stark, Iris von der Tann (in her way), Tom Topolski, Ron Topolski, Alex Topolski, Janine Tramontana, James Tunkey, Michael Tunkey, and many others for spending collectively hundreds of hours in conversation with me, sharing their memories and several shoves in the right direction; Scott Propeack, Tullis Johnson, Tom Holt, and Heather Gring at the Burchfield Penney Art Center, who spent several hours with me in conversation, showing me Andy's works in the vault, and allowing me to work with Andy's archive; Ed Cardoni and John Massier at Hallwalls for sharing their exhaustive knowledge of the Buffalo avant-garde and its diaspora; Mary Helen Miskuly at the Castellani Art Museum at Niagara University for sharing important records related to Armand Castellani; and Robert Pohl and Aaron Bartley, who together comprise most of the living memory and history of Buffalo poetics and the broader Buffalo avant-garde, roughly 1962 to the present. I am also indebted to numerous curators and registrars at museums holding Andy's work, including Caitlin Brague at the National Gallery of Art in Washington, DC, who allowed me to view Andy's work *Overground II* (along with my dear friend Joe Morra, who accompanied me there); Indira Abiskaroon and the whole staff at the Brooklyn Museum, who were able to welcome me into the vault and to set up a private, one-hour installation of Andy's sculpture *The 9th Power*; and Mara Gordon for assistance with cataloging works by Andy and Cindy. Countless others provided indirect aid. I am grateful to Roísín Ní Mhórdha at Nine River Road in Callicoon, New York, for her hospitality and conversation; to Yael/Jennifer Feinerman for welcoming me back to 69 Seminary Road, and for being a good steward of the property; to Joe Lin-Hill for his advice and support; to Bob Mecoy for suggestions on an early draft of the manuscript; and to Mark E. Dellas and Mark A. Dellas for their trust, talents, and artistic partnership; to Adam Kreutinger, for his charisma, uniqueness, nerve, and talent; to Max Crinnin and Sam Edwards, heart-companions, who have provided something like an artistic agenbite of inwit when I most needed it; and to Steven J. Coffed—more than a friend, more than a brother—one of the few true constants in my life for going on two decades. I have benefitted from the example and attention of many excellent teachers, too many to name; here I thank Mick Cochrane, for his mentorship, friendship, and generous example—for teaching me not only how to write, but how to be a writer in the world. Once the manuscript was (more or less) finished, another brilliant team assembled to bring it into the world. Thank you Jim McCoy for taking a chance on an unknown debut author and his little-known subjects and for imagining a reader at the end of each one of this book's vectors; thank you Alisha Gorder for helping to find them; and thank you Susan Hill Newton, Allison Means, Nola Burger, Nathan MacBrien, and the entire team at the University of Iowa Press for your creativity, energy, and genuine investment in this project. And I am grateful—every day—for Rachelle Toarmino, my first reader, last word, and love.

Finally, I am eternally grateful to Cindy and Andy, whose attention, encouragement, and example have kept me going all these years.

Notes

EULOGY.DOC

1. The quote is most commonly attributed to Maya Angelou. However, *Richard Evans' Quote Book*, a collection of aphorisms from prominent members of the Church of Jesus Christ of Latter-Day Saints, published in 1971, attributes it to Carl W. Buehner, a high-ranking member of the Mormon "Brethren" and 1968 Republican candidate for governor of Utah. (He lost to incumbent Democrat Cal Rampton.)

BEGINNINGS ON ESSEX

1. Hallwalls now occupies Ani DiFranco's Babeville, a concert hall and arts hub in a former church at the corner of Delaware and Tupper.
2. In 2021, Buffalo Institute for Contemporary Art (BICA) succeeded Big Orbit in what was originally the Hallwalls gallery space.

BYWAY: A FRACTIONAL HISTORY OF MONEY, IDEAS, AND ART IN BUFFALO

1. Born in the Eggert-Kensington neighborhood of Buffalo, Charlie had taken advertising art at Hutch Tech high school and dreamed of being an illustrator. By the time he got to Pratt for his foundations year in 1969, he realized the golden age of illustration was over. He flirted with conceptual art and earth art; he read *Walden* and *On the Road*; he sought a counterweight to the crits and their bullshit in the Craftsman scene. One year later he'd broken up with his girlfriend, moved back in with his parents in Buffalo, and sworn he'd make art without ever touching another paintbrush. In reality he spent much of his time looking for jobs at ad agencies, taking the bus to East Aurora to wait tables at the Roycroft Inn, and hitchhiking back to New York in an effort to stay "plugged in."
2. It was a symbol, a signal, a red herring. In his book *Art Will*, Clough describes it as a sacrament in St. Augustine's language—"an outward and

visible sign of my newfound inward and spiritual grace"—intended "to convince both myself and Buffalo's art-loving public that I was, in fact, an artist." Clough, *Art Will: A Fifty-Year Odyssey from Hallwalls to the Roycroft* (Warren, CT: Floating World Editions, 2021), p. 7.

3. Charlie is dating Diane; Michael is dating Nancy; Robert is dating Cindy. It was a "heterosexual" scene, one participant recalled in an interview for the retrospective publication *Consider the Alternatives: 20 Years of Contemporary Art at Hallwalls* (Buffalo: Hallwalls Contemporary Art Center, 1996).

4. The Goodyear family is not known for this address, and the house no longer stands. In 1903 the Goodyears moved into 888 Delaware Avenue, a Châteauesque estate built by E. B. Green at the center of the city's Millionaires' Row. Conger lived at 888 Delaware until his marriage in 1908, when he and his first wife, Martha Forman, built a house at 160 Bryant.

5. Conger's father, Charles W. Goodyear, left a thriving career in law—during which he replaced Grover Cleveland as a name partner at a Buffalo firm when Cleveland left to serve as New York State governor—to build lumber, coal, and railway businesses. He and his brother Frank had extensive lumber operations in New York and Pennsylvania, using new railroad technologies and rail spurs to access previously isolated areas of woodland. Establishing the Great Southern Lumber Company, they created the company town of Bogalusa, Louisiana, for their workers, developing everything from housing and hotels to churches and a YMCA/YWCA from the ground up. The mill at Bogalusa was the largest in the world. Meanwhile Charles remained active in politics as a close confidant of Grover Cleveland, helping to orchestrate his gubernatorial election and pave the way for his ascent to the White House, where Charles and his wife Ella were the Clevelands' first guests.

6. "An explosion in a shingle factory" remains the most memorable epithet leveled by the New York press at this high achievement of cubism.

7. The social history of Buffalo's aristocracy is a story of sometimes polite and sometimes rancorous schisms, much like the Presbyterian and Episcopalian churches to which the elite, for most of the city's history, exclusively belonged.

In 1867 a group of notable Buffalonians, including former US President Millard Fillmore, founded the Buffalo Club, the city's first social organization, eventually moving into the home of the postwar industrialist Stephen Van Rensselaer Watson at 388 Delaware Avenue, where it remains today. Reading the early membership rolls is like reading a city map: Richmond, Cary, Rumsey, Sidway, Statler, Spaulding, Porter, Fargo, Jewett, and so on.

A generation later, in 1885, the rising scions decided they wanted a less formal place to socialize. While many retained memberships in their "fathers' club," they formed a second fraternity based on the "university clubs" popular at the time, eventually building a Tudor-style clubhouse at 977 Delaware. They played bridge; they drank; they decorated their wood-paneled halls with literary mottoes: "And the best of all ways / To lengthen our days / Is to steal a few hours from the night"; and "Where the women cease from troubling and the wicked are at rest" (lately modified).

The wicked did rest a good long while under Saturn's protection—until Prohibition.

On August 29, 1923, William J. "Wild Bill" Donovan, district attorney of Buffalo, decorated World War I veteran, and future father of the CIA—and at the time a Saturn Club member—directed federal agents to raid the club, where they discovered, according to court documents, sixty quarts of whiskey, a similar amount of gin, five gallons of moonshine, and bottles of champagne, vermouth, and other liquors. These were not in the club's cellars but in the private lockers of prominent club members, among them the industrialist George A. Forman, banker (and future art collector) Seymour H. Knox II, poet and Congressman Peter A. Porter, Clarence Sidway, and the clubhouse architect, Duane Lyman.

The Saturn Club was no longer safe for merrymaking, and the mottoes on its walls rang hollow. Three years after Donovan's raid, grandsons of the Saturn Club's founders (and great-grandsons of the Buffalo Club's founders) split off to form a new and even more exclusive group, and sought a less conspicuous clubhouse where they might drink and play their cards unmolested.

Chuck Ramsdell, Bert Fenton, Joe Cary, and Frank Goodyear Jr. were among the founders of the Pack Corporation, or the Pack Club, in 1926, according to the few club documents that have, over the years, slipped out of members' possession. According to these documents, the club's purpose was for its members "to gather in the long winter evenings to play bridge and exchange current gossip and news of the day in secluded surroundings, 'far from the madding crowd.'"

Not too far, though. Once E. B. Green Jr. joined his father's famed architecture practice, he needed more than the modest trappings of his home at 164 Elmwood Avenue. But the apprentice architect's starter home was perfect for an exclusive club, a Prohibition-era watering hole for the second- and third- and fourth-generation elite, hidden in plain sight. So the Pack Club purchased it.

8. The Wilcox house had served as the inauguration site for Teddy Roosevelt after President William McKinley's assassination, cementing old Ansley in national and local memory. Wilcox would continue to exert an influence as the century matured, even departing the frontier to join in pitched battle with New York City's Bob Moses, as memorably chronicled by Robert A. Caro in *The Power Broker: Robert Moses and the Fall of New York* (New York: Knopf, 1974).

9. "Ostracized for a Picasso," Goodyear told a crowd at the University at Buffalo in 1951.

10. Knox's father raised horses on the family estate in East Aurora, where the younger Seymour learned to play. With the stature of a jockey—he was around 5'4"; close friends called him "Shorty"—Seymour took his team to the US championship in 1932 and went on to play at the highest levels in Europe and South America. He gave up polo in the '60s.

11. These trips were remarkably fruitful. Gordon Smith would typically visit a gallery first, often at Martha's suggestion, and if a work passed muster, he would set up a private viewing for Seymour. Consider these donations Knox made *in a single day*: Arshile Gorky's *The Liver Is the Cock's Comb*, 1944; Jackson Pollock's *Convergence*, 1952; Franz Kline's *New York, N.Y.*, 1953; Adolph Gottlieb's *Frozen Sounds II*, 1952; Sam Francis's *Blue-Black*, 1952; and Mark Rothko's *Orange and Yellow*, 1956. Some of these came from auction houses, some from galleries, and some from the artists themselves. Knox's purchases from Martha Jackson's gallery alone include works by Francis Bacon, Willem de Kooning, Richard Diebenkorn, Helen Frankenthaler, Grace Hartigan, Hans Hofmann, Jasper Johns, Lee Krasner, Roy Lichtenstein, Marisol, Agnes Martin, Joan Mitchell, Robert Motherwell, Bridget Riley, David Smith, Clyfford Still, and Andy Warhol.

12. The Knox-Smith-Jackson combo arguably played an even greater role than the CIA in cementing the global reputation—and value—of American abstract expressionist art and artists. In these movements Seymour's predecessor found the limits of the tastes he'd developed at the *Armory Show*: Conger worried about "the charlatan under the Modern mantle" and wasted no time on the "drip and scribble schools." Richard Huntington, "The Albright-Knox's 'A. Conger Goodyear Collection,' One Patron's Vision of the Future," *The Buffalo News*, August 4, 1996.

13. This is essentially a direct quote from Petr Kotik, who told me this in a phone call June 16, 2021. His estimation is unchallenged.

14. The phrase is sometimes attributed to Rockefeller and sometimes attributed to Martin Meyerson, president of UB during the turbulent years of 1966 through 1970.

15. Coincidentally, these two aspects came together in the person of Nelson Rockefeller, who would direct huge sums of money to the arts as governor of New York, as president of the Rockefeller Brothers Fund, and as a Rockefeller of considerable influence in the family foundation.

16. In addition to the College of Arts and Sciences, President Meyerson approved several more loosely defined "colleges" organized around collectivist or anarchist principles or disciplines and interests such as women's studies, lesbian studies, Black studies, and so on. See Jennifer Wilson, "The Unlikely History of Tolstoy College," *New Yorker*, January 19, 2016.

17. The quaint lanes of single-family homes had been built on former farmland before the Great War. It began on University, Radcliffe, and Larchmont; then in the '20s, propelled by automobiles built at Buffalo's Pierce-Arrow factory or Albert Kahn's Ford plant a few blocks south on Main Street, the neighborhood crossed Niagara Falls Boulevard northward to Pelham, Allenhurst, and Capen.

18. According to Linda Brooks in her book *Proximities*, the collective Ant Farm buried a Dodge Cruiser station wagon filled with artifacts of the mid '70s. They intended to dig up their time capsule in 2000, make any necessary repairs, and drive it to California. However, leaders at Artpark forgot about the car and only confirmed its existence with the help of local geology professors and their radar equipment in 2018. Artpark's board is still considering the cost and environmental impact of exhuming the station wagon, which now sits beneath a hill used for seating at summer concerts. Unfortunately, the same conservative legislators who championed Artpark were less enthusiastic about its early attraction for the avant-garde, and they influenced its movement toward outdoor concerts, family-friendly theater, and crafts. See Linda Brooks, *Proximities: Art, Education, Activism* (Minneapolis: TC Photo, 2020).

19. Dan Robinson, chair of painting at UB, and Duayne Hatchett, chair of sculpture, were early Essex Art Center tenants. Duayne brought two of his TAs, Joe Panone and Andy Topolski. Joe in turn brought his student Robert Longo.

20. In a nod both to the economic imperatives of student work and to the principle of site-specific material selection, Roger constructs one of his pieces from fence posts that had formed a retaining wall at the Crosby Loop on UB's South Campus, demolished to accommodate the southernmost metro stop.

21. Like Charlotta Kotik, Linda Cathcart would be a significant influence on Hallwalls and on local artists generally during her time as a

curator at the Albright-Knox. She went on to serve as executive director of the Contemporary Arts Museum Houston (CAMH) from 1979 to 1987; while there she put on the first solo museum exhibition of Cindy Sherman and her film *Stills* (1979). She later opened her own gallery in Santa Barbara and eventually founded and ran Casa Dolores: Center for the Study of the Popular Arts of Mexico, an institution built around her personal collection. She died in 2017 and was lauded by artists, curators, and civic leaders for her leadership, support, and open-mindedness.

22. Carol Kino, "Renaissance in an Industrial Shadow," *New York Times*, 2 May 2012, a feature on the Albright-Knox's show *Wish You Were Here: The Buffalo Avant-Garde in the 1970s*.

23. "[Other] people didn't really have ideas," Charlie explains to me. "Except Petr Kotik. He had all the fucking ideas in the world."

24. The concept allowed them to feature more work at a lower cost.

I BLAME YOU FOR ALL THE GOOD IN OUR FAMILY

1. As a teenager I did the simple math and realized the Donarumas and Manellas had operated a "tavern" during Prohibition. I pressed my great-grandmother on this point one Easter dinner, and she conceded the operation's questionable legality—and further confirmed that her earliest dates with John were often to the city's popular speakeasies.

2. I didn't think to read my great-grandfather's obituary until I began this project: "JOHN C. DONARUMA DIES AT 78; BARKEEPER KNOWN AS 'MY CARD.'" I hadn't realized that the joke became his nickname—well-known enough to make the obit's headline—but I did remember my father adding to the story that eventually, when too many friends and acquaintances were in on the joke, they would rebuff the offer. ("Oh, I've got your card, John. Wouldn't leave home without it"—maybe even retrieving the yellowed, crinkled thing from a moneyclip or a wallet.) John would protest ("No, no, my new card") until he'd forced a surrender and could hand over a crisp 3.5" × 2" note. Of course it read "My New Card."

3. Hengerer's would merge with Sibley's in 1981 and disappear completely by 1987, shoppers leaving behind the great nineteenth-century palaces of Buffalo's flush past for the Walden Galleria, the Boulevard, the Eastern Hills, the McKinley, stores like cooled shoeboxes with cluttered clearance sections at the back.

1. "I felt like I didn't want to fuck with Cindy, I didn't want to cross her," Jessica clarifies—though she can't remember any specific incident that gave her the impression. Still, it's consistent with other descriptions of Cindy, and consistent, too, with my mother: it's true to say of both sisters that one doesn't have to guess about their affection (or their distaste).

2. If Andy sought to explain—in his art—the role of urban planning in his collision with Cindy in 1980, he might have pulled a red thread taut around three pins, the first two at his and Cindy's childhood homes on McKinley and Claude in Buffalo, and the third some 400 miles away on the brown banks of the Potomac, near what is today the intersection of Thirty-First and K Streets NW in Washington, DC. It was there, on March 9, 1791, that the French engineer Pierre Charles L'Enfant rented a room from the innkeep John Suter and started work on his plan for the US Capitol, casting onto a slip of Chesapeake swamp an unprecedented vision of circles and "grand avenues" along the hypotenuses of tessellated right-triangles. The brothers Ellicott—Andrew, Benjamin, and Joseph—finished L'Enfant's work, and the youngest took this experience north to his next commission: Buffalo.

3. The placement of the Erie Canal's western terminus determined the fates of these two cities: Buffalo annexed Black Rock in 1853.

4. This, too, is an economic tale. The Iroquois Confederacy turned belligerent in an effort to control the European fur market. At the same time, the British and French vented their hostilities through proxy contests, enlisting numerous Native American allies on both sides, around the Great Lakes and St. Lawrence River Valley. The "Beaver Wars," initiated for territory and monopoly, descended into genocide, as the Iroquois eliminated or absorbed once-peaceful neighbors.

5. No living source could say why Andy left the program at Michigan, but in a notebook in the Burchfield Penney archives I discover what appears to be the longhand draft of a letter Andy intended to send to Michigan. Dated a few years after he had left, the letter contests the school's attempt to extract payment from him, and indicates that he departed very early after discovering the school would not grant him the financial aid that he had anticipated.

6. Bethune Hall was originally a plant of the Buffalo Meter Company—a "daylight factory" in the region's industrial vernacular, featuring an exposed concrete frame filled with transparent glazing. The style developed from progressive intentions to expose laborers to natural light. When the University at Buffalo acquired the building in 1970, the school

christened it after Buffalo's Louise Blanchard Bethune, the first female professional architect and the first woman named fellow of the American Institute of Architects. The school moved out in the mid-1990s, and the building became an underground (illegal) exhibition space for the city's graffiti artists. In 2010 Ciminelli Real Estate redeveloped the site into eighty-seven upscale loft apartments, with rents ranging from $950 to 2,000 per month.

7. McIvor was nationally recognized as a painter, though he taught printmaking at UB. This was a side gig: he chaired the graduate art program at Buffalo State, where Cindy would enroll in 1980.

EBMA

1. Joan's family dentist, Dr. Shelsky, had introduced her parents to the Mazurs when Joan was a child. By then J. C. and Steffe Mazur had moved from the East Side into an old stone mansion on West Ferry—"huge, gray, with high ceilings." She remembers the Mazurs as fascinating, full of life, unlike other adults she knew. Without children of their own, they doted on Joan. J. C. showed her his sketches for stained-glass commissions. In the front hall hung an arresting portrait of Steffe. Andy knew Steffe, too, perhaps through his aunt Genevieve.

2. Patti Smith, *Just Kids*. New York City: Ecco, 2010. p. 174

3. These are just a few of UB's contemporary classical heavyweights, the likes of which would never again assemble in one place. Lukas Foss, founder of the famed Creative Associates, would later orchestrate a laser show for the Grateful Dead. Morton Feldman, pioneer of indeterminate music, was developing wholly novel forms of musical notation during the same period that he frequented the Dom. Closest to Andy were the S.E.M. Ensemble cofounders Petr Kotik, who had emigrated in '69 from Eastern Bloc Czechoslovakia, and Julius Eastman, who would leave Buffalo after enraging John Cage (a frequent visitor to the University at Buffalo, collaborator with UB faculty member Morton Feldman, and June in Buffalo Faculty Composer beginning in 1975) with an explicitly homo-erotic interpretation of the latter's *Songbooks*. Eyewitnesses recount that Cage remained visibly rattled even the next day—uncharacteristically for the famous contemplative. See biographer Renee Levine Packer's *Gay Guerilla: Julius Eastman and His Music* (Rochester, NY: University of Rochester Press, 2018); and critic Jeff Simon's "Great American Classical Composers—Under Duress," *Buffalo News*, July 31, 2016.

4. See Dick Higgins, *Intermedia, Fluxus and Something Else Press:*

Selected Writings by Dick Higgins, ed. Steve Clay and Ken Freidman (Catskill: Siglio Press, 2018), esp. "Intermedia" (24–29) and "Intending" (36–41).

5. The "social problems that characterize our time, as opposed to the political ones, no longer allow a compartmentalized approach. We are approaching the dawn of a classless society, to which separation into rigid categories is absolutely irrelevant.... Castro works in the cane fields. New York's Mayor Lindsay walks to work during the subway strike. The millionaires eat their lunches at Horn and Hardart's. This sort of populism is a growing tendency rather than a shrinking one." (Higgins, "Intermedia," 23).

6. Dick Higgins, "Games of Art," *The Something Else Newsletter* 1, no. 2 (March 1966).

7. "Buffalo had a huge impact on who I became," Larry told me. He would go on to make a name as a film and TV art director and set designer, with credits including *ER* and *High Fidelity*.

8. The performers were Sally Rubin, Eberhard Blum, Donald Knaack, and Jan Williams, and the exhibition (for lack of a better word) included works by Hugo Ball, Raoul Hausmann, Marcel Duchamp, and Kurt Schwitters. https://www.hallwalls.org/perflit/287.html.

9. "Tony Bannon on Andy Topolski (1952–2008)," Burchfield Penney Art Center, Monday, July 8, 2013. https://www.burchfieldpenney.org/general/blog/article:07-12-2013-12-00am-tony-bannon-on-andy-topolski-1952-2008/.

10. Longo, Bannon told me, never hesitated to call Andy "the smartest one of us."

HARD CHOICES

1. The purchaser, "a long-standing client of Sotheby's," the auction house confirmed, had the last laugh, of course: the semi-shredded piece leapt in value at once. The purchase confirmed—and ratified by Pest Control, Banksy's authentication service—representatives of Sotheby's immediately began to crow about the piece's place, and theirs, in "the pages of art history." The work, since renamed *Love Is in the Bin*, was on loan to Staatsgalerie Stuttgart before selling in 2021 for $25.4 million, an auction record for Banksy.

2. If these troubling questions weren't clear enough when *Comedian* first made headlines, they would become starker still. The Georgian-American artist David Datuna waltzed into Perrotin, removed the banana from the wall, peeled it, and ate it. An accomplice filmed it for Instagram. The

action shocked most witnesses, but apparently not Emmanuel Perrotin: the French gallerist quickly reassured visitors and prospective buyers that the physical banana was not intrinsic to *Comedian*'s value. He was in harmony with Cattelan on this point: the artist issued certificates of authenticity to all three buyers (including Colette founder Sarah Andelman and Billy and Beatrice Cox), noting that they are free to replace their bananas as frequently as nature and their noses might require. The episode only ended after the gallery covered up a second "intervention": an unknown visitor, voicing one of the most popular memes of the day, took lipstick to the spot on Perrotin's wall where *Comedian* had hung, writing "Epstien [sic] didn't kill himself." Caroline Goldstein, "The Artist and Jeffrey Epstein Truther Who Vandalized Maurizio Cattelan's Banana Booth Defends Himself in Court," *artnet*, January 2, 2020.

3. This appears to be an aberration: Buffalo returned to form in the 2024 census, showing a modest decline of 1.3 percent.

4. Freudenheim was a lifelong friend and supporter of numerous nationally recognized artists with Western New York ties. Her death on April 12, 2020, at eighty-three, meant the closure of Buffalo's only major commercial art gallery and the end of an era of inestimable influence. Though I frequented her gallery between 2016 and 2020, Nina and I never exchanged more than a few words about my aunt and uncle. She had one solo show for Andy and "essentially represented him in Buffalo" after he left for New York, Peter Muscato told me, but several sources shared vague accounts of their eventual falling out. I began this project only three months after her death.

5. Robert "Mack" McCloskey Mahoney (1928–2003) is probably best described as a Buffalo cultural gadabout. The World War II Navy veteran, featherweight boxer, folksinger, coffee shop proprietor, chair of English at Buffalo Seminary, local Green Party leader, *Buffalo News* arts contributor, and antiwar activist was also father to the artist Lisa Toth and father-in-law to her husband, John.

6. The Park Slope Walsh describes to me is hard to imagine. Once a Gilded Age suburb, and today one of the wealthiest neighborhoods in New York, Walsh said that while he lived there, Park Slope was a pocket of violence and drug crime, where muggings and shootings happened nightly. Even then, though, the Italian, Irish, and African-American neighborhood gangs that warred with each other nightly were losing a different kind of battle to the young professionals, drawn by artists like Walsh, who were renovating the district's brownstones at an accelerating pace, casting themselves into the velvet past.

TANGENTS

1. Chris Kraus, "You Are Invited to Be the Last Tiny Creature," in *Where Art Belongs* (South Pasadena: Semiotext(e), 2011), 9–43.

MAGIC GEOMETRY

1. Schultz would lead the Albright-Knox for almost two decades (December 9, 1983–October 1, 2002), and he would do much to position it as a durable contemporary institution. His tenure saw the acquisition of some 1,200 contemporary works, the growth of the endowment by 400 percent, an $8.4 million renovation, and the addition of Clifton Hall to the campus. His was also a comparatively untroubled reign, despite coinciding with a decline in state funding for the arts. Schultz's successor, Louis Grachos, would spark a board revolt and ignite enduring controversy with a choice to sell off (at a poor price) the bulk of the museum's world-class collection of art not legibly "contemporary."

2. Eric had independent tastes and rigorous principles—the qualities that drove him to open his own gallery and then, after his partner left, to keep it going himself—but his pedigree was impeccable. He graduated from Colby College in 1969 (after a roving undergraduate career that saw him attempt to weld together the philosophy, politics, and economics and art history tracks at Oxford) and went on to Columbia. He had worked at the Guggenheim and served as director and curator at various smaller galleries before opening his own space.

3. Michael Brenson, "WHAT'S UP UPTOWN; Art: In Galleries, a Personal Touch," *New York Times*, May 10, 1985.

4. The *Times* "Spring Salutes" section, June 9, 1986, described a typical happening at the Oscarsson-Siegeltuch Gallery—a "cocktail buffet" featuring Carmen Cicero's jazz quartet, with tickets at $75 a pop, to benefit the Fine Arts Work Center in Provincetown, MA.

5. This interview is accessible in full at the Pollock-Krasner House and Study Center. Mary Gabriel reports this excerpt in her book *Ninth Street Women* (New York: Back Bay Books, 2018), 190.

6. Charlotta explained this in a filmed interview in her ground-floor Cobble Hill, Brooklyn, apartment on Friday, August 16, 2024.

EIGHTY PERCENT

1. I owe this insight and the "cocreator" label to my friend Joe Hassett and his book *The Ulysses Trials* (Dublin: Lilliput Press, 2016). See "Margaret Anderson's Gospel of Beauty Meets John Quinn," 26.

2. Wynn served as a special assistant in the Lindsay administration; as the mayor's representative on the powerful Board of Estimate he helped to consolidate an inefficient tangle of municipal agencies and institutions into what is today NYC Health + Hospitals. He opened a management consulting firm in 1970 but returned to government in 1975, when Carey picked him to head the state's human rights division. There, Wynn significantly expanded the scope of human rights protections statewide with his decisions in several pivotal discrimination cases—including, according to his *Times* obituary, "that a minimum height requirement for male prison guards was discriminatory; that the New York City Marathon must allow competitors in wheelchairs to participate; that tennis clubs could not offer discounts for married couples; and that job applicants could not be denied work simply for being obese or drug users in treatment." Sam Roberts, "Werner Kramarsky, Rights Official and Arts Patron, Dies at 93," *New York Times*, August 23, 2019.

3. Joachim Homann, "Remembering Drawings Collector Werner H. Kramarsky (1926–2019)," Harvard Art Museums, November 22, 2019. https://harvardartmuseums.org/article/remembering-drawings-collector-werner-h-kramarsky-1926-2019.

4. Andrew Russeth, "Wynn Kramarsky, Venturesome Drawings Collector and Arts Patron, Is Dead at 93," *ARTnews*, August 23, 2019. https://www.artnews.com/art-news/news/wynn-kramarsky-dead-13143/.

5. This was certainly true. Although they eventually drifted apart, in the early years after closing his gallery Eric made a new start with Eric Siegeltuch Fine Arts, a consultancy focused on career management and financial planning for artists. He continued to take an interest in Andy's work. As late as August 24, 1990, he would write to Wynn—"I just came from Andy Topolski's studio yesterday, and was bowled over by the new body of work. He is just irrepressible!" Though he wasn't Andy's agent, he thanked Wynn for his recent offer to put out a catalog of Andy's work—presumably the catalog that would accompany the touring show led by the Galerie von der Tann the following year.

6. As of this writing the record holder is Gustav Klimt's *Portrait of Adele Bloch-Bauer I*, which sold in 2006 for $135 million.

7. MoMA Archives, Werner H. Kramarsky Papers, I.555, Topolski, Andrew: Correspondence.

8. His daughter Laura sent me a detailed spreadsheet confirming this.

9. Letters indicate Wynn acted as Andy's agent in certain circumstances. As early as 1987 the record reveals him purchasing Andy's drawings on behalf of wealthy and influential friends, including Alexander "Sandy" Cortesi, an early software entrepreneur and New School of

Design trustee living at the posh 829 Park Avenue, and Robert Felner, a MoMA donor from the other side of Central Park, at 55 West Seventy-Fifth Street. MoMA Archives, Werner H. Kramarsky Papers, I.555, Topolski, Andrew: Correspondence.

INVENTING MOTION / MOVING TARGETS

1. The *Phoenix* went defunct in 1998. A partial archive exists at the New York State Library in Albany and the clip is available online at https://nyshistoricnewspapers.org/?a=d&d=pho19870903-01 (see p. 14).

2. Gabriel, *Ninth Street Women*.

ARRIVALS

1. His much closer resemblance to Mark Ruffalo would become obvious a few years later, when the latter appeared as the Hulk in *The Avengers*.

2. Patti Smith, *Just Kids*. New York City: Ecco, 2010. p. 152.

GIVE US BARRABAS!

1. Martino was an appointed NFTA commissioner, head of the local CWA union chapter, and later a member of the Buffalo Common Council for the South District. She served as a board member of the Buffalo Philharmonic Orchestra and head of the local arts council, then a political position distributing patronage from NYSCA.

2. There is no evidence of controversy at the time of the selection, but history has recognized the choice as representative of the region's conservatism. Reviewing Topolski's 2013 show at the Burchfield Penney, which included the airport proposal, *Buffalo News* art critic Colin Dabkowski called Andy's proposal "ambitious and beautifully rendered" and "meticulously plotted," compared to Calvo's "tamer concept."

AMERICANS ABROAD

1. The Museum Ostwall is housed at the top of the Dortmunder U—a former storage facility for the massive Union Brewery, characterized, as its name suggests, by a giant, four-sided "U" shape appended to the top.

2. My research in the Kramarsky files at MoMA suggest this refers to Patrice Landau, once proprietor of Gallery Lavignes Bastille at 27 Rue de Charonne in Paris. In February 1992 Landau approached Andy about producing limited edition prints of work he was then displaying at the

Elga Wimmer Gallery. Cindy handled the transaction with counsel from Wynn, who connected her with a lawyer. According to the agreement Landau would pay Andy $24,000 in monthly installments of $1,000 for the right to produce the limited-edition prints. It is unclear whether Landau ever produced these prints or whether Andy recovered the missing pieces from the Elga Wimmer Gallery.

3. See Museum of Modern Art Archives, Werner H. Kramarsky Papers, I.555, various correspondence among Wynn Kramarsky, Andrew Topolski, and Iris von der Tann, dated October through December 1991.

4. See Museum of Modern Art Archives, Werner H. Kramarsky Papers, I.555, letters from Andrew Topolski to Wynn Kramarsky dated October 15 and December 16, 1991.

OUT THERE

1. Julie L. Belcove, "A New Boone," *W*, November 1, 2008.

2. Peter C. T. Elsworth, "The Art Boom: Is It Over, or Is This Just a Correction?" *New York Times*, December 16, 1990.

3. This review earned a lengthy response from the curator behind the show, which survives in Topolski's archive in the Burchfield Penney:

> *4 March 1994*
>
> *To the Editor:*
> *The review of our recent exhibition Topolski: Recent Drawings and Sculpture ("Topolski exhibit at Albright raises a big question: Why?" by Marilyn Fox, 2/25/94) warrants a response. Let me say at the outset that any review, negative or otherwise, is a necessary byproduct of bringing art, especially contemporary art, to its community. Yet, as reviews themselves occupy the public forum, they are fair game for response.*
>
> *Leo Steinberg, a distinguished art historian, has described the discomfort to be had from modern art. He terms this the "plight of the public" and characterizes it as a state of perpetual anxiety, but one worth taking seriously. Indeed, I take seriously Marilyn Fox's state of distress when viewing Andrew Topolski's art. It can at first appear incomprehensible. Let me, on the other hand, put in a word for those who, like Ms. Fox, didn't get it. Steinberg explains that when "confronting a new work of art, one may feel excluded from something they thought they were part of." For Ms. Fox, this sense of loss comes in the form of boredom, a failure of aesthetic appreciation, and an inability to perceive positive values in Topolski's work.*
>
> *Suppose now that we consider these sacrifices worthwhile. For instance, Ms. Fox is bored because she finds Topolski's work too enigmatic. Let's*

*consider for a moment that Topolski was trying to make his art complex
in order to force us to recognize a different kind of system. By combining
references to mathematics, music, historic texts, and aesthetics Topolski
creates a composite language that focuses on the relations between all of
these systems. Complex, but potentially challenging and rewarding. Ms. Fox
also assumes that we are entitled to answers, but do we demand this kind of
justification from scientists or mathematicians whose occupations involve
the creation and mastery of intellectual puzzles? Then there is her criticism
on aesthetic grounds. In observing Topolski's connections to mathematics
and science, she finds it void of humanity or aesthetics. Here I believe Ms.
Fox constructs a false dichotomy, one that is most disturbing for a liberal
arts college. As a professor of art history, it is my greatest challenge to make
students aware of connections between art and science. Andrew Topolski's
art invites just this kind of contemplation.*

*Ultimately, one deals with the issue of taste. Topolski's conceptual art may
not be Ms. Fox's cup of tea. But to judge it as obscure, unrealized potential,
and sterile is to predetermine its positive value for a larger public. I stand by
my assessment of Topolski's work as one that provides a composite language
rich in form, feeling, and complexity.*

Jill Snyder
Director, Freedman Gallery

4. These quotes are from James Joyce, *Ulysses* (1922), ed. Hans Walter
Gabler (New York: Vintage, 1986), 31, 100, and 37, respectively.

5. "Die Grenzen meiner Sprache bedeuten die Grenzen meiner Welt."
Ludwig Wittgenstein, *Tractatus Logico-Philosophicus*, trans. C. K. Ogden
(1922; rpt. New York: Dover, 1986), §5.6.

6. "And given the nature of our intellectual commerce with works of
art, to lack a persuasive theory is to lack something crucial –the means
by which our experience of individual works is joined to our understanding of the values they signify" (*New York Times*, April 28, 1974). This
axiom spurred Tom Wolfe to write his book-length takedown of the critical contemporary art establishment, *The Painted Word* (New York: Farrar,
Straus & Giroux, 1975).

SEMINARIANS

1. "The little towns of the Catskills," as Christiane Fischer-Harling
called them, "boomed" after September 11, 2001. County records show
that Cindy and Andy were at the very crest of the coming wave. Curiously,

they had also been early, if minor, participants in the gentrification of Williamsburg; after 9/11, they would unwittingly lead the gentrification of the Catskills. The traditional benefits of such cycles were not to accrue to Cindy and Andy in either case.

SILENCE, EXILE, AND CUNNING

1. See "Final Report on the August 14, 2003 Blackout in the United States and Canada: Causes and Recommendations," by the US–Canada Power Outage System Task Force, April 2004.

2. Only Charlotta Kotik contested this view of a long break in Andy's studio practice. In a filmed interview in her apartment in August 2024, she said, "We all took a break [after 9/11]—we had to. But then we got back to work." While it's impossible to tell for certain whether and how long Andy may have stepped back from his previously prolific studio practice, I have chosen to privilege Don Metz's and Christiane Fischer-Harling's accounts in large part because they were in a better position to observe Andy during this period. Charlotta never visited Andy and Cindy in Callicoon. Don Metz visited multiple times and spoke to Andy on the phone frequently. Christiane spent long weekends and holidays just up the hill. However, Charlotta's countervailing opinion highlights an important insight into artistic process. While Andy's output of finished works notably fell off in the immediate aftermath of 9/11, he was still *working* in a sense—his conscious and subconscious minds were processing the trauma of his experience and dramatic changes in political discourse and culture that unfolded in their wake. He was reading, watching, thinking—and probably sketching, experimenting. This largely invisible gestation was a necessary part of the process that would lead to the explosion of work in a new register he produced in the last years of his life.

KILL ME A SON

1. I have no guess as to what happened to this message. I must have sent it from the same Hotmail account where I received Cindy's reply. I still occasionally use the account as a backup, and I have never received any notification about exceeding storage limits or automatic deletion policies. Being denied access to the origin of this email chain brought on acute, if muted, panic. For months I had been grappling with the degradation of memory (chiefly my own), and the innumerable dead ends of other people's recollections. Now I was discovering the decay of a

relationship in digital space. Thinking about how much of ourselves we give to each other online—how much this has changed since 2007—and how much we assume and rely on the documentary permanence of those digital signals, which often we forget as soon as we've released them—was terrifying.

2. Nearly everyone who knew Andy stopped speaking with him at some point, though almost none living today remembers—by choice or by chance—exactly why.

MINDS OF MY GENERATION

1. Several contemporaries tell me that the works in this series—which catapulted Longo to fame, and in turn inspired the stagecraft of the Talking Heads—were themselves inspired by Longo's teacher Joe Panone's portraits of galloping horses.

2. "The word 'generation' in the title is a bit tricky. The artists included here represent only one aspect of art being made at the time, though they are presented as if they were the whole story. No larger context for the work is suggested, though they shared a set of social and political experiences." Holland Cotter, "At the Met, Baby Boomers Leap Onstage," *New York Times*, April 23, 2009.

3. It's worth noting the role of state funding in supporting the New York communities included in the Met show. Both Artists Space and Hallwalls were possible because of NYSCA grants.

THE HUMAN CHAIN, THE HUMAN HAND

1. The Niagara Frontier Food Terminal opened in 1931 as a modern, sanitary, and spacious replacement for the cramped chaos of the former Elk Street Market. The NFFT was the result of a cooperative effort by sixty of Buffalo's major food merchants, who put up the equity in their own properties to fund its construction—$5 million then, what would be north of $80 million today. With help from the Erie and Nickel Plate Railroads, they connected the complex to a sizeable rail yard—nothing like the Frontier Yard to the north, but with receiving tracks for 198 cars; team delivery tracks for 236 cars; and hold, inspection, and icing tracks for another 133 cars. The terminal fed Greater Buffalo for a few decades. Eventually many of the tenants moved out; eighteen-wheelers started shipping food direct to mega-groceries like Wegmans and Walmart, and the region lost over half its population. Businesses closed and tenants

departed. The terminal's sixty acres and surrounding lots, also industrial, cracked off from Kaisertown in the collective consciousness and became its own, unofficial district: Ghost Town, locals called it.

Starting in 2019, though, the NFFT began to reemerge with a new purpose. It offered cheap space—industrial, retail, or studio, as needed—plentiful parking, easy access from Clinton or the Interstate, a nearby Tim Hortons, and a filling station on site. Western New York artists, priced out once again from other gentrifying areas, quickly caught on to Ghost Town. The spirit of Essex Street has taken up residence here—for now.

· · ·

TO SEE A SAMPLING OF ARTWORK BY ANDREW TOPOLSKI, VISIT
https://photos.app.goo.gl/x8pAB58wA3kqofwS8

TO SEE A SAMPLING OF ARTWORK BY CINDY SUFFOLETTO, VISIT
https://photos.app.goo.gl/8ax4LzXZVDuDPZfj6